Cleaning Painted Surfaces

Aqueous Methods

Richard Wolbers

Archetype
Publications

Published by
Archetype Publications Ltd
6 Fitzroy Square
London W1T 5HJ
www.archetype.co.uk

Tel: 44(207) 380 0800
Fax: 44(207) 380 0500

First published 2000
Reprinted 2003

ISBN 1 873132 36 0

International Academic Projects, sponsors of this volume, gratefully acknowledge support from the Samuel H. Kress Foundation.

Typeset by Kate Williams, Abergavenny.
Printed and bound in Great Britain by Henry Ling Ltd., The Dorset Press, Dorchester.

Contents

Acknowledgements vii
Foreword viii

1 Introduction 1
1.1 Introduction 1
1.2 Adhesion of soils 1
1.3 Traditional aqueous methods 5

2 Acids and bases 9
2.1 Chemical equilibria 9
2.2 Law of Mass Action 10
2.3 Acids and bases and the definition of pK and pH 13
2.4 Hydrolysis 15
2.5 Buffers 16
2.6 Acid–base titrations 18
2.7 Solubility product 20
Case History 2.1: James Peale, Portrait of Mary Morris Jones (oil on canvas, early nineteenth century) 21
Case History 2.2: F. Schoonover, The Prodigal Father (oil on canvas, 1932) 24

3 Surfactants and affinity surfactants 27

3.1 Surface activity and surfactants 27

3.2 Structural classification of surfactants 28

3.3 Properties of solutions containing surfactants 29

3.4 Critical micelle concentration (CMC) 30

3.5 Micelle size: aggregation number 35

3.6 Micelle size and charge 36

3.7 Krafft point: temperature versus solubility of surfactants 37

3.8 CMCs for nonionics 37

3.9 Affinity surfactants 39

Case History 3.1: E. Von Liebrach, Winterscape: Skating on the Pond (oil on canvas, nineteenth century) 40

Case History 3.2: Unattributed, Venetian Canal Scene (oil on canvas, nineteenth century) 44

Case History 3.3: Dean Wolstenholme the elder, The Death (oil on canvas, early nineteenth century) 48

Case History 3.4: Unattributed, German Student Model Violin Bow (composite object, pre-World War II) 49

Case History 3.5: C. F. Ryder, Paxsons Hollow (oil on canvas, nineteenth century) 52

4 Detergents and detergency 55

4.1 Detergency 55

4.2 Mechanisms of detergency 56

4.3 Laundry detergent compositions as models for detergency 58

4.4 Evaluation of detergency 58

4.5 Adsorption of surfactants on soil and substrate surfaces 61

4.6 Surfactant adsorption as a function of CMC, pH, and counter-ion concentration 63

4.7 Detergent systems design 66

Case History 4.1: Joan Brown, Kitchen Still Life (oil on canvas, 1964) 67

Case History 4.2: Unattributed, Corner Cupboard (composite object, Pennsylvania 1830–1840) 69

4.8 Detergency in non-aqueous systems 71

Case History 4.3: Unattributed, Massachusetts Hinged Writing Desk (composite object, 1750–1780) 74

Case History 4.4: William Naismith, Pastoral Landscape (oil on canvas, nineteenth century) 76

Case History 4.5: Frederic Remington, In Defense of the Barricade (oil on canvas, 1889) 80

Case History 4.6: Unattributed, Tilt-top Tea Table (composite object, Philadelphia c.1765) 81

5 Emulsions 85
- 5.1 Emulsions: definition 85
- 5.2 Hydrophile-lipophile balance (HLB) number 86
- 5.3 Macroemulsions 92
- 5.4 Phase inversion temperature (PIT) 95
- 5.5 Cloud point 96
- 5.6 A ternary system: xylene/water/Triton X-100 96
  - *Case History 5.1: Unattributed, Polychrome Trade Sign, Bust of George Washington (composite object, late nineteenth century)* 98
- 5.7 Microemulsions 102
  - *Case History 5.2: Unattributed, Gilded Frame (composite object, nineteenth century)* 104
  - *Case History 5.3: Elmer Garnsey, Architectural Decorative Paint (early twentieth century)* 107

6 Chelation 109
- 6.1 Chelation: definition 109
- 6.2 Metal displacement equilibria 116
- 6.3 Estimation of ion concentrations on paint films 116
  - *Case History 6.1: Albion Bicknell, Painting of a Prize Cow (oil on canvas, late nineteenth century)* 119
- 6.4 Chelate–chelate exchange equilibria 120
  - *Case History 6.2: J. L. Hansen, Portrait of Hannah Holbrow (oil on canvas, 1842)* 121
- 6.5 Metal buffering 123
  - *Case History 6.3: William Mason Brown, Landscape: View of a River (oil on canvas, c.1865)* 124

7 Enzymes 127
- 7.1 Enzymes 127
- 7.2 Classification of enzymes 128
- 7.3 Active sites on enzymes 129
- 7.4 Enzyme kinetics 131
- 7.5 Temperature and pH effects on enzyme reaction rates 132
- 7.6 Enzyme purification and isolation 134
- 7.7 Enzymes important to conservation 135
  - *Case History 7.1: Jacob Eichholtz, Portrait of Anne Ross Hopkins (oil on canvas, nineteenth century)* 139
  - *Case History 7.2: Unattributed, Christ Washing the Feet of the Disciples (oil on canvas, nineteenth century)* 143
  - *Case History 7.3: Unattributed, Wallpaper Fragment, Corbett-Sharp House, Odessa, Delaware (paper, early nineteenth century)* 146

Case History 7.4: Frederick Sandys, Portrait of Miranda (oil on panel, nineteenth century) *149*
7.8 Other enzymes of special note 155

8 Clearance 157
8.1 Clearance: an introduction 157
8.2 Properties of paint surfaces 158
8.3 Properties of varnished surfaces 160
8.4 The design of cleaning systems with clearance in mind 160
8.5 Residual material remaining after cleaning 163
8.6 Substitution of less toxic materials for cleaning 164
8.7 Specific clearance conditions 164

Appendix 1: Examining and staining paint cross-sections 167
A1.1 Carbohydrates 168
A1.2 Proteins 171
A1.3 Lipids, oils and fats 177
A1.4 Resins 180

Appendix 2: Suppliers of materials 184
Sigma Chemicals 184
Ethomeen and Carbopol products 184
Micromesh polishing materials 185
Shellsol T (mineral spirits) 185

References 187
Index 191

Acknowledgements

Special acknowledgements are to be made to the Winterthur Museum and Gardens and to the jointly sponsored program between Winterthur and the University of Delaware in Art Conservation (WUDPAC) for permission to allow objects and object treatments to be reproduced here in part or in full.

Grateful acknowledgement should be given to The Samuel H. Kress Foundation and Lisa Ackerman for support for this project.

Thanks also to Jan Brennan and the Sid Richardson Collection in Fort Worth Texas for permission to report and discuss the treatment of the *Defense of the Barricade* by Frederic Remington.

Special thanks are also to be given to the graduate students and faculty of WUDPAC for their contributions to this text, and their work on these projects. In particular Phillip Klausmeyer, Joanne Barry, Mark Lewis, Susan Buck, David Blanchfield, Ruth Barach Cox, Carolyn Tallent, Riki Bjarnhof, Melissa McGrew, Gini Rasmussen, and Lucy Wolfgang Smith.

I would also like to thank those special people in my professional life that have supported this and other my other endeavours, and without whom I would not have had such a wonderful and fulfilling career in art conservation: Joyce Hill Stoner, Debbie Hess Norris, Janice Carlson, Chris Stavroudis, Paolo Cremonesi, Alan Phenix, Andrea Rothe, Mark Leonard, Caroline Keck, Constance Silver, Perry Huston, Valerie Dorge, Dusan Stulik, Alberto Tagle, Herant Khanjian, Narajan Khandakar, and David Miller.

Finally, this book is dedicated to the loving memory of my grandfather Harry, who made magic happen in a simple garage workshop.

Richard Wolbers
July 2000

Foreword

There are three layers of paintings – the varnish, the paint and the canvas – about which there is insufficient knowledge of their physico-chemical properties and hence their response to conservation treatments. In other words, we cannot claim to be fully satisfied with our present state of understanding of the material structure, and the deterioration over time, of any layer of a painting. Most of the research carried out today into the materials of paintings is concentrated on trying to achieve a greater knowledge of the properties of all these areas, with the aim of furthering our understanding of the consequences of conservation treatments, both immediate and long term, and also the effects of earlier treatments.

This book contributes significantly to the selection of appropriate and controllable cleaning methods for varnished and unvarnished paint surfaces. It is a distillation of the author's practical experience over many years in formulating a cleaning treatment for a given object. Some of this material has been published previously as case histories, and some has been discussed in courses and lectures given by Richard Wolbers. The debate that his methods engendered has promoted research into, and evaluation of, more traditional methods of cleaning surfaces with solvents and alkaline reagents. This is still continuing: see for example *Traditions and Innovation: Advances in Conservation* (Burnstock and White 2000; Stulik *et al.* 2000). This text now gives a reasoned statement of the ideas underlying his methods by first illustrating chemical principles and then increasingly complex case histories – complex in the sense that the paintings and furniture that are used as illustrations have already been the subject of several campaigns of treatment, ranging from incomplete removal of varnish to the addition of a non-traditional coating material which has then interacted with the original coating.

The nature of soiling on painted surfaces is described first, followed by acid-base reaction, surfactants, detergency, emulsions, chelation, the use of enzymes, and general considerations on minimizing and then removing residual materials from the surface which has been treated. An appendix outlines the microscopical and staining methods which are used to characterize the surface to be cleaned, and which provide the information for treatment planning. With the exception of the appendices, the substance of the chapters following the introductory one has not previously been published in the conservation literature. Nor could it have been found in its completed form without some searching of the chemical and biochemical literature, even though the concepts themselves were mostly described some decades ago. Throughout the text there are insights into the behaviour of pigments in coatings, and into the environmental history of coatings, which generate the altered surface seen by the present-day conservator. Indeed, the most recent intervention might have had more impact even than the artist's original choice of material, on the surface encountered today. This book reports on work in progress and experience gained, but does not include the author's latest researches into the subject.

Aqueous cleaning methods add a further 'weapon' to the conservator's armoury of methods for the reduction or removal of disfiguring accumulations of dirt and varnishes on paint. They have been used – and studied – quite extensively over the past ten years or more, since Richard Wolbers first brought them to conservators' notice through his courses. Some methods, such as enzyme cleaning, are particularly poorly understood within conservation, because their original, biochemical use is rather different. While the case histories describe nineteenth- and twentieth-century paintings and furniture exclusively, and may emphasize the cleaning of never-varnished surfaces to an extent unusual in some conservators' experience, the general principles are applicable to the surface cleaning of both traditional and modern paint media. These, in fact, may be found on sculptures, ethnographic materials, and even textile and paper supports, as well as on paintings, gilded surfaces and furniture. Aqueous methods are certainly worth considering for those surfaces which cannot be cleaned safely by the more traditional methods based on the use of solvents. The idea of 'safety' may be applicable both to the artwork, and to the conservator, who may be faced with an oversized painting which responds either to treatment with a toxic solvent such as xylene, or to a carefully formulated xylene gel that offers less evaporation of the solvent.

This text provides much basic information on the properties of the detergents, surfactants, gels and soaps which Richard Wolbers has introduced to conservation, and rationalizes the choices to be made among them. To this end, the sequence of chapters, and also the index, has concentrated on materials (both in the paint and varnish surfaces themselves, and those used in cleaning) and concepts. The author's aim has not been to provide recipes, but instead tools for understanding, and a firm foundation for future research.

Joyce H Townsend
Consultant Editor
August 2000

The author and publisher wish to express the concern that while the methods and materials described in this book have proven useful to the conservation of the artefacts described in the case histories, they are merely illustrative of certain materials, techniques and their applications. All materials adopted from these case studies should be used with the greatest of caution and to local, state and federal guidelines that might apply to their safe handling and storage. No liability will be accepted on our part for their misuse, misapplication or damage to either the conservators who may use them or the artefacts they might apply them to.

1

Introduction

1.1 Introduction

Aqueous methods have been used, almost certainly since antiquity, as an aid in the removal of soiling materials from surfaces on which they settle and are retained. For painted or varnished surfaces in particular, water-based or water-containing preparations can and do form an impressive array of tools for the conservator of these materials to adopt for cleaning these surfaces as well. Although water-based preparations have most often been associated exclusively with the removal of soiling materials, it may well be that, with some simple modifications, these same or similar aqueous preparations can also be important in the separation or removal of more problematic materials (coatings, paints, adhesives, etc.) from fine and decorative paints and varnishes. The use of water as an agent in the removal of soiling materials from paint or varnish surfaces is a good place to start, partly because it allows for a review of the aqueous methods and materials that we are likely to encounter or adopt for these purposes, but additionally, as a way to review the nature of traditional film-forming materials, and how soils are retained on these surfaces. This text will essentially be divided into chapters describing first the theory underlying each aqueous material or method, but also case histories from actual treatments to illustrate and accentuate how 'theory' can be applied or integrated into an actual cleaning problem or situation.

1.2 Adhesion of soils

Usually, the properties of paint and varnish surfaces that can most often be cited as responsible for retaining soiling materials are: roughness; moisture resistance;

elasticity; relative hydrophobicity and hydrophilicity; tackiness; and electrical properties (Zimon 1969: 157). To understand how these properties might influence the retention of soiling materials, we shall review the types of soiling materials (solids) likely to fall on paint and varnished surfaces, some of their physical and chemical properties, and what forces are likely to be developed under normal conditions to attract and hold them on these surfaces.

Sources for solid soiling materials may be characterized as *point* or *collective*, that is, discrete sources such as factory smokestacks, or cumulative sources like the exhaust material from vehicles, respectively. Particulate soils may be formed by condensation or sublimation processes; disintegration (grinding, drilling); coagulation; or other chemical processes. Particle sizes may vary from 0.001–500 μm in diameter. Consider the size ranges associated with these sources (Table 1.1).

Whatever the source for the soiling material, some form of transport or *dispersal* system (due to atmospheric conditions – wind, temperature, rain, etc.) brings the material eventually to a paint or varnish surface. Real soiling materials are often a mixture of particle types, and can exhibit a wide range of particle sizes. The smaller a particle is, the longer it can be retained in the atmosphere; the larger it is, the shorter this time becomes. The *residence time* of a particle, how long it is airborne and, coincidentally, how far it will travel, is a function of size as well (Table 1.2).

In most actual soils a bimodal size distribution is typically evident; generally, the particle sizes fall into two distinct ranges, 0.03–0.5 μm and 5–100 μm for soils deposited in the exterior environment (Kroschwitz 1991a). This simply reflects the situation that normal soils tend to propagate from sources that are both far away (long residence time, small size) and close at hand (short residence time, larger size).

The retention of soils on surfaces may be due to a variety of interactions. The size of a soiling particulate is a critical parameter in estimating the forces likely to develop and retain it on any given surface. As a function of size, certain forces tend to predominate over others between particle and surface. For molecular forces (ionic, dipolar, hydrogen bonding, or Van der Waals interactions) the force of adhesion to a

Table 1.1 Source of particulate versus particle size range (Lapple 1961)

Source of particulate	Size range (μm)
combustion of coal	1–200
metallurgical	0.001–100
salt nuclei	0.03–0.5
pollens	10–100
cementitious dusts	0.1–300

Table 1.2 Size versus residence time (Willeke & Whitby 1975)

Size (μm)	Residence time
<1	100–1000 hours
1–10	10–100 hours
>40	limited, settles fast
500	seconds

surface can be expressed by the following general expression, if the adhered particle is assumed to be roughly spherical in shape (Zimon 1969: 14):

$$F_{ad} = \frac{Ar}{6H^2} \quad [1.1]$$

where A is a constant for the particulate, accounting for its individual dispersive effects, induction, the medium surrounding the particle and surface, etc.; here r is the radius of the particle and H is the distance between the spherical particle and the surface at any given point on the spherical particle. It is clear from equation 1.1 that the smaller the value for H, the greater the proximity of the particle to the surface, and the greater the molecular force generated. H is a minimum at the point of contact, and F_{ad} at its maximum. The greater the contact area, or the greater the number of *contact points*, the stronger the interaction of this type. For an absolutely smooth surface, the contact point would be minimal (Zimon 1969: 157); for a roughened surface, the number of contact points between particle and surface might increase, as well as the F_{ad}. Typically, F_{ad} is minimal on extremely smooth or an extremely rough surface; surfaces of only moderate roughness tend to exhibit the greatest F_{ad}s.

Molecular forces or interactions of the type described above are, of course, only one type of force that can adhere a particle to a surface. Electrical interactions or forces (where a *potential difference* exists between particle and surface, and electrons can flow from one to the other) can also exist (Zimon 1969: 169). Electrical interactions are only really operative at relatively short distances (limited to contact points themselves), as are molecular forces, but can exceed in some cases the magnitude of molecular forces. Furthermore, electrical forces really exist only between conducting materials, and are proportional to $r^{2/3}$ for a hypothetical particle of radius r. For surfaces that are non-conducting or are made non-conducting, these types of interactions can be minimal. Where water is present, electrical interactions may be eliminated altogether.

F_{ad} can also be a function of coulombic forces (attractive, static electrical forces, where opposite charges on surface and particle attract one another); these forces are relatively more predominant the smaller the 'gap' between particle and surface, and are not a function of the number of contact points. Coulombic forces vary with the inverse square of the r of a particle (in other words $1/r^2$) (Zimon 1969: 170). As particle size decreases, this force tends to predominate. Again, as with electrical forces or interactions, water can disrupt or preclude this type of interaction. At very high relative humidities (RHs) (usually > 65%), and relatively low r values, water can condense between particles and a surface, and act as a direct (liquid) adhesive between surface and particle. These capillary forces tend to increase as particle size decreases by the factor $r(1 - r^n)$, where r, again, is the particle radius and n is an integer (Zimon 1969: 170).

In relatively dry air as the surrounding medium, any one or all of the forces possible (e.g. molecular, electrical, coulombic, and capillary) may exist to secure a particle to a surface, at the same H, or distance, from the surface, then:

Component force:	coulomb	electrical	molecular	capillary
Size relationship to component force:	$1/r^2$	$r^{2/3}$	r	$r(1 - r^n)$

In summary, as particle size decreases, generally speaking, molecular, and electrical forces will decrease as well; at very small particle sizes coulombic and capillary forces tend to predominate more. If the medium around the particle/surface changes to include moisture all forces may still exist; but if condensed water is present (or if the surface is wetted during washing) only limited molecular forces and liquid/surface interactions are possible, and electrical and coulombic forces are eliminated altogether.

The moisture permeability of films will contribute to their equilibrium moisture content, and relative ability to develop certain types of surface interactions. Generally, the more moisture permeable a film is, the more hygroscopic the surface, and the more easily water can be absorbed onto and even condense there affecting the types of forces possible to secure soil particulates. Conversely the more hydrophobic, or less water permeable, the less role water will play in either disrupting electrical or coulombic forces, and as an adhesive by condensation. In Table 1.3 the relative permeability of film-forming materials is given for comparison.

Paraffin would essentially be the least permeable of the materials listed here, the most hydrophobic, and the most difficult to condense water onto at very high RHs, or to wet with water.

The hardness of paint and varnish films can also affect the type and magnitude of the interaction contributing to the overall force of adhesion of a soil particulate (Zimon 1969: 166). The greater the contact area the stronger the molecular, electrical, and to some extent, coulombic, interaction will develop on a surface. If the paint or varnish surface is easily distendable, or elastic, a larger contact area will result as the surface is deformed slightly with a lesser impact force (whatever the dispersal force specifically). Several standardized methods are available for measuring film hardness, but generally the most widely used is the pendulum method (impact tester). Film hardness is also a function of temperature. Specifically, the film hardness is much reduced above the glass transition temperature (Tg), and measurements of Tg yield information on the film hardness at ambient temperature (Schilling 1989). Waxes, oils, and silicone-based polymers have been advanced as modifiers of paint and varnish materials, either as direct constituents or additives, or as separately applied surface treatments, to modify the electrical properties, and hygroscopicity, of these surfaces. But the addition of any material that modifies (plasticizes or leaves tacky) these surfaces has led to increased soil particulate retention for lower impact or dispersal agent forces. Dispersion paints such as

Table 1.3 Moisture permeability of various film formers (Zimon 1969: 160)

Film type	Permeability (μg water passing through in 120 hours)
Skin glue	3900
Gelatin	730
Linseed oil	570
Linseed oil (polymerized)	286
Rubber	232
Tung oil/ natural resin	200
Tung oil/phenolic resin	107
Paraffin	10

latexes (emulsion paints in the UK) that are formulated with high amounts of plasticizers and surfactants generally form films which have surfaces that have a disproportionate concentration of these materials, and yield more elastic surface characteristics than films cast from non-dispersion resin counterparts.

Water as a solvent can play a central role in reducing significantly the amount of work needed to overcome the force of adhesion for many soil particulates. As a highly dielectric medium, water is especially good at separating charged particles from one another, and can reduce or eliminate entirely interactions based on electrical and coulombic forces. It has been estimated that on steel plates as model surfaces for instance, the force of adhesion for adhering glass bead particles of various sizes could be reduced by as much as three orders of magnitude with water as opposed to air as the surrounding medium (Zimon 1969: 115).

It must also be stated that although water alone can be helpful in cleaning surfaces, some retained materials will still be held by surface interactions that must be overcome by additional methods or materials in concert with the solvent properties of water. Consider for a moment the following characterization of a typical soiling mixture from an exterior surface in an urban environment (Cutler & Kissa 1987):

water-soluble material	15.9% (w/w)
solvent-soluble material	7.1%
inorganic (ash)	56.3%
moisture	3.0%
pH (10% slurry)	6.7

Surprisingly, only a small portion of the soiling material is potentially water soluble (15.9%) outright; the remainder would have to be dispersed in water to be removed effectively. The solvent-soluble fraction is probably hydrocarbon-like in nature (machine oils, lubricants, etc, dispersed in the atmosphere), and would be hydrophobic in character. The inorganic, or 'ash' material left after ignition of the soiling mixture was characterized further and shown to contain (Cutler & Kissa 1987):

SiO_2	26.4% (w/w)	MgO	1.7%
Fe_2O_3	11.1%	carbon black	0.55%
CaO	7.7%		

These materials undoubtedly reflect the composition of modern urban soils that contain a significant amount of debris from construction. The particular metals associated with these compounds (Ca^{+2}, Fe^{+3}, and Mg^{+2}) may also complicate the use of dispersing or chelating agents in aqueous solutions.

1.3 Traditional aqueous methods

A variety of aqueous methods has long been applied to paint and varnish surfaces for their advantageous cleaning effects. Wine, ammoniated solutions, solutions of potash or lye, various soap preparations, and a host of sliced foodstuffs (potatoes, onions, garlic, etc.) have all been reported at one point or another as being useful cleaning aids. Physiological fluids have also been used as cleaning agents: urine, blood, bile fluids, and saliva have been suggested at one time or another for their cleaning properties. Saliva, for instance, is still used for surface soil removal on a variety of substrates, and can be characterized by the aqueous materials or conditions shown in Table 1.4 (Long 1961).

Table 1.4 Aqueous materials and conditions characterizing saliva

water	
pH	6.8–7.4 – both hydrogen phosphate and carbonate as buffers
proteins	chiefly albumin
amino acids	most of the 20 or so commonly found ones
Na^+	in substantial amounts, with traces of K^+, Ca^{+2}, Mg^{+2}, Cu^{+2}, Co^{+2}, SO_4^-, SCN^-, NH_4^+ and Cl^-
diammonium citrate	(0.01% w/v)
enzymes	amylase, lipase, protease, lysozyme

While saliva is a complicated mixture of materials, at its heart water is still the primary component, and without water as a solvent, none of the other materials would have any additional effect. The water contained in saliva is buffered to a particular pH range (6.8–7.4) with essentially two materials, carbonate ion (CO_3^{-2}) and hydrogen phosphate ion ($H_2PO_4^-$). It is also full of an impressive array of ionic materials, the chief of which is sodium (Na^+). We sometimes associate the particular effectiveness of saliva for cleaning certain surface soils with the enzymes that are present in it. Actually, their concentration (and more importantly, their ability to catalyze the breakdown of specific materials) is so low that they may in fact play only a minor role in observed surface-cleaning effects. Citrate, as the diammonium salt, is a metal ion complexing material that can separate and solubilize metallic ions that would otherwise form intractable salts or complexes on surfaces. Some of the proteins like albumin and the amino acids present in saliva can be described as having a weak surfactant effect; that is, an ability to reduce the surface tension between water and oily substances, and thereby allow water and whatever is dissolved in it to act more effectively on the oily substance. While mucin, in particular, gives saliva its particular slippery feeling, as a polymeric material it both slightly thickens saliva, and helps suspend soils that are removed from surfaces thus facilitating their removal.

There really is nothing *magic* about how and why saliva works; it simply is the effect of water and a series of materials present in water that makes it seem so effective in surface cleaning some soils. For clarity's sake, we might simply refer to the materials present in saliva by *effect* rather than by specific name. Our list might then be generalized to read as in Table 1.5.

All of the materials present in saliva can be fitted into one or more of the categories listed above. In fact, most aqueous surface-cleaning preparations contain materials that can also be assigned to one or more of these categories. This list is, in effect, our list of the tools we might adopt for designing an aqueous cleaning system

Table 1.5 Effect of materials present in saliva

water	solvent
pH/buffer(s)	hydrogen ion concentration or control
surfactant(s)	wetting, emulsifying, dispersal, solubilization
ion or specific ionic effects	dissolution and formation of certain salts
chelation	metal-complexing agents
enzymes	materials that can effect a chemical change or modify a material to change solubility
adjuvants	thickeners, suspension aids, solvents, corrosion controllers, preservatives etc.

for any given situation. The primary effects of water itself, pH (and the buffering materials that allow us to control the pH of aqueous solutions), surfactants, specific ion effects or concentrations, chelation (or metal complexing effects), and the use of enzymes (and their ability to modify or break down natural biopolymers in particular to render them soluble in water) will be the primary effects that will be examined in this text. While the last category, *adjuvants*, admittedly embraces a wide range of effects, these will only be touched on it the present text as part of the case histories presented with the theoretical sections. Lastly we shall consider the best choice of clearing or rinsing agents for a given aqueous cleaning treatment. The use of fluorochrome and reactive dyes to characterize paint and varnish films while a treatment is being planned will be discussed in Appendix 1.

2

Acids and bases

2.1 Chemical equilibria

Water, as a solvent, is especially effective at dissolving ionic materials. The dissolution of electrolytes into their component ions is facilitated to one degree or another because water is a very *polar* solvent, but also because it exhibits a high dielectric constant or ability to separate oppositely charged ions, despite their tendency to be strongly attracted to one another, to form stable or neutral salts. The dissolution of a given electrolyte or salt may be thought of as a sequence of two chemical reactions or steps; bonds (ionic) are broken, and new bonds are formed (with water, by virtue of its strong dipole moment). But occasionally, some of the ionic bonds are reformed again (as the oppositely charged ions recombine to form the starting neutral electrolyte or salt). Immediately on placing an electrolyte in contact with water, the dissolution reactions predominate, but in time, and especially as more and more ions of opposite charge are dissolved in water, recombination of the individual ions takes place to one degree or another. This latter recombination 'reaction' catches up with the rate of the initial dissolution reactions. At this point, it would appear as if no new ions were being dissolved in the water solution. In other words, at some point, an equilibrium is reached between dissolution and recombination of the ions. When both 'reactions' are more or less occurring at the same rate, an equilibrium, or steady state, is established, and the overall concentration of any ionic species at any one moment appears as if it is constant. An example of this is the dissolution of acetic acid in water. A 0.01 M solution of acetic acid is ionized approximately 4% at room temperature. This means that, at equilibrium, about 4% of the total number of acetic acid molecules will appear to have separated into individual acetate and hydrogen ions, and the rest remain in the un-ionized form as free acetic acid. It is interesting to note how little of the acetic acid (4%) appears to be dissociated at equilibrium. Acetic acid is a relatively weak electrolyte, i.e., it tends to remain more in the un-ionized form than separated into its individual ionic species. Common salt, NaCl, on the other hand, is an example of a very strong electrolyte, and almost completely dissociates in aqueous solution into Na^+ and Cl^- ions. The *position* of an equilibrium, or the extent of dissolution of any given salt can be affected by:

- the nature of the substances involved
- temperature
- pressure
- concentration

If the temperature is increased even slightly, more dissociation occurs. An increase in temperature tends to shift an equilibrium reaction in the direction of the process or reaction absorbing or requiring energy; in this case energy is required to separate the ionic species from the neutral salt. Le Chatelier's principle is a traditional, and general, statement of the effects of most factors that influence the position of equilibria:

> *A system in equilibrium, when subjected to a stress resulting from a change in temperature, pressure, or concentration, and causing the equilibrium to be upset, will adjust its position of equilibrium to relieve the stress, and re-establish the equilibrium.* (Smoot *et al.* 1983: 482).

2.2 Law of Mass Action

The effect of concentration on equilibrium reactions is expressed in the Law of Mass Action (Smoot *et al.* 1983: 482). It states that:

> *The speed of a reaction is proportional to the product of the molar concentrations of the reacting substances, taken to proper powers, the powers being the coefficients of the reactants in the balanced equation for the reaction.*

In the dissolution of acetic acid in water, the acid combines with water to form two oppositely charged ionic species:

$$CH_3COOH + H_2O \Leftrightarrow CH_3COO^- + H_3O^+ \qquad [2.1]$$

(Note: hydrogen ions (H^+) rarely exist as isolated species; they tend to associate with water to form hydronium ions (H_3O^+)). If we assume that an equilibrium has been established between the substances on the left and those on the right, the forward (dissolution) reaction just matches the backward (free acid formation) reaction. According to the Law of Mass Action, the rate of the reaction forward can be expressed as

$$r_1 = k_1 \times [CH_3COOH] \times [H_2O] \qquad [2.2]$$

and the rate of the backward reaction as

$$r_2 - k_2 \times [CH_3COO^-] \times [H_3O^+] \qquad [2.3]$$

where the square brackets denote the concentration of each species expressed in moles. The constants k_1 and k_2 are constants of proportionality for the individual reactions. Since, at equilibrium, r_1 should equal $r_{2,}$ by definition, then

$$k_2 \times [CH_3COO^-] \times [H_3O^+] = k_1 \times [CH_3COOH] \times [H_2O] \qquad [2.4]$$

or

$$\frac{[CH_3COO^-]\times[H_3O^+]}{[CH_3COOH]\times[H_2O]} = \frac{k_1}{k_2} = K \qquad [2.5]$$

In this case K is a combination of the individual proportionality constants for convenience and is, as they are, a function of temperature. Constant K is generally called the *reaction constant*, and in this particular case, the *ionization constant* for the acetic acid reaction. By convention, the products of an equilibrium reaction are usually expressed as the numerator in these expressions, the reactants as the denominator. Most equilibrium reactions can be expressed in the general form:

$$m[A] + n[B] \Leftrightarrow p[C] + q[D] \qquad [2.6]$$

or

$$\frac{[C]^p \times [D]^q}{[A]^m \times [B]^n} = \frac{k_1}{k_2} = K \qquad [2.7]$$

where $[A]$ and $[B]$ are the molar quantities of the reactants, while the quantities m and n represent the numbers of each molecule in the overall balanced reaction shown in equation 2.6. Likewise $[C]$ and $[D]$ are the molar quantities of the products; and again, the quantities p and q represent the numbers of each molecule in the overall balanced reaction.

For acetic acid at room temperature, it was suggested above that about 4% of the acid was dissociated in a 0.01 M solution. Using equation 2.7, we can calculate the reaction or ionization constant for the acid at room temperature:

$$\frac{[CH_3COO^-]\times[H_3O^+]}{[CH_3COOH]\times[H_2O]} = \frac{k_1}{k_2} = K \qquad [2.8]$$

Assuming the concentration of water $[H_2O]$ is constant for all aqueous reactions, equation 2.8 becomes:

$$\frac{[CH_3COO^-]\times[H_3O^+]}{[CH_3COO^-]} = K \qquad [2.9]$$

and

$$\frac{0.0004\times 0.0004}{0.0096} = K \qquad [2.10]$$

$$1.66 \times 10^{-5} = K \qquad [2.11]$$

This K value is true for all reactions of acetic acid at room temperature (25°C). As a known value, it can help in estimating the amounts of $[CH_3COO^-]$, $[H_3O^+]$ (or $[H^+]$), and $[CH_3COOH]$ relative to one another. If, for instance, the amount of $[H_3O^+]$ (or $[H^+]$) should be increased with the addition of some other acid to the acetic acid solution, the amount of $[CH_3COO^-]$ would drop slightly, and the amount of $[CH_3COOH]$ would therefore rise as well, to yield the same K value. In other words, raising the amount of acid in the acetic acid solution would tend to drive the reaction backwards slightly, favouring the reformation of the reactants CH_3COOH and H_2O.

In the most general sense, then, the concentration of the reactants or products of an equilibrium reaction can affect the position of the overall equilibrium at any given temperature. By raising the concentration of reactants, we tend to favour the formation of products. The opposite is also true; by increasing the amount of product, we tend to drive an equilibrium reaction towards favouring reactants, or non-reaction. Actually, it should also be added that by *removing* products from a reaction system, we tend to drive a reaction forward towards producing more product; by letting them accumulate, we slow the forward direction or formation of more products in an equilibrium reaction.

Many of the materials found in soiling layers, as well as many that comprise the constituents of varnish and painting materials on fine art and decorative surfaces, contain weak electrolytes. Consider linseed oil itself as a binding material for paints. Depending on how it is processed and prepared for use as a paint-binding medium, a small, but measurable amount of free fatty acid material is present in the films formed from this natural product (triglyceride). Palmitic and stearic acids may be present in significant quantities in a linseed oil containing paint film, both from the outset, and, as the film is subjected to ageing (exposure to light and oxygen) (Mills & White 1994). While they respond slowly to water, in terms of swelling or dissolution, paint films containing these fatty acids do react with water, however slightly:

$$CH_3(CH_2)_{16}COOH + H_2O \Leftrightarrow CH_3(CH_2)_{16}\,COO^- + H_3O^+ \qquad [2.12]$$

As an electrolyte, stearic acid can dissolve in water, to form both a stearate ion and a hydronium ion (equation 2.12). At room temperature, this reaction, at equilibrium, would go in the direction of the formation of the two separate ions in water (first swelling, or taking on water, would occur, and then the actual dissolution of a portion of the available stearic acid would follow). If however, the amount of hydronium ion (acid in other words, or $[H_3O^+]$) was raised significantly, by adding some additional acidic material to the water (i.e. lowering the pH), the reaction would tend to go more towards the left, favouring the formation of free palmitic acid, which is a solid at room temperature. In this case, by increasing the amount or concentration of a product, we can 'push' a reversible reaction in the direction of forming (or slowing the dissolution, at least) of a film-forming material. By controlling the $[H_3O^+]$ concentration in aqueous solutions on linseed oil paint films, we can, in effect control the solubility of at least this one (and by analogy, the other similar fatty acid materials found in films formed from drying oils).

2.3 Acids and bases and the definition of pK and pH

According to the traditional Arrhenius definition of an acid (Smoot *et al.* 1983: 496–8), an acidic material is a substance that can give up or yield a hydrogen ion $[H^+]$ in solution, while a basic material can yield a hydroxide ion $[OH^-]$. Strong acids like HCl completely ionize, and yield one $[H^+]$ for each molecule of HCl dissolved; weak acids tend to ionize only partially, and tend to dissociate reversibly. As with any reversible reactions, the dissolution of weak acids in water may be described by an equilibrium constant, usually designated as K_a. Again, using acetic acid in water as an example:

$$CH_3COOH + H_2O \Leftrightarrow CH_3COO^- + H_3O^+ \qquad [2.13]$$

$$\frac{[CH_3COO^-] \times [H_3O^+]}{[CH_3COOH]} = K_a \qquad [2.14]$$

In the Arrhenius scheme, weak bases in water could similarly be assigned reaction constants. The Brönsted-Lowry definition (Smoot *et al.* 1983: 498) modifies the Arrhenius concept to include the specific role of (and allow for a different) solvent (or material) in the transfer of a hydrogen ion for defining an acidic material. Here it is proposed that acids be defined more generally as any substance that can transfer a hydrogen ion (or proton) to another substance, not just water. Generally, then, the reaction of a Brönsted-Lowry acid could be written as:

$$HA + B \Leftrightarrow A^- + BH^+ \qquad [2.15]$$

where HA is the hydrogen ion or proton donor, and B the hydrogen ion or proton acceptor. For weak acids then a reaction constant would be written as:

$$\frac{[A^-] \times [BH^+]}{[HA] \times [B]} = K_a \qquad [2.16]$$

And similarly a K_b could be derived for a weak base:

$$\frac{[HA] \times [B]}{[A^-] \times [BH^+]} = K_b \qquad [2.17]$$

Since, in the Brönsted-Lowry scheme, the species that remains after an acid has transferred a hydrogen ion, or proton, is also a base (it could take the hydrogen ion back on to form the initial acid again), Brönsted and Lowry also defined the term *conjugate acid and base*; the deprotonated or protonated form of an acid or base, respectively. The strength of acids can be compared in terms of their K_a values: the stronger the acid, the higher the K_a value. The strongest acids would have K_as that approached a value of 1. Very strong acids are completely ionized in water and generally cannot be described or differentiated by equilibrium K_a values. But while some acids may behave as strong proton donors in water, when the carrier solvent is changed to some other material, i.e. methanol or ethanol, they may behave as weaker acids in those solvents. Because of their relatively lower dielectric constants compared to water, it is much more difficult to ionize strong acids in these solvents, than in water. Consequently, the observed K_a values are much higher in water. HNO_3 is a good example; in water its K_a value is essentially 1; in ethanol it behaves more as a weak acid with a measurable K_a (= 1×10^{-8}).

Water itself is an example of an *amphoteric* material; it can act as weak acid or base. In Brönsted-Lowry notation, water, as a weak acid, can be described by the equilibrium expression:

$$2H_2O \Leftrightarrow H_3O^+ + OH^- \qquad [2.18]$$

$$\frac{[H_3O^+] \times [OH^-]}{[H_2O]^2} = K_w \qquad [2.19]$$

By convention, the concentration of water is constant, so the expression simplifies to:

$$[H_3O^+] \times [OH^-] = K_w \qquad [2.20]$$

At 25°C, $K_w = 1 \times 10^{-14}$. When the individual concentrations of the $[H_3O^+]$ and $[OH^-]$ ions are equal, each would therefore be 1×10^{-7}. A *neutral* solution is defined as a solution where the concentrations $[H_3O^+]$ and $[OH^-]$ are equal. An *acidic* solution is defined as a solution where $[H_3O^+]$ is greater than 1×10^{-7} ; a *basic* solution is defined as a solution where $[H_3O^+]$ is less than 1×10^{-7} . Remember that the product of the $[H_3O^+]$ and $[OH^-]$ concentration at any given temperature is equal to the constant, K_w. As $[H_3O^+]$ rises, $[OH^-]$ falls reciprocally. Rather than using the cumbersome scientific notation, based on powers of 10, by convention, $[H_3O^+]$ and $[OH^-]$ concentrations can be expressed as their negative logarithmic equivalent for simplicity's sake. The pH scale (0–14) is the expression of $[H_3O^+]$ concentration as a negative logarithm, which is equivalent to the logarithm of the reciprocal of $[H_3O^+]$:

$$\text{pH} = \log\left(\frac{1}{[H_3O^+]}\right) \qquad [2.21]$$

and likewise

$$\text{pOH} = \log\left(\frac{1}{[OH^-]}\right) \qquad [2.22]$$

and that

$$\text{pH} + \text{pOH} = \log\left(\frac{1}{K_w}\right) = 14 \qquad [2.23]$$

It is also convenient to refer to the equilibrium or ionization constant, K_a, of an acid in logarithmic notation as well. The pK_a of any given acid is defined as:

$$pK_a = \frac{1}{\log K_a} \qquad [2.24]$$

Similarly, pK_b is:

$$pK_b = \frac{1}{\log K_b} \quad [2.25]$$

Weak acids such as acetic acid, with a K_a of 1.66×10^{-5} would therefore have a pK_a, at room temperature, of

acetic acid:

$$pK_a = \frac{1}{1.66 \times 10^{-5}} = 4.77 \quad [2.26]$$

In other words, the higher the pK_a value for any acid, the weaker it is; the lower, the stronger. A similar statement could be made for the pK_b of a base; the lower the number, the weaker the base, and the higher, the stronger.

2.4 Hydrolysis

A salt comprising at least one ion which is a conjugate of either a weak acid or base can undergo with water a reaction of a general acid-base type. If we were to dissolve sodium acetate in water, the reaction that would occur could be written as:

$$CH_3COO^-Na^+ + H_2O \Leftrightarrow CH_3COOH + OH^- + Na^+ \quad [2.27]$$

where the acetate ion acts as a conjugate base; that is, it accepts a proton from water itself, or undergoes hydrolysis. A K_b could be expressed for this reaction. Since the net outcome of this reaction is to raise the $[OH^-]$, the solution would appear to be more alkaline on completion. If equations 2.27 and 2.13 from above are added together, the net reaction is equation 2.18. It follows that the net reaction constant for water K_w can be described, in this case, as the product of the two individual constants K_a and K_b:

$$K_w = K_a \times K_b \quad [2.28]$$

For many such conjugate bases of weak acids, their hydrolysis can be described by the relationship expressed in equation 2.28. Restated in a simpler way: equation 2.28 expresses a reciprocity between the relative strength of weak acids, and the hydrolysis of their conjugate bases. The weaker the acid (the higher the pK_a), the stronger the hydrolysis (or basicity) of the conjugate base derived from the acid.

Ammoniate ion can, in a similar fashion, act as a weak acid on hydrolysis. If we were to dissolve ammonium chloride in water, the following reaction would occur:

$$NH_4 + Cl^- + H_2O \Leftrightarrow NH_3 + H_3O^+ + Cl^- \quad [2.29]$$

The K_a for NH_4^+ can be obtained from the K_b for NH_3; using equation 2.16 again, the K_a for the ammoniate ion can be easily calculated.

Many heavy metal cations can be hydrolyzed to some extent in water. Fe^{+3} can combine with water in an acidic reaction to produce ferrous hydroxide:

$$pKa_1 = 7.2 \quad [2.39]$$

and
$$HPO_4^{-2} \Leftrightarrow PO_4^{-3} + H^+ \quad [2.40]$$

$$K_2 = \frac{[PO_4^{-3}]\times[H^+]}{[HPO_4^{-2}]} \quad [2.41]$$

$$pKa_2 = 11.5 \quad [2.42]$$

With polyacidic substances, the secondary ionization constant is always smaller than the primary ($K_2 < K_1$) and if a third were possible, it would be smaller still, etc. An overall reaction constant for the formation of phosphate ion from dibasic phosphate can be written by combining the individual constants K_1 and K_2:

$$K = K_1K_2 = \frac{[HPO_4^{-2}]\times[H^+]}{[H_2PO_4^-]} \times \frac{[PO_4^{-3}]\times[H^+]}{[HPO_4^{-2}]} = \frac{[PO_4^{-3}]\times[H^+]^2}{[H_2PO_4^-]} \quad [2.43]$$

2.6 Acid–base titrations

When small amounts of base are added incrementally to an acid solution, the pH rises with each additional increment; a plot of pH versus amount of base added would look in many cases like the curve marked *A* illustrated in Fig. 2.1 for acetic acid. Close to the pK_a for acetic acid (4.77), and the titration curve tends to exhibit an inflection point (the direction of curvature changes), that is, as more base is added, no concomitant rise in pH seems to occur. Acetic acid forms a strong buffer pair with

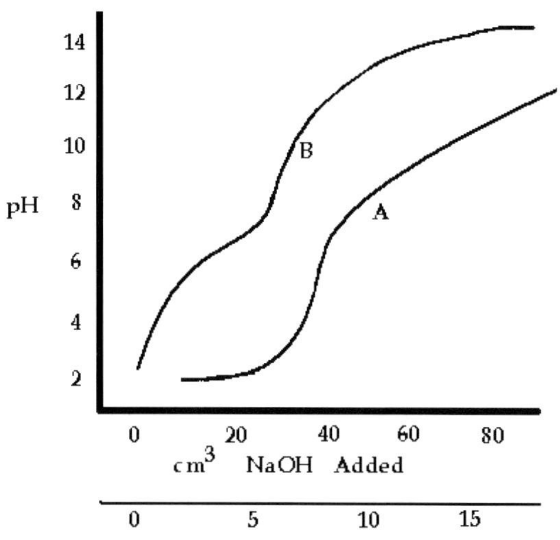

Figure 2.1 Titration curves for acetic acid (A) and linseed oil (B)

its conjugate base at or about its pK_a. Within about a pH unit or so, above and below the pK_a for most acids (and the pK_b for basic materials), an acid (or basic) functional group will exhibit some degree of buffering ability (see Table 2.1).

For the 'titration' curve for a relatively fresh linseed oil film (Wolbers n.d.) (a solid material, marked *B* in Fig. 2.1), where swelling (film thickness) is plotted against the amount of base added (rather than a simple change in pH) to a solution in contact with the film, at least one inflection point is also evident on or about nearly the same pH as the acetic acid curve. The observation can be explained by the presence of free fatty acid groups on, and in, the oil film. Even though the film is a solid material, and while the specific pK_as of the constituent fatty acids vary slightly, most have a limiting pK_a value of about 4.9. Below that value, these fatty acids are virtually un-ionized, and insoluble (and in this case unwetted) in water. But as the pH is raised slowly, and approaches 4.9 more closely, more ionization occurs in these materials. As these weak fatty acids become increasingly ionized, they take on more water, especially at the carboxylate end of their structures, and the linseed oil film swells slightly with water. As more base is added to the solution applied to the linseed oil film, at a certain point, above a pH of about 8.5 or so, the film thickness expands almost exponentially, and never seems to form a definite inflection point. At pHs above about 8.5, another kind of chemical reaction takes place; the hydrolysis of ester groups within the general triglyceride structure:

$$\left(CH_3(CH_2)_{16-18}CO_2\right)_3(CH_2)_2CH + H_2O \Leftrightarrow \qquad [2.44]$$
$$\left(CH_3(CH_2)_{16-18}CO_2\right)_2CH_2CHCOH + CH_3(CH_2)_{16-18}CO_2H$$

Above a pH of 8.5, the oil film is simply disrupted (and eventually solubilized) by the splitting off of constituent fatty acids from the parent triglyceride that forms the backbone of the polymerized oil film.

Natural resins that contain an ionizable group also exhibit a sharp increase in swelling (and dissolution) at or near the pK_as of the ionizable groups in contact with aqueous solutions. Abietic acid, one of the main constituent materials in rosin that has been heated, has a single carboxylic acid group in its structure (at the C3 position) (Mills & White 1994: 98). The pK_a of this acidic group is 6.73; while this means that the group is very weakly acidic, it does suggest that if the pH were raised to 6.73, the group would be half ionized (half deprotonated or anionic in character). At higher pHs (say, a unit or so above the pK_a) the carboxylic acid group would be fully ionized and, generally, most of the abietic acid molecules would be substantially hydrated, or soluble in water at that point. If the pH were to fall well below the pK_a (again, say a pH unit below the pK_a), abietic acid would remain minimally hydrated, and would remain a solid material in contact with aqueous solutions.

Proteinaceous binding materials also exhibit an interesting response to aqueous conditions, and specifically changes in pH. The protein fraction of whole milk has been exploited as a paint-binding system; by allowing bacteria to grow in whole milk, a curd, or protein-rich fraction from the milk can precipitate, and be collected as a separate fraction. While the exact composition of such preparations may vary from preparation to preparation, the major or bulk proteins that constitute the curd exhibit iso-electric points at various pHs throughout the acid range. As an *amphoteric* molecule, a protein carries both acidic and basic functional groups, and can act as either acid or base. At the iso-electric points, the number of ionized acidic groups exactly balances the number of basic groups that are protonated, and the protein molecules appear electrically neutral, and, coincidentally, least soluble in water. The major proteins that form the curd in acidified milk exhibit a net iso-electric point at or about 5.5 (Long 1961). At this pH, they tend to precipitate, and remain minimally soluble in aqueous solutions. If the pH is raised substantially above or below this point, the proteins start to dissolve in water (or at least swell) as they become increasingly anionic or cationic, respectively, in character.

2.7 Solubility product

For sparingly soluble electrolytes in water, equilibrium conditions can exist between whatever ionic species can dissolve to a point of saturation, and the remaining undissolved electrolyte. Similarly to the Law of Mass Action, at any given temperature, for sparingly soluble electrolytes in saturated solutions, the equilibrium relationship can be stated as a general principle: *At saturation, the product of the molar concentrations of the ions of the electrolyte, raised to the proper powers, is a constant* (Smoot *et al.* 1983: 496). As with the general Law of Mass Action, the powers are the coefficients of each ionic species in the balanced equation for the dissolution reaction. For the hypothetical electrolyte A_mB_n, the ionization reaction would be:

$$A_mB_n \Leftrightarrow mA + nB \qquad [2.45]$$

and the solubility product expression would be:

$$[A]^m \times [B]^n = \mathrm{K_{sp}} \qquad [2.46]$$

where the square brackets indicate the molar concentrations of the separate ionic species A and B. As an example, $CaCO_3$ (as aragonite in seashells for example) is sparingly soluble in water, to approximately 0.013 g l^{-1}:

$$\mathrm{CaCO_3 \Leftrightarrow Ca^{+2} + CO_3^{-2}} \qquad [2.47]$$

The K_{sp} can be calculated from the product of the molar amounts of each species in solution (the molecular weight of $CaCO_3$ is 100.09; for each species this would be 1.29×10^{-4} moles of each species), so

$$[1.29 \times 10^{-4}] \times [1.29 \times 10^{-4}] = \mathrm{K_{sp}} = 1.66 \times 10^{-8} \qquad [2.48]$$

Again, since expressing K_{sp}s in scientific notation can be cumbersome, the negative logarithm K_{sp} or pK_{sp} may be more useful for solubility product data:

$$-\log \mathrm{K_{sp}} = -\log(1.66 \times 10^{-8}) = 8.22 \qquad (2.49)$$

Calcium carbonate is useful as another example of an aspect of equilibrium reactions; an electrolyte which is only sparingly soluble in water may be put into solution if its ions can be converted to other species of weak electrolytes. If an acid is added to the calcium carbonate solution, the added hydrogen ions will react with any carbonate ion present in solution to form carbonic acid H_2CO_3. The equilibrium between the solid calcium carbonate, and the small portion of it soluble in water is displaced by the removal of CO_3 ion, and the net effect is to bring more carbonate ion into solution, dissolving a bit more of the solid until a new equilibrium position is reached. In other words, by reacting an acid with the $CaCO_3$, we can effectively dissolve more of it than might otherwise go into solution at any given temperature. Acids are good 'solvents' for carbonates. In Chapter 6 another application will be introduced – the idea of increasing the solubility of low K_{sp} electrolytes or salts by complexing (sequestering) the metal ions they contain.

Case History 2.1: James Peale, *Portrait of Mary Morris Jones* (oil on canvas, early nineteenth century)

The portrait came to the studio because it had sustained a rather large and jagged tear to the primary linen support. The portrait was glazed, and, when the single nail which fixed the frame to the wall failed, the glass shattered, tearing the portrait. On examination in the studio, it appeared under near ultraviolet light that the portrait carried a single application of a natural resin varnish on its surface. The varnish was still relatively continuous, and only lightly discoloured (yellowed) with ageing or exposure. Evidence of minor abrasion to the paint film, as well as brushmarking in the varnish, suggested that the present clear coating was not the original varnish applied by the artist. The varnished painting surface was substantially soiled, and apart from the difficult structural stabilization and repair required by the tear to the primary support, the cleaning requirements for the painting were minimal. Since the present varnish was still forming a continuous film, and was only lightly discoloured, it was decided that the painting was to be surface cleaned of soiling materials only, and that the present varnish coating was to be maintained. Cross-sectioned samples that were removed from the painting were stained with fluorochrome dyes to aid in the characterization of binding media. The results suggested that the painting was principally constructed from oil-bound paints, and it, indeed, had only a single natural resin coating (estimated by its autofluorescence colour in the near UV) that gave a weak staining for an oil component as well. The painting was consolidated along the tear it had sustained. Temporary adhesive strips were used to secure the tear until it could be mended in a more permanent fashion. The painting was then surface cleaned with the following mixture:

water (deionized)	100 ml
acetic acid (glacial)	0.5 ml

the pH of this solution was adjusted with 1 N NaOH added dropwise with stirring, to bring the pH up to 5.5; a portion of this solution was set aside (50 ml), and then the following ingredients were added to the remainder:

Triton X-100	0.3 ml
methyl cellulose (4000 cps grade)	1 g

Typically, this gelled mixture (with all four ingredients) was applied to the varnished painting surface, stirred with a soft sable brush (00), and then wiped from the surface almost immediately with a dry cotton swab. The cleaned, varnished paint surface remained clear and unblanched after cleaning; the treated area was rinsed with the portion of the acetic acid/water pH 5.5 solution that was set aside initially. Again, a dry cotton swab was used to clear and dry the rinsed surface. The rinsed surface was then allowed to air dry, given a final rinse with mineral spirits, and dried with a soft cotton pad.

Commentary

An aqueous solution can be used to surface clean a varnished oil painting if certain precautions are taken. Natural resins like dammar and mastic which have been traditionally used for varnishes on easel paintings age and oxidize on exposure; they inevitably form weakly acidic resin acids that often exhibit pK_as in the range of about 6.5–7.5 (abietic acid, as a diterpene acid, has a pK_a as high as 7.6). By lowering the pH to 5.5 it is below the range in which many of these resin acid materials would be substantially ionized. Water is a powerful solvent for these materials, and would wet onto them, swell and disrupt them, or even solubilize or extract portions of films containing these materials if the cleaning were carried out at or above their pK_as. Water, at a pH of 7, is high enough in pH to disrupt these film-forming materials if they contain substantial numbers of acidic groups initially, or as they age on exposure. We also have to consider the response of the materials in the paints underneath this surface coating; the pK_as of the fatty acids that comprise a linseed oil binder in a paint film would also certainly swell or be affected by water at a pH of 5.5, although the effect may be slow, and, practically speaking, of small consequence if we do not expose the paint/varnish surface; that is, as long as the varnish itself is undisrupted by our treatment, and remains more or less the 'surface' we actually contact during cleaning (see Figs 2.1.1 and 2.1.2). At a pH of 5.5 we are working below the pK_as of many resin acids, and may, if the varnish layer is continuous enough, avoid even minimally contacting the underlying paint surface. There is really no advantage in dropping lower than 5.5 in terms of pH; the more acidic the solution, the less risk we run of swelling directly the varnish or oil-binding materials, but we have to consider the other likely components in a paint film as well. Recall from above that acidic solutions can be powerful solvents for hydrolyzing certain salts like carbonates. Certain pigments, extenders, and the like might be affected by increasingly acidic solutions. As a general rule, natural resin films will always be cleaned more successfully at slightly acidic pHs (say in the 5.5–6.5 range); oil-bound paint surfaces may be cleaned in the range 5.5–8.5. The contact time in this case was minimal and restricted: the cleaning solution was applied as a gel and wiped from the surface almost immediately, rinsed, and then dried with a second rinse of mineral spirits. All of the components of the cleaning mixture are certainly water soluble and should be rinsed with the acetic acid/water pH 5.5 rinse. Water alone as a rinsing aid might be inappropriate because the pH would undoubtedly rise on the cleaned surface to 7 as the acetic acid/acetate buffer created in the cleaning mixture was removed by

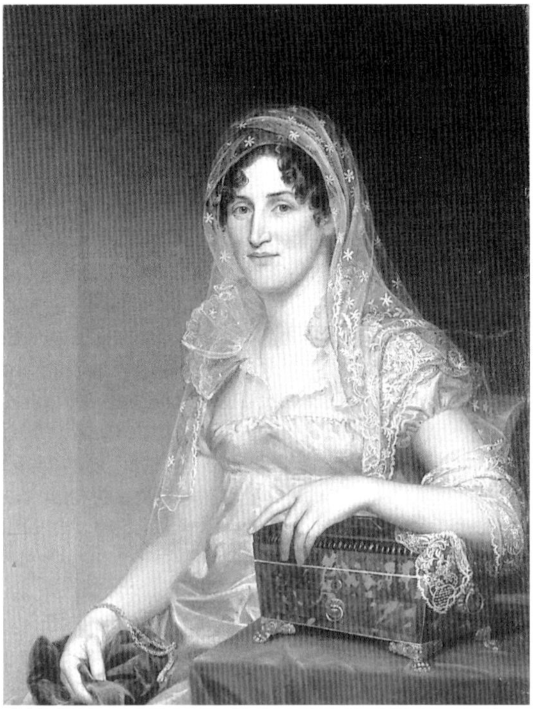

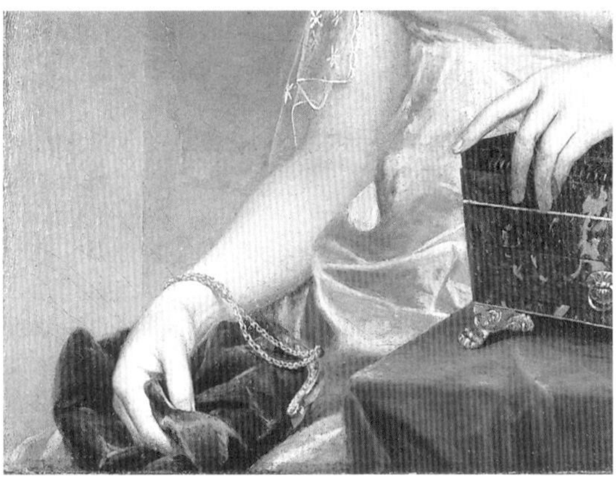

Figures 2.1.1 and 2.1.2 James Peale, *Portrait of Mary Morris Jones* (oil on canvas, nineteenth century) (see colour plates)

dilution. We might run the risk of blanching or disrupting the cleaned varnish surface at even that slightly higher pH. Triton X-100 is a mild nonionic surfactant that is included as a general soil dispersant; however, it is simply and more efficiently rinsed with mineral spirits than with repeated water rinses (see especially Chapter 4 for a broader discussion of detergents and detergency). The inclusion of methylcellulose (4000 cps) raises the viscosity of the cleaning mixture to help restrict or limit its application to small areas, and its inclusion is a general aid in suspending solubilized soiling materials (again see Chapter 4, 'suspension aids'). The heart of the cleaning mixture here is an acetic acid/acetate buffer (pK_a 4.77) in a water solution. 0.5 ml of glacial (or concentrated) acetic acid in 100 ml of water is equivalent to approximately a 50 mM solution of the acid. By itself, the pH of the acid in water would be quite low;

it is adjusted upwards to 5.5 with the addition of a base (1 M NaOH), to create a nearly balanced amount of acetic acid and acetate ion in solution. Alternatively, we could have simply weighed out and added nearly equimolar amounts (25 mM each) of acetic acid and sodium acetate to water for the same effect. Interestingly, the amount of buffer used was determined largely by the surface pH of the varnished painting; a surface pH electrode was touched to the dampened painting surface and indicated a surface pH of 6.5 (in other words, on wetting, a $[H_3O^+]$ concentration of 3.3×10^{-6}M was measured). If this represents the amount of acid our buffer must absorb and still maintain a 'balanced' equilibrium, an excess of both buffer acid and conjugate base are needed; at least substantially greater than the anticipated amount of acid added on contact. Usually three orders of magnitude greater is sufficient; here, at 25 mM each, buffer acid and conjugate base are about 7000 times greater in concentration than the amount of acid being added on contact. There are basic materials besides NaOH for raising or adjusting the pH. Bases such as KOH, NH_4OH, or organic amines like triethanolamine might be useful if raising the pH were the only issue, but the choice of base, and more specifically, cation ($Na+$, $K+$, etc.) will also affect the condition of the surface we leave behind after cleaning. The acid groups present in the resin varnish can be left in the free acid form after rinsing at a pH of 5.5, or as a salt, if a sufficient amount of a monovalent cation is available to form a salt with them. Certain cations are more effective at maintaining electrical neutrality on the cleaned surface. In this case, without some sodium ions (however few) left behind on the cleaned surface, the cleaned resin surface would be quick to pick up an electrostatic charge, and attract more airborne soiling materials on its surface.

Case History 2.2: F. Schoonover, *The Prodigal Father* (oil on canvas, 1932)

On initial examination, *The Prodigal Father* appeared to be an oil painting on a pre-primed canvas, and looked as if it did not carry a varnish or clear coating material on its surface. Its surface was weathered and soiled, but additionally carried a deposit of white, waxy, rather intractable, crystalline material which was especially disfiguring in the darker passages of the painting. It was originally painted to serve as the source image for a photo-engraving, to be used as an illustration for a magazine short story, and later to be discarded. The painting survived as a valued object in its own right, and was now in need of conservation and cleaning. Under near UV light, the painting appeared to be unvarnished; the soiling material 'masked' what little auto-fluorescence was present on the painted surface. A small sample was removed from one of the darkest areas on the male figure, mounted, cross-sectioned, and examined with the microscope – this again suggested that the painting was not varnished. Staining of the cross-section with a lipid-soluble dye helped characterize the paint-binding material as a drying oil. The cross-sectioned sample also revealed a relatively unweathered surface to the oil paint, but did give the hint of the presence of another, whitish crystalline material on the paint surface. To characterize the whitish material further, a second sample was removed by scalpel from the painting's surface with the aid of a stereo microscope. The sample material was pressed in a diamond cell and its infrared spectrum obtained using an FTIR microscope. The spectrum suggested that the material was a fatty acid salt. A simple microchemical spot test for lead (KI in a weakly acidic solution) suggested that the fatty acid material was a Pb^{+2} salt of the material. The painting was cleaned with the following mixture:

water (deionized)	100 ml
triethanolamine	0.75 ml

the pH of this solution was adjusted with 1 M HCl added dropwise with stirring, to bring the pH down to 8.5; then the following ingredients were added to the remainder:

Triton X-100	0.6 ml
methyl cellulose (4000 cps grade)	2 g

Typically, this gelled mixture was applied to the painted surface, stirred with a soft sable brush (00), and then wiped from the surface almost immediately with a dry cotton swab. The cleaned paint surface remained clear and unblanched after cleaning; the treated area was rinsed with a dilute solution of NaOH in water (0.002M, pH 8.5). Again, a dry cotton swab was used to clear and dry the rinsed surface. The rinsed surface was then allowed to air dry, and given a final rinse of mineral spirits, and patted dry with a soft cotton pad.

Commentary

As with Case History 2.1, it was possible to clean the surface of this painting using an aqueous system. Generally, the pH can be raised to 8.5 on an oil film, and, given the relatively short contact time involved, will remove soiling material from an oil paint without disrupting it. Raising the pH above 7 will always have a general surface-cleaning effect; most of the weakly acidic materials in soils will be fully ionized at that point and will come into solution in water. At higher pHs, cleaning will also occur, but with the added disruption of the oil surface itself as it is saponified or broken down. It was suggested above that most surface cleaning on oil films can safely occur between a pH of 5.5 and 8.5, however, we should apply certain qualifications. If there were other water-soluble components in the paint film; if it was extremely weathered or oxidized itself; or if the paint film was 'leanly' bound (in other words, far above the critical pigment-binder ratio for a serviceable coating), then we might forego an aqueous method. The other interesting aspect of the soiling or disfiguring material on this surface is the likely presence of a fatty acid salt of Pb^{+2} (or metal soap). Lead stearate (and palmitate) can be present on the surface of a weathered oil-bound paint, and is a normal feature of its deterioration. It can also be present in substantial quantities by itself as a drier and pigment dispersal aid in some more modern paints (i.e. those made from the later nineteenth century onwards). It seems significant that it was present everywhere (especially the darker, non-white areas or passages) on the painted surface (see Fig. 2.2.1). It was suspected that this material was present in large quantities simply because the artist had chosen an inexpensive and/or poorly made artist's tube colour, one that carried an excess of the metal soap. Metal soaps are extremely insoluble in water, so the inclusion of a surfactant in this cleaning mixture was more to effect its removal than any other component. Again, the mixture

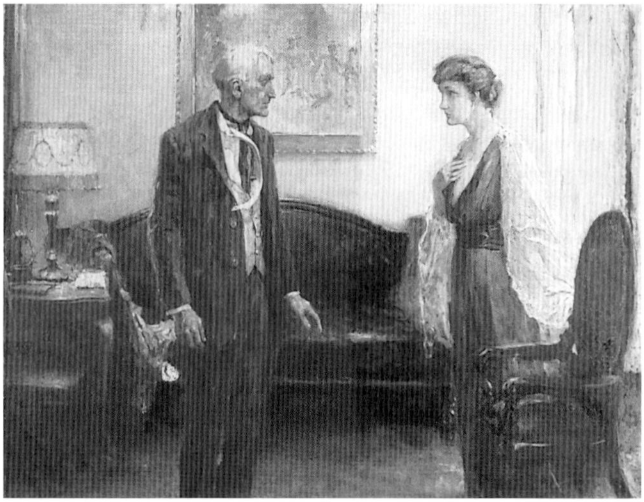

Figure 2.2.1 F. Schoonover, *The Prodigal Father* (oil on canvas, 1932) (see colour plates)

was gelled with methyl cellulose (4000 cps) to help restrict its application, and facilitate its removal. In this case the pH was adjusted to 8.5, using triethanolamine (pK_a 7.8) as the buffer. A solution of 0.75 ml triethanolamine in 100 ml of water represents about a 50 mM amount of the buffer altogether. Again, as with Case History 2.1, the amount of buffer is largely determined by the amount of acid (or base) present on the surface of the painting that we are likely to encounter when we wet the surface. Triethanolamine has a pK_a in the relevant range, but it also exhibits two other features that might be useful in this case (and might recommend it over other potential buffering compounds). Triethanolamine is a weak metal-complexing agent (and there was a predominance of Pb^{+2} salts on the painting surface; metal-complexing agents will be examined later in Chapter 6), and it has a slight solvency effect (it is an alcoholic amine) that might aid in the roll-up or dispersal of the metal/fatty acid salt present (see Chapter 4 on detergency). The rinsing in this case was done at a slightly elevated pH; all four of the components are water soluble of course, but again, the surface was rinsed to remove the majority of the water-soluble residual materials first, allowed to air dry, and then rinsed a second and final time with mineral spirits to remove the last traces of Triton X-100 that might have remained on the surface. A very dilute solution of NaOH was used as the water rinse, because at the concentration used (2 mM) enough Na^+ ions would be left on the cleaned paint surface to leave it electrically neutral. It has been estimated from conductivity measurements (300–1000 μS is a typical value to observe) on oil-bound paint surfaces that a 2–3 mM amount of a monovalent ion such as Na+ or K+ in solution may equal the normal ion concentrations on these surfaces; here we are simply leaving the surface at about the same ion concentration at which we found it.

3

Surfactants and affinity surfactants

3.1 Surface activity and surfactants

Surface activity is generally defined as the tendency of a solute to collect at an interface (Osipow 1962: 144). Surfactants are molecules that, by and large, demonstrate a propensity towards surface activity because of structural disparities that exist intrinsically in these molecules. Generally, one portion of the surfactant is polar, while another is decidedly non-polar or only hydrocarbon-like in character. In an aqueous solution for instance, the polar end of the surfactant is usually so strongly attracted to the surrounding water that the entire molecule remains in solution, despite the hydrocarbon moiety attached to it. But at a sufficiently high concentration, a surfactant will collect at an interface or surface (usually one less polar than the water itself) spontaneously, oriented in such a way as to arrange all of the hydrocarbon portions of its structure away from the water, and onto the surface or interface, and the polar portions towards the surrounding water. Thermodynamically, this is the least energy-demanding arrangement for the surfactant to take on – grouping non-polar hydrocarbon portions away from water, where little secondary bonding can occur, and orienting the polar portions towards the water, to create stabilizing dipolar or hydrogen bonding interactions.

Conventional soaps behave as surfactants in water, in just the way described above. A fatty acid soap such as palmitic acid (Fig. 3.1) is soluble in water, as long as the carboxylic acid group at the end of the molecule is substantially ionized. This single carboxylate ion is sufficiently attracted to the surrounding water molecules so as to keep the entire molecule in solution, despite the rather long (C16) hydrocarbon chain attached to it. At sufficiently high concentrations, palmitic acid collects at oily (hydrocarbon) surfaces or interfaces, and orients itself spontaneously at the boundary between water and the oily surface or interface, with the hydrocarbon 'tail' of the molecule attracted to the oily surface, and the carboxylate end pointed

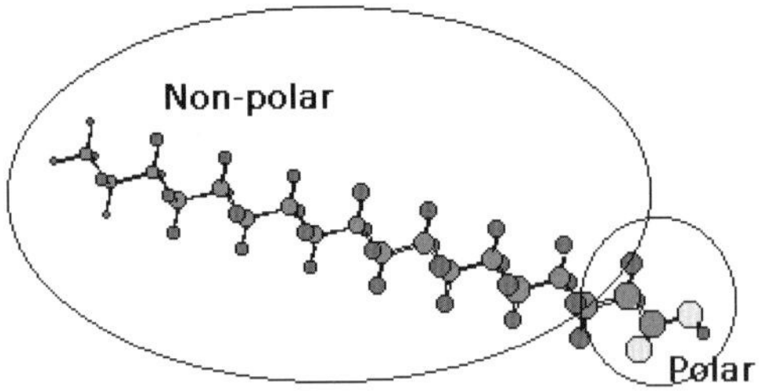

Figure 3.1 Palmitic acid

towards the water. However, depending on the relative polarity of the surface or interface with respect to water, this orientation might change. A palmitic acid molecule in solution in water would align itself to a metal surface with the polar end (carboxylate ion) attracted to the metal surface, and the hydrocarbon chain pointed out into the water, because in this case the metal would hold a greater attraction for the carboxylate end of the molecule than would water. Surfactants generally exhibit polar and non-polar tendencies in the same molecular structure, and it is this disparity or dual character inherent in them that is the driving force for their collection on surfaces or at interfaces between materials of equally disparate character in terms of polarity and non-polarity.

3.2 Structural classification of surfactants

In the present context, surfactants will be considered as primarily water-soluble compounds that exhibit some *relative* degree of surface activity towards hydrocarbon-containing materials or surfaces (oils, waxes, fats, resins, and aliphatic solvents). The word relative is emphasized because, depending on the exact structure of the surfactant and certain conditions in the water surrounding it, a range of surface activity can be manifested in these structures. For convenience, the following definitions will be used throughout this text: the polar end of a surfactant structure will be referred to as the *hydrophilic* (Greek for water-loving) end of the molecule; the hydrocarbon end of the molecule will be called the *lipophilic* (oil-loving) end or portion of the surfactant. Hydrophilic functional groups can be characterized by the types of weak secondary bonds (hydrogen or dipolar) they can establish or form with water. Alcohols, thiols, amines, carboxylate, sulfates, sulfonates, etc. all have polar groups that would be considered hydrophilic. Linear, branched, cyclic or even aromatic hydrocarbons would comprise the usual range of lipophilic groups or structures. For convenience, a list of surfactant structures is presented in Table 3.1 to show the breadth of structural types and combinations possible. The structures are grouped according to similarity in terms of the polar or hydrophilic functional groups. Thus, all acid polar groups are placed under the general category of *anionic* structures, basic polar groups are categorized as *cationic* structures, and non-ionizable structures like alcohols, etc. as *nonionics*. *Amphoterics* are structures that are either anionic or cationic in character, depending on the pH of the surrounding water. *Miscellaneous* structures are those odd materials like certain polymers or fluorine-containing structures that show surface activity under certain limited or special conditions.

Table 3.1 Examples of surfactant structures/types

Detergent	CMC (mM)	Aggregation number	Molecular weight
Anionic			
Caprylic acid, Na salt	351	–	166.2
Cholic acid, Na salt	14	2–4	430.6
Deoxycholic acid, Na salt	5	4–10	414.6
Lauryl sulfate, Na salt	8.27	62	288.5
Cationic			
Dodecylrimethylammonium chloride	14	–	308.4
Cetylypyridinium chloride	0.9	–	274
Amphoteric			
CHAPS	8	10	614.9
CHAPSO	8	11	630.9
Nonionic			
Nonidet P-40	0.29	–	602.8
Triton X-100	0.24	140	624.9
Aerosol OT	0.23	–	725.3
Miscellaneous			
Surynol 61	0.1	–	127
FC-176	0.1	–	1000–2000

3.3 Properties of solutions containing surfactants

Lowering the surface energy of a liquid has the effect of allowing the liquid to wet and spread over surfaces more easily. The surface energy of a liquid like water depends on the potential energy of the electromagnetic field which extends outwards from the outermost surface layer of water molecules. The surface energy is greatest when the *activity* (or the energy associated with the weak secondary forces between the surface water molecules) is maximized in this surface layer of water molecules. For the potential energy (and therefore the surface energy) of this field to be at a *minimum*, the water molecules (and any solute dissolved in the water for that matter) have to orient themselves so that the least active portions of their structure are pointed outwards. When a surfactant, in particular, is dissolved in water at room temperature at a sufficient concentration to begin to affect appreciably the outermost boundary layer of water, the surfactant molecules collect at the air/water interface with the hydrocarbon (least active) portions of their structures pointed towards the air, and the more active portions of their structure (polar groups) pointed inwards towards the water itself.

This arrangement is simply a consequence of the 'work' required to insert or dissolve the surfactant molecule into water at the water/air boundary; the least amount of chemical 'work' is expended (and the reaction is likely to occur, in this case, to form a solution) when the energy gained by forming new water-to-hydrophilic group interactions nearly offsets the energy lost or expended in breaking water-to-water bonds, and the work to exclude the lipophilic portions of the surfactant from water. In the bulk solution, the chemical 'work' in dissolving a surfactant is minimized by forming aggregates of the surfactant (*micelles*) where the

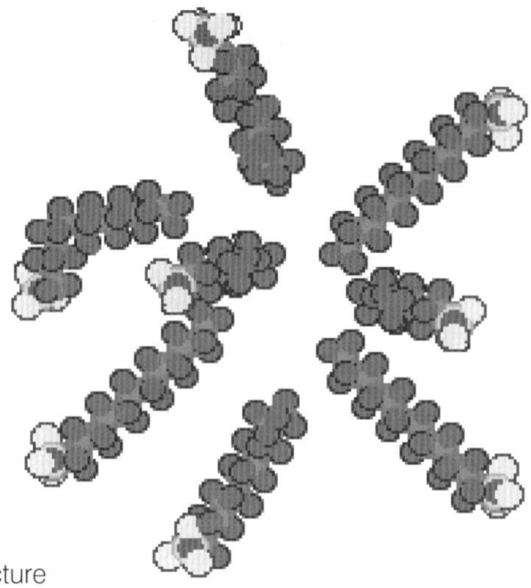

Figure 3.2 Micelle structure

lipophilic ends of the surfactants tend to collect together, and the hydrophilic ends tend to point outwards into the water (see Fig. 3.2). Here the work of dissolving the surfactant, i.e., breaking water-to-water bonds, is more than offset by the energy gained in creating new water-to-hydrophile, and lipophile-to-lipophile interactions in the micellular arrangement.

3.4 Critical micelle concentration (CMC)

Aqueous solutions of surfactants can exhibit marked changes in their physical properties over a very narrow range of surfactant concentration. Below a certain minimal concentration, the dissolved surfactant behaves as if it were any solute dissolved in water; lowering the freezing point, raising the boiling point, lowering the vapour pressure, and, if it is an ionic structure, increasing the conductivity of water. At the point where enough surfactant molecules are in solution effectively to lower the surface energy, and begin to form internally in the solution into micelle-type structures, most of the physical properties of the solution will appear to change dramatically. Conductivity (σ), viscosity (η), refractive index (n_0), and surface tension (γ), to name just a few, all change as a function of micellular formation or aggregation (Osipow 1962: 185). The concentration at which this dramatic change takes place in solution properties is called the *critical micelle concentration* (CMC) for the surfactant, and it is a characteristic and fundamental property of each individual surfactant structure (see Figs 3.3 and 3.4). As an example, for an anionic soap like sodium palmitate, the critical concentration is 3.4 mM. If we were to start with deionized water at room temperature, and slowly build up the palmitate concentration to just below this critical amount, as we increased the palmitate ion concentration in solution the conductivity of the water would increase linearly as a function of the amount of palmitate ion in solution (an anion). At the critical concentration for palmitate, micelles would begin to form; these aggregates or

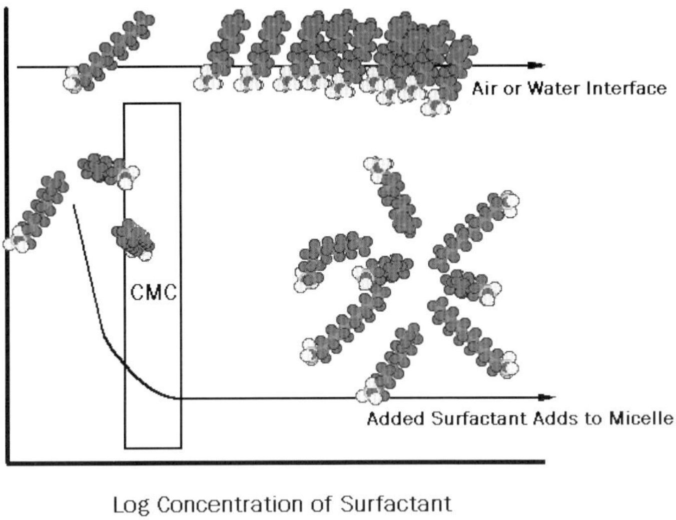

Figure 3.3 Formation of micelles and surface activity at the CMC.

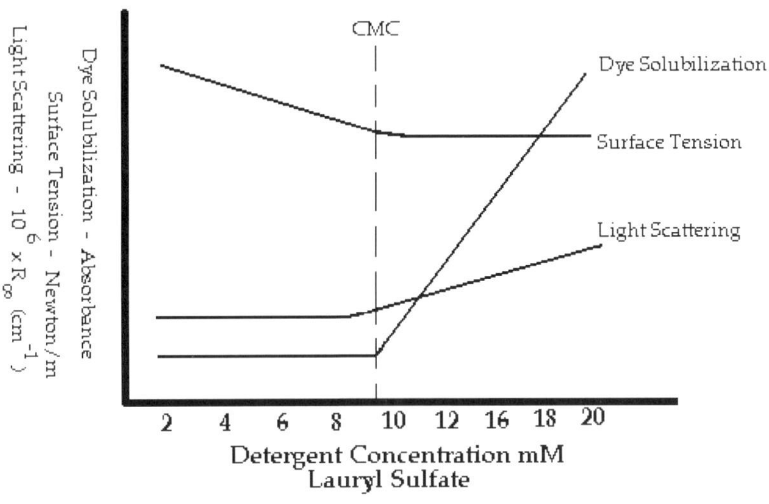

Figure 3.4 CMC determination by dye solubilization (ds), surface tension (st), or light scattering (ls) methods.

clusters would group the palmitate molecules in such a way as to make it harder generally to conduct electricity through the solution. The surface tension would decrease as we approached the critical concentration, but then would level off or remain fairly constant with additional palmitate, as most of the palmitate would be held in a micellular arrangement.

The critical micelle concentration for a surfactant is intimately tied to its structure. Remember, the 'work' required to dissolve it in water involves breaking and reforming weak secondary interactions or bonds. The longer the hydrocarbon chain or structure associated with the surfactant molecule the more 'work' will be required to try to insert it into water. If this energy is not offset by what is gained by forming new interactions between the hydrophilic group and water, the surfactant is less likely to be held or dissolved in water, and would, at very low concentrations, want to arrange itself, or form micelles (where the hydrocarbon portion of the structure is oriented away from the water) at increasingly lower concentrations. This relationship between hydrocarbon chain length and critical concentration can be expressed mathematically in the form of the Shinoda equation (Klevens 1948):

$$\log(\text{CMC}) = A - BN_c \qquad [3.1]$$

where B is a constant, A is a constant for any given temperature and homologous series of surfactant (same structural type), and N_c is the number of carbons in the hydrocarbon portion of the surfactant structure. As examples, the various values for A and B are given in Table 3.2.

For any homologous series of normal hydrocarbon-chain surfactants, the CMC value is halved for each carbon added to the chain. In actuality, when the absolute *chain length* of the hydrocarbon portion of many linear hydrocarbon surfactant structures is compared, similar CMCs are observed between them (Table 3.3).

It follows that the Shinoda equation can be modified to predict the CMCs for a wider range of linear surfactant structures from

$$\log(\text{CMC}) = 2.26 - 2.31L \qquad [3.2]$$

where L is the overall molecular ion length in nm.

Table 3.2 Values for the constants A and B for various ionic surfactants (Osipow 1962: 165)

Surfactant	Temperature (°C)	A	B
Sodium fatty acid soaps	25	1.92	0.290
Potassium fatty acid soaps	45	2.03	0.292
Alkane sulfonates	40	1.59	0.294
Alkane sulfonates	50	1.63	0.294
Alkyl sulfates	45	1.42	0.295
Alkyl ammonium chlorides	45	1.79	0.296

Table 3.3 CMC versus chain length of hydrocarbon portions of various surfactants (Osipow 1962: 166)

Surfactant	Hydrocarbon group	Length (nm) of group	CMC (mol l^{-1})	Temperature (°C)
Fatty acid	$C_{11}O^-$	1.53	0.050	25
Sulfonates	$C_{10}SO^-$	1.58	0.041	25
Sulfate	C_9OSO^-	1.56	0.052	25
Amine·HCl	$C_{10}NH^+$	1.51	0.048	25
Fatty acid	$C_{15}O^-$	2.04	0.0034	45
Sulfonate	$C_{14}SO^-$	2.07	0.0030	45
Sulfate	$C_{13}OSO^-$	2.07	0.0033	45
Amine·HCl	$C_{14}NH^+$	2.02	0.0031	40

3.4.1 *Effects of salts on CMCs*

It has been observed that ions of an opposite charge (*counter-ions*) to the charge on an ionic surfactant will depress the surfactant's observed CMC (Osipow 1962: 167). Ions of the *same* charge have no apparently similar effect. This can be explained by the fact that micellular arrangements of ionic surfactants generally have a very high surface charge density, with the arrangement and concentration of the ionized group outwards towards the water at the micelle surface. This increased charge density is usually much greater than if individual (unaggregated) similarly charged ions were in solution separately, and at about the same concentration. Consequently, counter-ions are attracted more strongly, and similarly charged ions are repelled with substantially more force at the micelle surface, than under normal ionic solution conditions. It is the increased association of counter-ions in this case that tends to depress the CMC. The relationship between counter-ion concentration and CMC can be described by the Hobbs equation (Hobbs 1951):

$$\log(\text{CMC}) = -0.50 \log[M^+] - A \qquad [3.3]$$

where M^+ is the counter-ion concentration, and A is a constant derived for each surfactant structure. Note that in the Hobbs equation, the specific monovalent counter-ion does not affect the CMC, and that A is essentially determined by the size (length) of the surfactant ion in solution.

3.4.2 *Effects of surfactant variations in structure on CMC*

In section 3.4, the relationship between CMC and hydrocarbon chain length was pointed out. It has also been demonstrated that other structural variations can influence, in a predictable way, observed CMC values. Some of the most important structure/CMC relationships are summarized below.

- The position of the hydrophilic group in the overall surfactant molecule will influence the observed CMC; as an example, when the sulfate group in a linear alkyl sulfate is located in the middle of the hydrocarbon chain, rather than at an end position, the CMC is increased.

Table 3.4 Effect of branching on CMC (Osipow 1962: 169)

Carbon no. of SO_4Na group	CMC (mM)	CMC of equivalent straight chain hydrocarbon (mM)
C1	1.65	1.65 (C14)
C2	3.26	3.30 (C13)
C3	4.52	5.8 (C12)
C4	5.76	12.0 (C11)
C5	7.95	25.0 (C10)
C6	12.3	52.0 (C9)
C7	15.8	100.0 (C8)

The observed increase is not nearly as great though, as for the equivalent linear surfactant structure of the longest hydrocarbon length section.

- The effect of one double bond in the hydrocarbon structure can increase the CMC by two to three times from the observed value for the equivalent *n*-alkane structure.

- Benzene rings (as in linear alkyl aryl sulfonates), also have the effect of raising the observed CMC. If a surfactant hydrocarbon structure were to include a benzene ring in its arrangement of carbon atoms, the CMC would increase by an amount equivalent to a linear structure of a slightly shorter hydrocarbon length (about 3.5 carbons shorter).
- The substitution of additional polar groups on the hydrocarbon chain of an *n*-alkane structure, will increase both the solubility and the CMC for the substituted structure. As an example, aleuritic acid (10,11,16-trihydroxy palmitic acid) has a CMC at least 20 times greater than that of sodium palmitate.
- Branched hydrocarbon structures exhibit a fourfold reduction in CMC if carbons are added to both branch ends.
- Additional methyl groups substituted directly on a primary amine will not substantially change the observed CMC from that predicted for the free amine.

3.4.3 Effects of other surfactants on CMC

It is often a common practice to blend one surfactant with another for a variety of reasons (cost, HLB modification (see section 5.2.3), detergency synergism, etc.). Harkins *et al.* (Harkins 1946) have described the effects of mixtures of ionic surfactants, and their effect on the observed CMCs for the individual surfactant components. When there are pronounced differences in the individual CMCs of the surfactants, the *higher* CMC surfactant will generally act, at low concentrations (lower than *its* CMC), as if it were a salt or electrolyte in solution, and depress the CMC of the other surfactant. This effect becomes even more pronounced at concentrations of the higher CMC surfactant, well above *its* CMC. When both surfactants have the same CMC they behave as if there was only a single surfactant structure present, and the theoretical CMC for both is observed for the mixture as well.

3.4.4 Effects of polar compounds and temperature on CMC

Solvents that are miscible with water, and in particular long chain fatty alcohols and amines, will act to generally depress the CMC of a surfactant. In the case of the latter, as the hydrocarbon chain is lengthened, or as the amount of polar groups increases in solution (by increasing the amount of amine or alcohol), this CMC depression is increased as well. This effect on the CMC is often exploited in shampoos and other proprietary surfactant-containing products. As the CMC is depressed (through surfactant blends, higher counter-ion concentrations, added polar compounds), less surfactant is needed in the overall cleaning system to reach the CMC and achieve the same effect (detergency, wetting, etc.) as if the surfactant were used alone. In the case of temperature in particular, the effects on CMC are more complicated. A surfactant alone will usually exhibit a higher than predicted CMC if the temperature is raised; as the free energy of a surfactant-water system is increased by heating, more 'work' is required to form micelles and more surfactant is needed to do so. When surfactants are blended with polar compounds – long chain alcohols for instance – the observed CMC may be increased or decreased depending on the temperature and the relative solubility of the alcohol in water.

3.5 Micelle size: aggregation number

The aggregation number for a surfactant is, like the CMC, a basic property for each individual surfactant, and describes a unique characteristic. It can be defined as the minimum number of surfactant molecules that is required to form a micellular structure. Surfactant micelles are dynamic structures; there is a constant exchange between surfactant molecules dissolved in the bulk solution surrounding a micelle with the surfactants that are incorporated in it, making a determination of an absolute size sometimes very difficult. Temperature, ionic strength, and other factors, including the concentration of the surfactant itself, can affect the absolute size of a micelle. Aggregation numbers are usually determined by light scattering, sedimentation rate, or low-angle x-ray scattering techniques used to determine the molecular weights of large polymers or other complex macromolecules in solution (Wennerstrom & Lindman 1979). In this case the aggregation number is simply the *time* averaged molecular weight (determined by one of the above methods) of the macromolecular complex or micelle, divided by the individual surfactant's molecular weight. Table 3.5 gives aggregation number data for a selected list of surfactants used in the present text. Deoxycholic acid, as the Na^+ salt has an aggregation number of between 3 and 12 molecules per micelle at Na^+ concentrations less than 0.1M; above 0.1M and the number increases slightly from 5 to 19. By contrast, Triton X-100 has a much greater aggregation number, between 100 and 150, at low Na^+ (< 0.01M) concentrations.

Table 3.5 Aggregation numbers for selected surfactants at two solution conditions (Neugebauer 1988: 25–7)

Surfactant	0–0.1M Na^+	0.1–0.2M Na^+
Deoxycholic acid, sodium salt	3–12	5–19
Triton X-100	100–150	–
Brij 35	40	–
Lauryl sulfate, sodium salt	62	101
Tween 80	58	–

The relationship between aggregation number and CMC can be expressed as follows (Neugebauer 1988: 41):

$$N = \frac{[S]-[CMC]}{[M]} \qquad [3.4]$$

or

$$[CMC] = [S] - N \cdot [M] \qquad [3.5]$$

where N is the aggregation number; S is the bulk surfactant concentration in mol l^{-1}; M is the micellular concentration of surfactant in mol l^{-1}; and CMC is the critical micelle concentration in mol l^{-1}.

Low aggregation number surfactants are especially important in the solubilization of certain types of materials. Low aggregation number surfactants will be discussed below in relation to polymer/surfactant systems (solvent gels, for instance) where low surfactant-to-dispersed-material ratios are important.

3.6 Micelle size and charge

A number of methods have been used to estimate micelle size (these are listed in section 3.5). Micelle size can vary specifically, though, as a function of counter-ion concentration. Not surprisingly, as the counter-ion concentration goes up, micelle size will increase, but will approach a maximum value. Concomitant with this limiting value for size will be a limit in the net number of charges (charge density) associated with its surface. Light-scattering experiments have been used to determine both micelle size and charge density. With light-scattering experiments in particular, usually plots of light scattering (or *turbidity*) versus concentration for a given surfactant (at concentrations well above the surfactant's CMC) will yield a linear plot that has, as its ordinate intercept, a specific value A (see Fig. 3.5). Now the derivation of this relationship is beyond the scope of the present text, but suffice it to say that the intercept A can be related to micelle size and charge through the following formula (Osipow 1962: 177):

$$A = \frac{q}{mM} \qquad [3.6]$$

where q is the number of charges on the micelle (charge density), m is the aggregation number, and M is the molecular weight of the surfactant. This relationship generally holds true for varying counter-ion concentrations; although a different intercept value will result at different counter-ion concentrations, as micelle size and charge are both modified (see Fig. 3.5). Table 3.6 below illustrates how charge

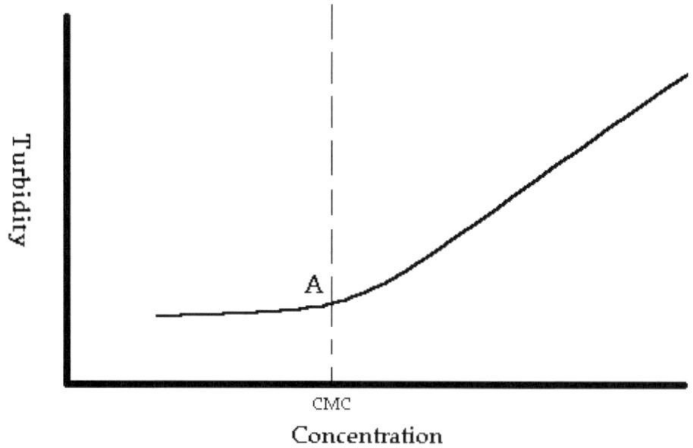

Figure 3.5 Turbidity versus surfactant concentration

Table 3.6 Charge versus aggregation number for cetylpyridinium chloride at varying NaCl concentrations (Osipow 1962: 179)

NaCl (mol l^{-1})	No. micelle charges	Aggregation number
0.01754	13	95
0.05843	16	117
0.4382	28	135
0.7304	35	137

density/counter-ion concentration/aggregate number can vary for a specific surfactant. Again, at high counter-ion concentrations, a limiting value will be reached for micelle size and charge density.

3.6 Krafft point: temperature versus solubility of surfactants

At concentrations of ionic surfactants well below the critical concentration, surfactants generally behave as any solutes might in water. Their solubility is limited, but can be increased by heating. If temperature versus solubility (molality) is plotted, up to a point, a linear relationship will be demonstrated between temperature and amount of surfactant that can be dissolved in the water. However, at some specific temperature (or more aptly, over a very narrow temperature range), the slope of the temperature versus surfactant solubility curve will increase dramatically (see Fig. 3.6). At this point micelles begin to form (since they are energetically favoured structures), and the solubility of the surfactant increases dramatically. This is the so-called *Krafft point* for a surfactant (Osipow 1962: 189); the temperature at which the solubility increases dramatically (i.e. the point at which micelles predominate). The specific concentration of surfactant at this temperature is the CMC for the surfactant at this particular temperature. It has been demonstrated (Raison 1957) that the Krafft point increases linearly as the chain length of a straight-chain hydrocarbon surfactant increases.

3.8 CMCs for nonionics

Hsiao *et al.* (1956) determined, by surface tension data, the CMCs for a series of alkylphenol nonionic structures which contained varying size polymers of ethylene oxide attached to them. The results are summarized in Table 3.7.

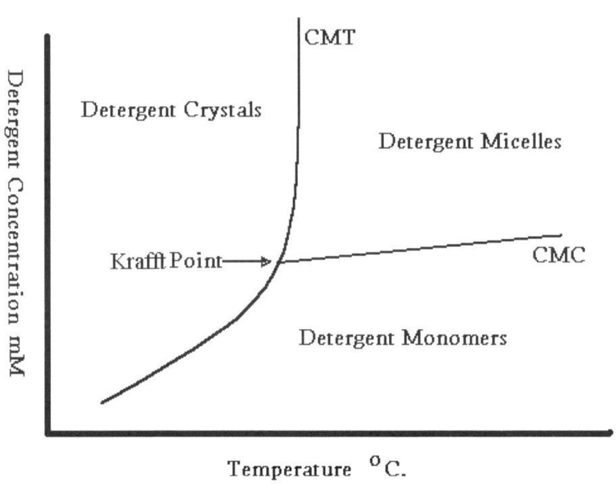

Figure 3.7 Temperature–composition phase diagram for detergent solutions

Table 3.7 CMCs of selected nonionics

Phenol	Mole ratio of ethylene oxide	CMC (mM)	Phenol	Mole ratio of ethylene oxide	CMC (mM)
octyl*	8.5	0.18–0.23	nonyl	20	0.135–0.175
nonyl	9.5	0.07–0.092	nonyl	30	0.250–0.30
nonyl	10.5	0.075–0.09	nonyl	100	1.0
nonyl	15	0.11–0.13			

*Triton X-100

The CMCs observed were nearly all of the order of 10^{-4}M; by comparison, the average ionic surfactant has a CMC in the range of 10^{-2}M (see Table 3.3, p. 32). Hsiao proposed that for ethylene oxide derivatives of nonylphenol, the equation 3.7 could be used to relate structure to observed CMC:

$$\log(\text{CMC}) = A + BR \qquad [3.7]$$

where R is the number of ethylene oxide units per mole of lipophile or hydrocarbon, and A and B are constants experimentally determined; A is 3.67 ± 0.05 in this case, but is a common value to many ethylene oxide derivatized structures; B depends on solution conditions, including counter-ion concentration, etc. The Hsiao equation basically states that the CMC increases as the size of the ethylene oxide chain increases. It is also interesting to note that, while ionic surfactants' CMCs generally increase with an increase in temperature, ethylene oxide derivatized structures of an equivalent hydrocarbon moiety tend to *decrease* in CMC as the temperature is raised; this is probably due to the increased dehydration of the ethylene oxide chain at higher temperatures (see section 5.5 on cloud point).

Water is thought to be associated with the ethereal oxygens on the ethylene oxide chains; salts (Na^+ in particular), and dilute bases tend to disrupt this hydration, and in general lower the solubility of these ethylene oxide derivatives in water. Dilute acids on the other hand, tend to increase the solubility of these surfactant structures possibly by the formation of oxonium compounds with the ethereal oxygens. Solubilized materials can apparently affect the solubility of ethoxylated structures as well. Weiden and Norton (1953) found that Triton X-100 separated from water above 60°C to form a surfactant-rich phase (cloud point); however, this temperature could be lowered by 5–50°C with the addition of aromatic solvents to the system (0.1–1% benzene, benzaldehyde, diethyl benzene, dibutyl phthalate).

In general, the ratio of ethylene oxide weight percentage of a nonionic structure to its hydrocarbon weight percentage can be used as a predictor of its solubility. At very low polyoxyethylene (POE) weight percentages, these structures are virtually insoluble in water. As the POE content increases the water solubility in general increases, until, at very high ratios of POE to hydrocarbon, these structures become insoluble in solvents and essentially only water soluble.

In the present context, both the lowering of the solubility of nonionics with certain solvents, the decrease in their CMCs with temperature, and the relative solubility of nonionics depending on their POE content, will immediately impact on such practical issues as surfactant choice, and clearance methods from paint film surfaces.

3.9 Affinity surfactants

Many compounds can show surface active properties: any 'dual character' i.e. partially hydrophilic, partially lipophilic structure will act in this way. The fundamental, and measurable, physical and chemical properties associated with each surfactant are manifestations of the specific dual nature of these types of molecules, and reflect the disparate structural properties that coexist side by side in these compounds. Linear alkyl-sulfates, -sulfonates, -carboxylates, -alcohols, and -amines especially behave predictably in terms of relating these fundamental properties to precise structural arrangements; the Shinoda equation 3.1 typifies this relationship between, for instance, CMC and hydrocarbon chain length.

When more complex hydrocarbon structures are present in a surfactant, though, or when the size and shape of the hydrocarbon moiety associated with a particular surfactant structure is large and bulky, wide deviations can occur in terms of relating the absolute structures of these types of materials to a particular ability to stabilize, for example, an oil and water interface. Take an abietic acid (Fig. 3.7) (Mills & White 1994: 98). Structurally, this diterpene acid ($C_{20}H_{30}O_2$) embraces in the same molecule both a large hydrocarbon structure and a single polar functional group at one end of the molecule.

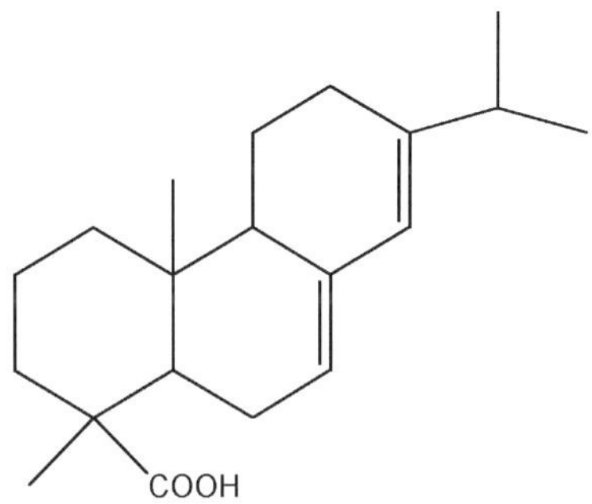

Figure 3.7 Abietic acid

When the single carboxylic acid group is fully ionized (at a pH approximately a unit above its pK_a, 6.7) abietic acid exhibits all the characteristics of an anionic surfactant (soap), in that it has a CMC (around 1 – 2 mM), and an HLB number of about 8.2 (see section 5.2.2 for a definition of the HLB system for describing surfactant strength or efficacy at solubilizing linear hydrocarbons of low molecular weight, e.g. paraffin oil). Consider though that the equivalent C30 linear fatty acid should, from the Shinoda equation, predictably have a CMC of the order of about 0.1 mM. The heterogeneity of this material as a natural product, the cyclic ring structures in the abietic acid molecule, and the units of unsaturation, all tend to raise the observed CMC and can, in some ways, account for the deviation from the ideal or predicted CMC. Abietic acid is a relatively weak surfactant for oily materials (again, see section 5.2.2). It does, however, exhibit a strong capacity for solubilizing other diterpenoid and triterpenoid structures (natural resins), largely because of the similarity in shape, or similarity in stereochemistry, to these other materials.

Structurally, the internal rings of the abietic acid molecule are in a 'chair' conformation; the hydrogen atoms and methyl groups substituted on these rings are equatorial, and both conditions allow for close associations of abietic acid to other terpenoid structures, through increased London or Van der Waals types of interactions. This added stability due to the 'fit' of one molecule to another gives abietic acid a strong ability to solubilize other terpenoid resins in particular. In other words, it is the strong affinity for one hydrocarbon structure to another that accounts for the specific solubilizing effect in this case.

Case History 3.1: E. Von Liebrach, *Winterscape: Skating on the Pond* (oil on canvas, nineteenth century)

The painting had been treated badly, as was evident from its precarious physical state when it was brought to the studio. At some point, it had been cut away from its original mounting system and lined with a glue-like adhesive onto a similar weight and structure of linen fabric. The lined painting had torn away from the stretcher and separated from it through time and neglect. Pinpoint flake losses had resulted in some loss of design materials. Its most immediate need was for structural stabilization. The darkened and discoloured resin varnish on the painting's surface also suggested a cleaning problem (see Fig. 3.1.1).

In cross-section, only a single continuous surface coating was evident, although there were what appeared to be remnants of a prior (or even original) varnish layer beneath the current continuous coating. The upper continuous varnish layer showed a positive reaction with antimony pentachloride, suggesting a wholly resinous content. The remnants of the older coating tested positively for both resin (antimony pentachloride) and oil (Rhodamine B). The paint layers themselves appeared to be bound in oil (they showed positive for Rhodamine B), and the white priming layer beneath appeared to be a combination of oil and protein (a so-called 'emulsion' ground, positive for both Rhodamine B and Lissamine Rhodamine sulfonyl chloride).

The painting had obviously undergone at least one restoration prior to its arrival at the studio. Removing the continuous coating was straightforward. Its solubility was consistent with that of a simple soft natural resin coating like dammar or mastic. A mixture of acetone and mineral spirits in a 1:1 ratio appeared to solubilize the varnish coating while leaving the oil-bound paint layers unaffected.

Once the continuous varnish coating was removed with the acetone/mineral spirits blend, the remnants of the earlier coating were more prominent. Bits of the coating remained lodged within the hollows of the brushmarks (see Fig. 3.1.2). Since the residual coating apparently contained some small portion of oil, it resisted swelling and solubilizing with solvents and solvent blends that were deemed safe for the underlying paints. And considering that it had been cleaned once in a previous restoration attempt (and not all that successfully), it had already been subjected to solvents of one form or another, and had resisted solubilization. Now, as it was further aged, it could be anticipated that this residual coating had oxidized still further and

Figure 3.1.1 E. Von Liebrach, *Winterscape: Skating on the Pond* (oil on canvas, nineteenth century), varnish partially removed (see colour plates)

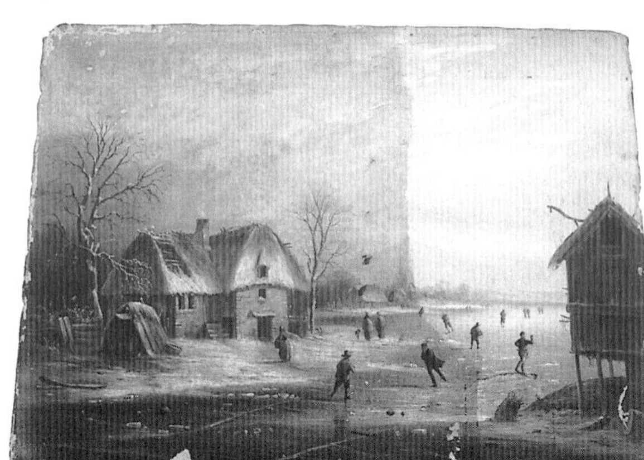

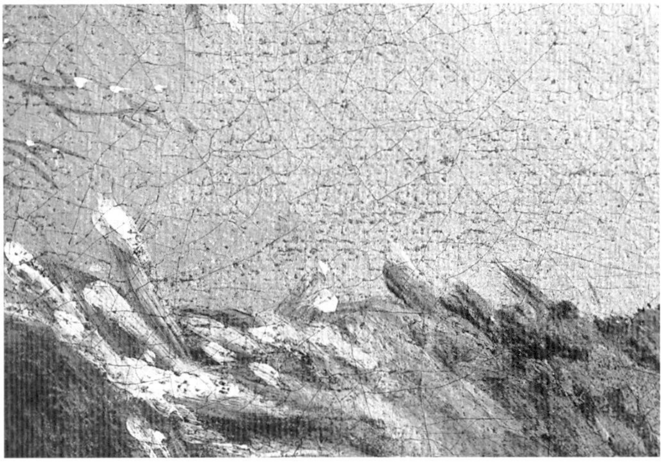

Figure 3.1.2 E. Von Liebrach, *Winterscape: Skating on the Pond* (oil on canvas, nineteenth century), coating in the brushmarks (see colour plates)

would be even more difficult to remove this time than it had been during the first restoration attempt. It was not surprising then, that very polar solvents and mixtures were necessary to resolubilize the residual coating. In spot tests, alcohols, alcohol/ketone blends, pyridine, and DMF-containing mixtures removed the residues but clearly at the expense of the surrounding oil paint as well.

A resin soap of the following formulation was made to address the residual coating material:

water (deionized)	100 ml
abietic acid (free acid)	2 g
triethanolamine	5 ml

1 N HCl was added dropwise to adjust the pH to 8.5, then the following was added:

Triton X-100	1 ml
hydroxypropylmethyl cellulose (4000 cps)	2 g

The preparation of the triethanolamine abietate resin soap was as follows. The abietic acid (technical grade, approx. 85% pure), as the free acid, was dissolved in 100 ml of water with the rapid addition of 5 ml of triethanolamine (the free acid of abietic acid is only sparingly soluble in water; its pK_a is approximately 6.7) with stirring on a magnetic stirrer. Any undissolved materials were filtered out of the solution after 1 minute of stirring. Dilute hydrochloric acid (1N HCl) was used to bring the pH down to 8.5 for the filtered solution. Triton X-100 was then added to the resin soap solution, and allowed to dissolve. Lastly, the hydroxypropylmethyl cellulose was added and the resulting mixture stirred until a uniform clear yellowish gel was formed. Typically, the mixture was applied to areas with residual coating using a small (00) sable brush. It was allowed to remain for a moment before a dry cotton swab was used to roll it off the paint film surface. The area thus treated was cleared with saliva, allowed to dry, and then rinsed with mineral spirits. The cleaned paint film was quite saturated in appearance, and showed no signs of added abrasion in the area of cleaning (see Fig. 3.1.3).

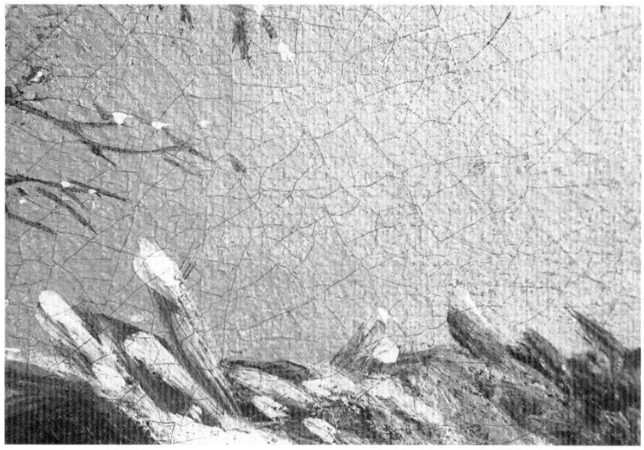

Figure 3.1.3 E. Von Liebrach, *Winterscape: Skating on the Pond* (oil on canvas, nineteenth century), detail, after cleaning (see colour plates)

Commentary

The residual coating material on the surface of this portrait is typical of certain picture varnishes in that it contained a small amount of a drying oil component. Drying oils such as linseed oil were typically added to dammar to give it added strength and flexibility. The oil resisted swelling and/or solubilization even with polar solvents, due largely to its polymerization. The previous restorer chose to leave material in the deeper recesses of the brushmarks rather than using a solvent that would 'scrub away' at the surface of the paint film, but clearly, this initial coating was difficult to dissolve even at that point.

With age, these residues from this previous surface coating had grown more oxidized, and therefore, more polar than at the time of the first restoration. In addition, the material had been extracted twice with relatively non-polar solvent blends – once during the original restoration (cleaning) and now with the acetone/mineral spirits blend during the removal of the continuous coating over it. At this point, it was all the more difficult to dissolve this material in a solvent blend without also risking removal of the underlying paint film.

There is a point where many organic materials, including natural resins, become so oxidized or weathered in their serviceable life that they are undoubtedly substituted with enough carboxylic acid functional groups to be potentially dissolvable in aqueous systems, when the pH is well above the pK_a of the acid-containing moieties. At a pH of 8.5, an aqueous solution will dissolve any weakly acidic material with a pK_a one pH unit below 8.5. A good part of the resin-oil mixture which was left on the painting surface after the first restoration could probably be dissolved in water if the pH were raised only slightly. Considering the rate and pHs at which oil-bound paints are swollen or dissolved, a pH of 8.5 in the present system was certainly high enough to dissolve acidic natural resin portions of the residual coating, but not high enough to swell rapidly the underlying oil paint film materials themselves. The pK_a's of acid groups substituted on resin structures probably fall in the range of 5–7, so raising the pH to 8.5 would certainly dissolve these materials. The question was; what buffer should be used to hold the pH at 8.5 in the present system?

The choice of triethanolamine (TEA) in the cleaning mixture really serves several purposes. As a base, its pK_b is 8.0, and it could be used easily as a buffer to hold the pH at or close to this value. But as a buffer, only about a 0.05M solution would be required to maintain the pH of the system. Now a 5% solution of TEA is equivalent to a 0.33M solution; why the excess? Some of the TEA went towards dissolving the abietic acid. About 85% of the 2 g of abietic acid was free acid material; this would be equal to about 0.05M abietate ion in solution, if it were completely neutralized, and it would consume an equivalent molar amount of TEA, or 0.05M. Some of the triethanolate ion would therefore be associated with the abietate ion in solution. The additional amount of TEA represents a fivefold excess of additional TEA, over the amount needed to neutralize (ionize) the abietic acid and dissolve it. At this excess, TEA could well still function as a buffer at a pH of 8.5. Triethanolamine was an important component in this cleaning system for two major reasons: (1) it created a soluble counter-ion to help dissolve the abietic acid and (2) in a sufficient excess, raised the pH of the system and held it there as a buffer ($pK_b = 8.0$). TEA is of course an alcoholic amine, and may exert a slight solvent (alcoholic) effect at the concentration used; it is also a weak complexing or chelating agent for certain divalent metal ions, and may also act in this system in that capacity.

Abietic acid has a diterpene acid ($C_{20}H_{30}O_2$) structure, and was used in this context as an affinity surfactant (soap), to help solubilize and disperse the resinous (and limited oily) materials that could not be dissolved directly into water by raising the pH alone. While it might be difficult to measure its CMC experimentally for a number of reasons, including the lack of purity or homogeneity of structure, etc., it can be estimated using the Shinoda equation (see section 3.4 above). Fig. 3.7 (p. 38) gives the structure of abietic acid. If it were the equivalent linear fatty acid (C20), its CMC would be:

$$\log \text{CMC} = 1.92 - (0.29) \qquad \text{(Feiser \& Feiser 1959: 59)}$$
$$\log \text{CMC} = -3.88$$
$$\text{CMC} = .000013 \text{ M}$$

Now considering that it contains two units of unsaturation (each of which would raise the calculated CMC two to three times); the branched and cyclic structure to abietic acid; and the presence of a high amount of TEA (an alcoholic amine) in this cleaning system, the observed CMC probably would be on the order of 0.001M or slightly higher. At this value (0.001M), if all 85% of the technical grade abietic acid were dissolved during the preparation scheme outlined above, the effective CMC in this system would be approximately 50 times the calculated value (this is not really true, but there is enough excess abietic acid in solution to act, and continue acting, as a surfactant). The HLB for abietic acid can also be estimated by group number (see section 5.2.1) at about 8.2. Combined with Triton X-100, the HLB for the system (combination of surfactants) would be 8.97 (see section 5.2.3). Triton X-100 is a nonionic surfactant which can be blended with abietic acid without precipitating it. If the net HLB in this system is 8.97, it is just high enough to form O/W types of emulsions. But remember, abietic acid is being used as an affinity structure, to help solubilize resinous materials in particular (and is not required for a high HLB value for the system). If more oil solubilizing were required, the net HLB of the system could be raised by adding more Triton X-100 (to approach the requisite HLB of 15 for minimum solubilizing effects on oils; again see section 5.2.2).

It should be noted that hydroxypropylmethyl cellulose (4000 cps) in this system is used as a thickener, but it may also be regarded as a suspension aid for oily materials.

Case History 3.2: Unattributed, *Venetian Canal Scene* (oil on canvas, nineteenth century)

Two surface coatings were present, but the uppermost presentation varnish was extremely darkened and discoloured with age, and this had prompted the owner to bring it to the studio. This second coating had been applied to the painting after a general crack system had formed in the paint and its first coating, and had travelled through the cracks to stain the fabric support on its reverse, mimicking the fracture pattern in the paint (see Fig. 3.2.1). This second coating had apparently been applied while the painting was still in its frame (the varnish extended nearly to the edge of the composition).

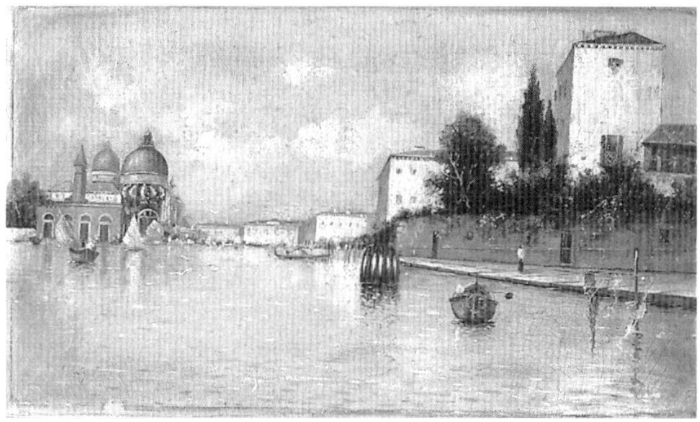

Figure 3.2.1 Unattributed, *Venetian Canal Scene* (oil on canvas, nineteenth century), before treatment (see colour plates)

The initial, older, coating was also present on the surface of the painting but was rather discontinuous. It appeared that an attempt had been made to clean the older varnish off the surface of the painting, but unevenly. This older coating appeared broken or partly cleaned at some points, especially on the right half of the composition. Some abrasion to the paint film in the 'broken through' areas was also evident, as was considerable damage to the area surrounding the signature in the lower left. A sample was removed from near a small tear in the lower left corner. It was evident from the cross-section that, indeed, two surface coatings were present on the painting (see Fig. 3.2.2, taken in UV light during removal of the top varnish), and that the paint and ground were bound in oil (shown by staining with Rhodamine B). The older coating seemed to be the original surface coating. Age, discolouration and the compromise

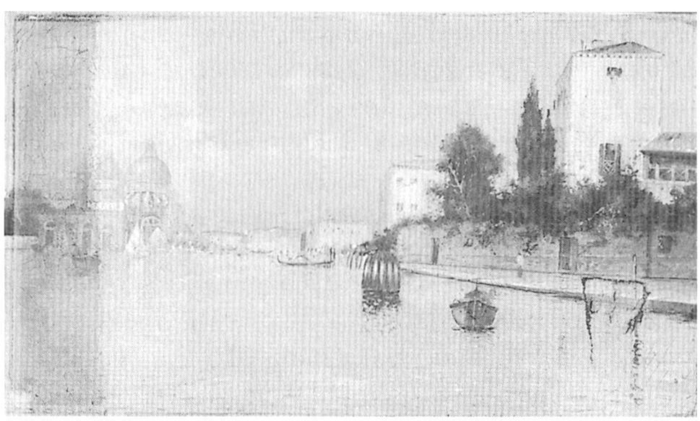

Figure 3.2.2 Unattributed, *Venetian Canal Scene* (oil on canvas, nineteenth century), taken in UV light during removal of the top varnish (see colour plates)

of its integrity during the prior cleaning attempt warranted its removal. Both the original and the second coating were tested for solubility in traditional solvent blends. Both required fairly polar (alcohol or stronger) solvents or very alkaline reagents to dissolve them. At best, the solvents 'broke through' the coatings very unevenly. And to complicate matters still further, they had virtually no effect on a band of the initial coating at the composition edges, which had been protected by the frame rabbet.

The focus of the cleaning was, of course, to recover the best possible presentation surface to the painting. Both coatings appeared to contain a small amount of oil (they stained positive with Rhodamine B). The uppermost layer appeared to be more affected by raising the pH; the lower, older layer seemed to be only slowly affected (swollen) by increasingly alkaline preparations. Empirically, it seemed that the upper layer of varnish might contain a higher percentage of alkaline extractable materials, i.e., it might contain a significant acidic fraction through increased oxidation or weathering. A 'resin soap' preparation could certainly be formulated that, even at a mildly alkaline pH, would solubilize a good deal of the acidic material in this uppermost coating, and disperse those other fractions of it that might not be quite water soluble, with the surfactant or soap moiety. The focus of the cleaning shifted from simply the removal of the two complicating surface coatings, to an 'unpacking' of the two coatings; the selective removal of one coating, while minimally disturbing another. Ideally, this would permit a stop midway in the cleaning process to appraise the condition of the older coating, and to consider leaving it if necessary.

The uppermost coating was removed with the following mixture:

water (deionized)	100 ml
abietic acid	4 g
triethanolamine	10 ml

The pH was adjusted with 1N HCl to 8.5, and the following added:

water (deionized)	100 ml
Brij 35	1 g
methyl cellulose (4000 cps)	3 g

The triethanolamine abietate soap was prepared exactly as described in the previous case history, with the exception that the Brij 35 (a waxy solid at room temperature) was weighed out separately, placed in 100 ml water on a stirrer hot plate, heated until it dissolved, and was then added to the soap solution. Typically, the mixture was applied to small areas of coating using a (00) sable brush. It was allowed to remain for a moment before a dry cotton swab was used to roll it off the paint film surface. The area thus treated was cleared with saliva, allowed to dry, and then rinsed with mineral spirits.

The discontinuous nature of the older coating layer, once the uppermost coating had been removed, warranted its removal as well. It was solubilized with the following:

water (deionized)	100 ml
abietic acid	2 g
triethanolamine	5 ml

The pH was adjusted with 1N HCl to 8.5, and the following added:

Triton X-100	1 ml
1-methyl-2-pyrrolidinone (N-Pyrrole®)	2 ml
methyl cellulose (4000 cps)	1.5 g

This mixture was prepared as was the initial resin soap but with the additional step that the 1-methyl-2-pyrrolidinone was added at the same time as the Triton X-100, and before the solution was gelled with the methyl cellulose. Typically, the mixture was applied to small areas of coating using a (00) sable brush. It was allowed to remain for a moment before a dry cotton swab was used to roll it off the paint film surface. The area thus treated was cleared with saliva, allowed to dry, and then rinsed with mineral spirits.

Neither of the soap preparations described above seemed to affect the oil-bound paint film of the recovered surface, but nor were they particularly effective in solubilizing the small portion of original coating that had been protected by the frame rabbet. Even the most polar of solvents such as DMF, pyridine, and morpholine failed to break into this edge material. A solvent gel, however, which seemed effective, consisted of:

Carbopol 954	2 g
Ethomeen C-25	8 ml
ethanol	75 ml
xylene	12 ml
water (deionized)	12 ml

The preparation of this solvent gel is similar to the procedure described more fully in case histories 4.5 to 4.7 (later). Essentially, a smooth paste was made of the Carbopol and Ethomeen. Ethanol and xylene were added to make a milky, but even, suspension. As the mixture was stirred with a variable speed, high torque stirrer (with a spark-arrested motor), water (12 ml) was added very slowly until a clear viscous gel formed. Typically the solvent gel was applied by brush to the painting's edge, stirred for a moment on the coating surface, and then wiped clear with a dry cotton swab. The area thus treated was then rinsed with a solvent blend of xylene:ethanol (10:1) and allowed to evaporate to dryness.

Commentary

This treatment protocol called for three distinct cleaning systems to complete the work. Ironically, the materials removed from the surface of the painting were all quite similar superficially. The original varnish layer had shown some indication of an oil content and was indistinguishable under the microscope from the later varnish layer, which also apparently had a low oil content. To further complicate the situation, where the original coating was protected from ageing and weathering by the frame rabbet, a decidedly different solubility was exhibited by the original coating material.

The order and rationale for each cleaning system might make more sense if we consider the presence of drying oil to be just one of the complicating factors in the removal of an otherwise soft or natural resin film. Another factor, of course, is the weathering (oxidation) of the natural resin itself. Take the uppermost coating first; raising the pH slightly (to 8.5) would encourage acidic resinous materials to be solubilized. Adding an affinity surfactant (abietate) would also help disperse resinous materials from the coating. Adding the Brij 35 has the effect of increasing the HLB of the system with another surfactant (nonionic) which is compatible with the abietate soap (the HLB of Brij 35 is 16.9; at the weight % used this gives a net HLB for the system of 11.3) for the oily material that might be present in the coating. As an aside, triethanolamine abietate (pH 8.5) alone was tested for its ability to remove the upper coating but was not at all effective. Once the Brij 35 was added to the mixture, however, it was quite effective in removing the upper coating material.

The older, initial coating also appeared to be a natural resin varnish with a small amount of oil, but this layer was not apparently affected by the first resin soap preparation. At a pH of 8.5, the rate of swelling (and concomitantly, the amount of acidic resinous material that might be present in the coating) was extremely slow.

An option would be to raise the pH, but that would have a serious undermining effect on the oil-bound paint beneath this coating. A higher HLB surfactant could be chosen for this particular system (greater than its value of 8.97), but at 15 or higher, greater solubilizing effects would occur, probably at the expense of the oil-bound paint beneath. With a surprisingly small amount of N-Pyrrole, the resin soap preparation at a pH of 8.5 was effective at removing the older coating.

The process of 'rolling up' can be advanced dramatically with a surfactant if swelling (the uptake of water) in a layer is facilitated. In this case, only a small shift in the net solubility parameter of water, with the addition of a less polar, but miscible solvent was effective in accomplishing this. Remember though, that additions of solvents to water and surfactant systems tends to raise the observed CMC for a given surfactant. The amounts used here of abietate, and Triton X-100 were at 50 and 40 times the CMC of each surfactant, respectively; so the small addition of solvent probably would not have much effect on their surfactant ability. The high amount of TEA might boost the CMCs as well, at a pH of 8.5, but again, the system contains an excess of each surfactant, so this is not important.

Since the band of insoluble original varnish at the composition edges had apparently not suffered as much oxidation or weathering as the exposed original surface coating material, the coating was still too non-polar ever to be solubilized efficiently by even a heavily modified water-based preparation. A solvent gel was the more appropriate way to solubilize this material. Carbopol, Ethomeen C-25, and a small amount of water were used to gel the ethanol/xylene/water solvent mixture. Ethomeen itself is a weak cationic/nonionic surfactant which aided in the solubilization of any polar components that may have been present in the coating at the edges. Solvent gels (see section 4.7 below) are essentially surfactant/solvent systems, and find their best use in solubilizing or dispersing polar materials, polymeric fractions, and the like into relatively non-polar solvent blends. A viscous gel in this case also allowed for the restriction of the area of application and an increase in the contact time of the applied solvents.

Case History 3.3: Dean Wolstenholme the elder, *The Death* (oil on canvas, early nineteenth century)

When *The Death* arrived at the studio, it was in excellent structural condition. It had been relined at some point onto a linen of similar weight and construction to the original support. A glue lining held the painting securely in place – taut and well attached to a keyable wooden stretcher. During the initial examination, a small sample was removed from a break at the tacking margin and examined under the microscope. At least four distinct applications of varnish were evident on the painting's surface. The initial varnish layer appeared to be resin only (it gave a positive result with antimony pentachloride), while the subsequent three revarnishing layers appeared to be resin and oil (both antimony pentachloride and Rhodamine B gave positive results) mixtures. The uppermost two layers, in particular, gave only slight positives for an oil component in them. The owner was interested in having the painting cleaned, and it was proposed that some, but not necessarily all, of the varnish layers could be removed to represent the painting in its best possible light. Two issues were of concern: this painting was one in a series of hunting scenes depicted by the artist, and the others might not be treated in the immediate future. And any cleaning at this point would eventually need to be reconciled with the remainder of the paintings in the group: a fully cleaned individual painting might easily overpower the others. Yet, not to clean the painting seemed to compromise its aesthetic appearance. A cleaning that could restore or recover the original varnish was the most desirable, but the condition of the original seemed to preclude the recovery of a full and integral original varnish layer. It was decided to remove the upper two layers of varnish and re-evaluate the appearance of the painting at that point.

The painting was cleaned with the resin soap mixture:

water (deionized)	100 ml
abietic acid	2 g
triethanolamine	5 ml

The pH was adjusted with 1N HCl to 9.0, and the following added:

Triton X-100	1 ml
hydroxypropylmethyl cellulose (4000 cps)	1.5 g

Typically, the soap solution was applied to the varnished painting surface using a sable brush (00) and allowed to stand with occasional stirring. The soap was then cleared with a dry cotton swab, saliva, and then allowed to air dry. A final rinse in mineral spirits of the area thus treated was carried out. After cleaning, the recovered surface appeared uniformly greenish-yellow under near UV light. The original crackle pattern remained in the recovered varnish surface. A cross-section after cleaning indicated that only the two uppermost varnish layers had been removed during cleaning.

Commentary

Treating this painting would have been a fairly routine example of the use of a 'resin soap' type of affinity surfactant, save for two aspects of the cleaning. First, the resin soap preparation used above apparently violates the rule of thumb not to treat oil-bound paints with any aqueous solutions above a pH of 8.5 – above this an oil-bound paint film can be rapidly and easily saponified (solubilized). In this case, however, rather than acting on an oil-bound paint directly, there were intervening resin and oleo-resinous layers as barrier materials on the paint surface. The immediate need was to solubilize specifically the two uppermost oleo-resinous coatings. Solvents polar enough to start to swell or dissolve them would undoubtedly have dissolved the initial varnish layer more rapidly (this actually happened in solvent tests on the surface). The surface might be cleaned of varnish materials but it would be at the expense of all four coatings through a form of 'undercutting' process, as the solvents would affect the lowest layer first. The triethanolamine abietate soap at pH 9.0 wet onto and into the two uppermost resin coatings, solubilizing weakly acidic materials, and dispersing, via the two surfactants in the preparation, many of the other resinous materials present. At this pH, there is an increased likelihood of breaking down the small amount of oil in the coatings as well, rapidly effecting a general dissolution of that problematic component. The ability to treat the surface quickly with a gelled preparation helped in this case to control the application, speed of penetration, etc., and to effect a controlled reduction of the uppermost surface coatings only.

The second unusual aspect of this cleaning concerned the recovered surface. After cleaning, it still had a crack system. In some areas of the painting, the cracks were visually distracting and prompted a light recoating overall with a fresh dammar layer. But the survival of the cracks also demonstrated that the recovered two layers of varnish had not been substantially reformed (i.e., swollen or disrupted) by the cleaning process.

Case History 3.4: Unattributed, German Student Model Violin Bow (composite object, pre-World War II)

One of the salient cleaning problems associated with violins, and other similar bowed musical instruments, is the accumulation of rosin and soiling materials on the top of the sound board, and bow elements in particular, with use. This accumulated material is blackish, disfiguring, and is often removed with either proprietary solvent, or highly alkaline preparations, usually at the expense of the oleo-resinous finishes that characterize the clear coating materials on these instruments. The following mixture was formulated to remove the accumulated rosin/soil material from the bow of a German pre-World War II violin:

water (deionized)	100 ml
Ethofat 242/25	1.3 g
acetic acid (glacial)	1 ml
benzalkonium chloride (10%)	150 μl

The pH was adjusted with 1N NaOH to 6.0 and then the following was added:

methyl cellulose (4000 cps) 1.5 g

Typically, the mixture was applied to small areas of the oleo-resinous coating on the bow handle (and horse hair) using a (00) sable brush. It was allowed to remain for three minutes before a dry cotton swab was used to roll it off the coating surface, along with the solubilized rosin. The area thus treated was cleared with water, allowed to dry, and then rinsed with xylene.

Commentary

The two features of note in this cleaning system are the low pH (6.0), and use of Ethofat 242/25 (Akzo Chemie) as the surfactant. The material to be solubilized (rosin) is essentially abietic acid. As a diterpene acid ($pK_a = 6.7$), rosin could quite easily be solubilized at a pH of 8.0 or higher, and along with a high HLB surfactant for the other general soiling materials (sebum, airborne particulates) that might be present with it, its routine cleaning or removal would be trivial. But on the historic finish, any loss of surfacing material is to be avoided, since it cannot be periodically replaced as it might during the serviceable life of the instrument. These finishes are by and large oleo-resinous coatings. By lowering the pH to 6.0, we avoid solubilizing any weakly acidic organic materials and minimize swelling in the coating (but without tending to solubilize the rosin itself). How can we pick up the rosin?

Ethofat 242/25 is an ethoxylated ester of abietic acid (abietic acid with 25 moles of ethylene oxide added to it). In other words Ethofat 242 is a nonionic resin soap, or a nonionic resin affinity structure, and as a nonionic moiety it can function as a surfactant independently of pH. The CMC is probably quite low (in the range 0.1–0.4 mM) and its HLB (by calculation) would be about 15.6. The HLB is relatively low, but remember we are not trying to solubilize an oily material. On the contrary, we are seeking a low HLB, as long as our surfactant structure has enough affinity for our particular target substrate (rosin) to be effective (which of course, it does). The amount of Ethofat used in this system is about 0.1 mM, just at the CMC probably for this surfactant; the low pH will probably act to increase the solubility of the surfactant in water, and also aid in its rinsing.

Gelling with the methyl cellulose (4000 cps) helps to restrict its application to the applied surfaces. The benzalkonium chloride is simply a general biocide or preservative to confer reasonable shelf life for the cleaning preparation once it is made.

Deoxycholic acid is another example of an affinity structure of sorts. As a bile acid secreted by the pancreas, deoxycholic acid is one of the materials that allow for lipid transport through membranes and in the bloodstream. From its structure (Feiser & Feiser 1959: 59), it can be seen (Fig. 3.8) that it carries a single acid group at one end of the molecule (at the C_{24}), balanced against at the other end a larger hydrocarbon, four-ring steroid structure. Again, the CMC for deoxycholic acid is 5 mM, and the HLB number (from group number) is 17.6 (see section 5.2.1 below). An equivalent C24 linear fatty acid should predictably have a CMC of 1.2×10^{-5}M. The 400-fold deviation between the observed CMC and the ideal value can be explained, as with

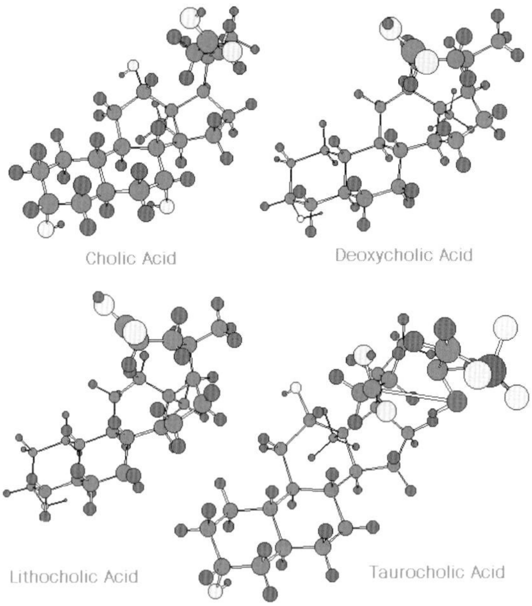

Figure 3.8 Structures of common bile acids

abietic acid, by the cyclic structure inherent in deoxycholic acid, and the added hydroxyl groups present in the structure. The HLB number of 17.6 suggests that deoxycholic acid can have some limited solubilizing effect on oily materials in general, but the surprising aspect of this molecule is its ability to bind with fatty acids in particular with a great deal of affinity (very high log *Ks* of formation). At pHs a unit or so above the pK_a for deoxycholic acid (6.6), dimers tend to form between two deoxycholic acid molecules (Fig. 3.9) in such a way that a long narrow hydro-

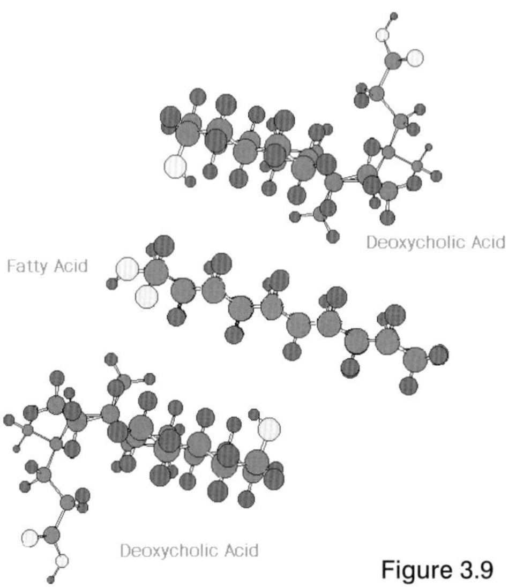

Figure 3.9 Deoxycholic acid micelle around a fatty acid

phobic 'pocket' or space is formed between them. Linear fatty acid molecules conveniently fit into this pocket, and are held there through increased London or Van der Waals force interactions. The pocket of two pairs of deoxycholic acid molecules end to end form a structure that is long enough to accommodate C_4–C_8 length fatty acids; C_9–C_{14} with six; and C_{15}–C_{29} with eight. Xylene, naphthalene, and acenaphthelene all combine with dimers of deoxycholic acid to form similar inclusion arrangements with these aromatic compounds in particular, and with very high log *Ks* for formation. Nominally, the aggregation number for deoxycholic acid is given as between 3 and 12, but clearly this depends on the specific nature of the compounds associated with it in solution. Deoxycholic acid has been used as a surfactant to remove soiling layers from weathered oil paint surfaces (in concert with chelating materials), that contain substantial amounts of Pb salts of fatty acids (stearate, palmitate) released from the films on weathering, or added as driers or dispersal aids in bulk to paint films. Deoxycholic, and taurocholic acids in particular, show some marked affinity towards other methyl steroid structures over linear fatty acid structures of approximately the same hydrocarbon content.

Case History 3.5: C. F. Ryder, *Paxsons Hollow* (oil on canvas, nineteenth century)

On initial examination, it appeared that the painting was unvarnished and had simply collected a substantial soiling layer on its surface. Small, limited, solvent tests were carried out, along with a series of aqueous tests, to determine the solubility of the soiling material on the painting's surface, as part of the initial routine condition report. The soiling layer seemed only to respond to saliva in testing, and the results from even this cleaning material were not entirely satisfactory. A tenacious gray layer of absorbed material seemed to come away only unevenly from the painting surface.

Cross-sections revealed, as suspected, no surface coating on the painting. To complicate matters, the paint was oil bound (it was positive with Rhodamine B), and dispersed pigment samples suggested the artist's palette chiefly consisted of lead white, ultramarine, a green earth, carbon black, and yellow ochre. The painting was cleaned with the following mixture:

water (deionized)	100 ml
deoxycholic acid (free acid)	2 g
Trizma·HCl	0.75 g
ammonium chloride	1.5 g
diammonium citrate	1.5 g

The pH was adjusted with 1M NH_4OH to 8.5, then the following was added:

methyl cellulose (4000 cps)	1.5 g
benzalkonium chloride (10%)	150 μl

Typically the gelled preparation was applied to the paint surface, stirred with a small brush (00), and then wiped away with a dry cotton swab. The area thus cleaned was rinsed with a 0.75% solution of Trizma-HCl in deionized water, pH 8.0, and then followed with a second rinse of deionized water alone. The cleaned and rinsed surface of the painting was then allowed to air dry. The recovered clean paint surface appeared saturated, and unblanched or unbraded on drying.

Commentary

This cleaning system features a moderately strong surfactant (HLB 17.6); a weak chelator (citrate), a slightly elevated ionic strength in a specific counter-ion (NH_4+), and a slightly alkaline pH (8.5) to effect the removal of a soiling layer. At the stated pH deoxycholic acid is fully ionized (pK_a=6.6), and this surfactant exhibits a strong affinity for fatty acids in particular. One of the likely materials present in the 'grey' soiling material is an appreciable Pb stearate or Pb palmitate concentration. These materials are not water soluble, but can be made so by complexing the Pb with citrate and dispersing the fatty acids with the deoxycholate. Solubilizing effects for oily materials become apparent at HLBs of 13 or greater, so the choice of deoxycholate is still at the 'weak' end of the HLB system. The oil film in this case was approximately 100-years-old, and this amount of natural ageing or weathering should have yielded an oil film that still would not be appreciably swollen at a pH of 8.5. The buffer choice in this case was Trizma-HCl for its pK_a (8.1), and for its water rinsibility from the paint surface (in fact, all of the components chosen in this case are water soluble, including deoxycholate with a CMC of 5mM). The water-Trizma rinsing system was simply used to keep the pH slightly alkaline (8.0) during the removal of the cleaning system components, but in particular, to facilitate the removal of deoxycholic acid. With a pK_a of 6.6, a water rinse alone at a pH of 7 (or 6.8, realistically, in unbuffered deionized water), would have precipitated deoxycholic acid on the paint surface, rather than remove it. One of the other odd features of this bile acid soap/surfactant is, that at pHs at or slightly below its pK_a, it forms a clear gel (a kind of pseudo-polymer of helically stacked free acid molecules of deoxycholate).

The author has used aleuritic acid (9,10,16 trihydroxy palmitic acid) as an affinity surfactant for degraded shellac surfaces. Proteins (collagens in particular) esterified with fatty acids have also been used as affinity surfactants for leather and hair-conditioning products, and, in the present context, for increased wetting of glue-based adhesives onto resin- or oil-loaded surfaces (wood).

The notion of exploiting surfactants for their particular affinities for certain hydrocarbon structures has been used extensively for the separation and isolation of biologically important compounds. Affinity chromatography using specific surfactants immobilized on solid supports to isolate and then release targeted compounds has led to the purification of even racemic mixtures of materials (Kahane *et al.* 1958). Concomitantly, the post-chromatographic separation and detection of trace amounts of surfactants from these preparations has been advanced considerably in the last few years.

The 'dual' character of surfactant structures as either hydrophilic or lipophilic has been extended somewhat to include structures that have *any* small disparity between one portion of the structure and another, in terms of *relative* lipophilic tendency. Short acrylic polymer chains have been coupled to linear hydrocarbon structures to act, in essence, as nonionic 'acrylic' affinity surfactants. Troysol CD1 is an example of such a structure used in the paint manufacturing industry as a dispersal aid for pigments in acrylic polymer solutions (*McCutcheon's Emulsifiers and Detergents* 1991). The author has used Troysol CD1 to increase the rate of wetting, swelling, and dissolution with aliphatic hydrocarbon solvents of acrylic films (n-butyl methacrylates) that otherwise would have required higher solubility parameter solvent systems.

4

Detergents and detergency

4.1 Detergency

Surfactants find their greatest practical use in the solubilization of specific materials, i.e. soils deposited on various substrate surfaces. Usually, *detergency* is defined as the functional use of surfactant structures in this regard (Osipow 1962: 377); that is, their *relative* effectiveness in the separation of a soiling material from a given substrate, as a function of concentration, and other solution conditions and materials. It should become clear from the outset that the nature of the soiling material, its specific interaction with a substrate surface, and the nature of the substrate surface itself (its physical and chemical makeup) all contribute to defining how effective a surfactant may be in separating one material from the other.

As has been pointed out in Chapter 1, soiling compositions can vary tremendously depending on the specific use, environment, etc. associated with an object or substrate. In the case of fine art or decoratively painted surfaces, presumably most of the deposited soiling material is through airborne transmission, and the character of the soiling materials usually collected on these types of surfaces reflects the normal atmospheric range of particulates associated with interior (or in some cases, exterior) conditions.

But these surfaces are complicated by the normal range of materials and conditions associated with paint and varnish-containing materials: pigments, dyes or colourants, binders, extenders, driers, dispersal aids, rheology modifiers, etc. can be found in endless permutations on these surfaces. And ageing, restoration practice, etc. all modify these surfaces further still, leaving us with the problem of defining the exact nature of these surfaces when we are presented with them (and attempt to clean them), and the nature of the soil interactions on them that may have been established over time. It will be helpful to examine detergency first as a general phenomenon, and then to return to its specific description on painted surfaces to gain a better understanding of how we can use it as a cleaning tool.

4.2 Mechanisms of detergency

Generally, the forces retaining soils on most surfaces can be summarized (from Chapter 1) as: physical, coulombic, ionic, or weak secondary interactions (hydrogen bonding, dipolar, or London (Van der Waals) forces). For large size particulates (greater than about 1 μm in diameter), coulombic (or electrostatic) forces are predominant. Usually coulombic forces can be overcome by water by itself, as a high dielectric constant medium. For particle sizes much less than 1 μm, weak secondary types of interactions tend to predominate and retain soiling materials on surfaces. The force of retention for soiling particles in this size range can be so great, for instance, that all of solvent, surfactant, and mechanical agitation may be required to dislodge particulates effectively. Ionic interactions can occur at all particle sizes, and usually require additional ions or complexing agents to undo or take apart. The physical entrainment of soiling materials on substrate surfaces may require a variety of techniques to overcome it, including physical and chemical methods.

The first requirement for detergency is the displacement of air on the substrate surface, and the effective wetting of the soiling materials by the detergent (surfactant) solution (Osipow 1962: 413). Maximal wetting on low-energy surfaces or materials depends on the surface tension of the detergent solution, and the value of the critical surface tension of the specific surface or material. When the surface tension of the detergent solution is equal to, or less than, the critical surface tension (g_c) of the substrate surface, wetting and spreading will occur. For surfaces that can be characterized as substantially oily or hydrocarbon in nature, critical surface tensions on the order of 0.03–0.04 N m^{-1} at 20°C are commonly encountered (Osipow 1962: 251). Enough surfactant has to be dissolved in water to depress its surface tension (for water the critical surface tension is 0.073 N m^{-1}) below this range to allow the water to wet and spread effectively on the low-energy surface. Usually, at or above the critical micelle concentration, a surfactant will have maximally lowered the surface tension of water to the point of causing wetting and spreading to occur; quite often it is the case that this 'breakpoint' is actually reached at concentrations of certain surfactants much lower than their CMC.

The subsequent removal of soiling material can occur in a number of different ways, but the most likely mechanisms are (Adam 1937):

- The soil can be 'rolled up', i.e. swollen with water, surrounded by adsorbed surfactant, and displaced from the substrate surface by the detergent solution (see Figs 4.1 a and b).
- The soiling material can be removed in repeated increments or 'thin layers' by direct emulsification.
- The surfactant can penetrate the soil to form 'reverse' micelles where small amounts of water surrounded by surfactant become dispersed in the soil, and on becoming more and more hydrated, invert to form a traditional micellular structure of dispersed soil in water (this has been referred to as a so-called *cryoscopic* effect).
- Particularly strong interactions or bonds (divalent metal salts, hydrogen bonds) that complicate soil-from-substrate release are overcome with adjuvants or conditions (compexing agents, solvents, pH) first, so that the detergent solution can then disperse the soil.

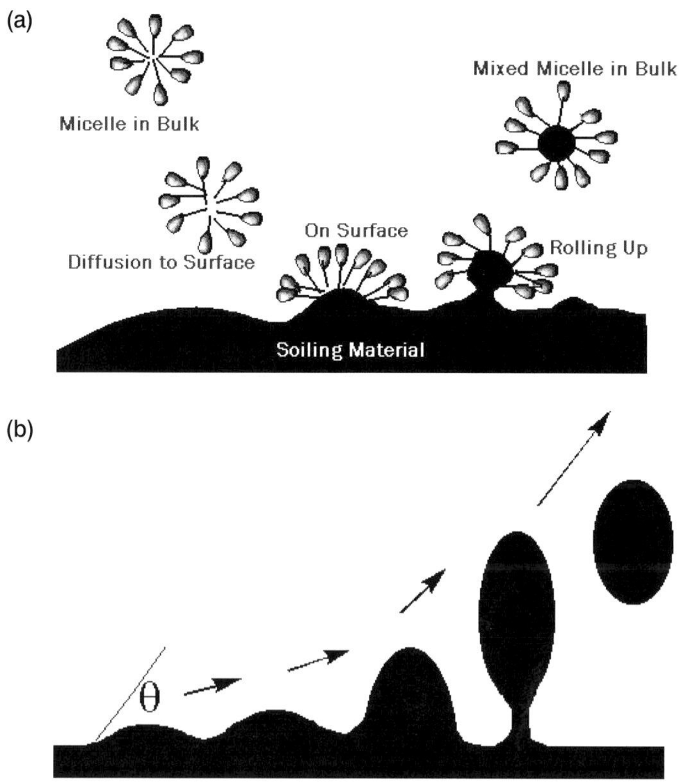

Figure 4.1 (a) Steps in the process of detergency. (b) The process of "rolling-up" a soil by a surfactant

Again, depending on the specific substrate, the type of soil, and the interaction between them, any one of the above models might aptly describe the general process of detergency. Regardless of the exact mechanism, adsorption of surfactant onto the soiling material and the substrate surface must occur first, and is an important aspect of detergency; but adsorption can deplete surfactant from the bulk detergent solution, and concomitantly, result in a rise in surface tension, and poor wetting. To avoid this, generally an excess of surfactant is dissolved in water to overcome what might be absorbed onto low-energy surfaces, and specific weights or amounts of soiling material. The adsorption of surfactant depends on the surfactant structure, temperature, and a variety of other solution conditions (Osipow 1962: 405). Here, for instance, the effect of salts (counter-ions in particular) at depressing the CMC of a surfactant has the advantage of increasing detergency. Raising the temperature generally will decrease adsorption, and therefore depress detergency.

One important final step or stage in detergency is soil suspension through the use of a 'suspension aid' (a colloid, polymer, etc., dissolved along with the surfactant in the water) to prevent the solubilized soil from being redeposited on the substrate surface during cleaning or rinsing (surfactant dilution) operations. High salt concentrations generally interfere with these types of suspension aids, however, by precipitating soils back onto cleaned surfaces.

4.3 Laundry detergent compositions as models for detergency

A traditional laundry soap formulation, say before the Second World War, might have included a substantial amount (85% by weight) of Na^+ or K^+ salts of common or easily obtained fatty acids (palmitate, stearate, oleate); an alkali, to raise the pH to between 10.5 and 11 (trisodium phosphate, sodium carbonate, sodium silicate); and a complex phosphate (sodium hexametaphosphate, tetrasodium pyrophosphate, sodium tripolyphosphate) (Schwartz 1949). The fatty acid soap was the surfactant in this traditional system. The alkali raised the pH to maximize the hydrolysis (and dissolution) of oily soiling materials (sebum, for instance), and increase the solubility of weakly acidic soils. The complex phosphate was used as a suspension aid, and as a metal-complexing agent in hard-water applications. After the Second World War, synthetic surfactants became cheaper replacement materials for traditional soaps, with improved soil solubilization properties. Wartime difficulties in terms of the availability and transportation of soap or soap precursor fats had spurred on the development of these alternative materials. The combination of complex polyphosphates and synthetic anionic surfactants were particularly effective in laundry detergent preparations on cottons and many of the new post-war synthetic fibre types (Hatch & Rice 1939). Again, a typical laundry preparation (up until fairly recently) may have included synthetic surfactant (15–40% by weight), complex phosphate (30–50%), sodium sulfate (5–15%), sodium silicate (4–8%), and sodium carboxymethyl cellulose (0.5–1.5%) (Osipow 1962: 381). The list now might contain optical brighteners, enzymes, perfumes, dyes, etc., but the 'heart' of the laundry cleaning system has changed very little. The model of a surfactant/alkali/complex phosphate system worked well on many different fibre types, and is often emulated in other cleaning situations because it addresses each of the steps outlined above for detergency to occur effectively.

4.4 Evaluation of detergency

Harris has reviewed various testing procedures for evaluating detergency in a variety of laundry cleaning operations (1959), but generally, many of these tests involve applying a standardized soiling mixture (something like carbon black/mineral oil) to a test fabric substrate. The soiled test fabric is immersed in a solution of surfactant and/or other aqueous materials or conditions, agitated in a controlled fashion, rinsed, dried, and its reflectance measured and compared to the initial reflectance of the soiled test fabric. Photometric methods have therefore been used extensively to evaluate detergency on fabric substrate materials. In summary, the nature of the synthetic soiling mixture, the type of fabric used, the washing conditions, etc. usually determine the results in these sorts of tests.

The same type of experiment has been done on test oil paint films with a synthetic soiling mixture (Wolbers 1992). For instance, the curves plotted in Fig. 4.2 were obtained in one such experiment. The test substrates in this case were 40-year-old oil paint films that had been applied to plywood substrates and aged under ambient conditions in a painting conservation studio. The soiling mixture (a mixture of organic and inorganic components, but largely composed of carbon, iron

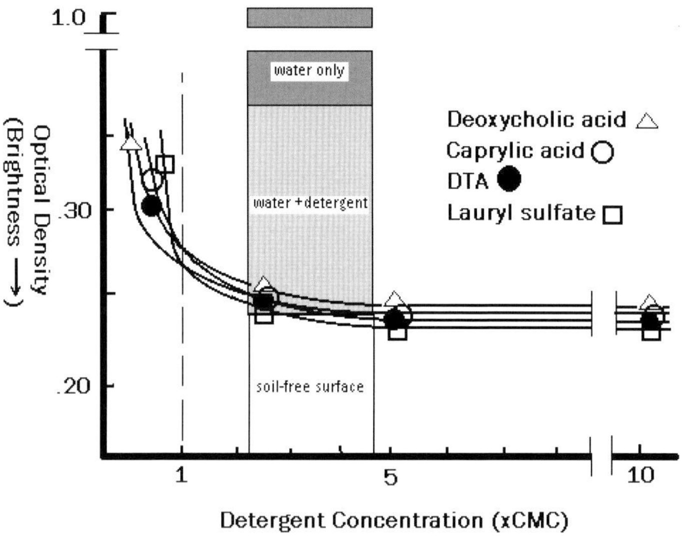

Figure 4.2 Soil desorption versus surfactant type and concentration

oxide, and mineral oil) was applied in each case to give an overall optical density of 1.0 unit on the paint surfaces; each surface was washed with deionized water, dried, and the reflectance measured. The detergent solutions were then applied to the test films to see what effect varying the amount of surfactant would have on the rate of solubilization of the remaining absorbed soiling materials.

The four detergents tested (sodium caprylate, sodium lauryl sulfate, sodium deoxycholate, and dodecyltrimethylammonium bromide, DTA), all exhibited increased solubilization of the synthetic soiling mixture at essentially the CMC for each surfactant. The pH was 8.0 for the anionic surfactants, and 6.0 for the cationic surfactant; counter-ion strength was kept low in all four cases (close to the stoichiometric amount to solubilize each ionic surfactant). The pH and the counter-ion (Na^+, Br^-) in all four cases apparently had little effect on the solubilized soiling material. More importantly, at only a slight excess (3 × the CMC for each) all four of the surfactants had essentially removed *all* of the soiling mixture that had been applied to the test film.

The same experiment was repeated again (Fig. 4.3); but at this point the paint films were soiled, rinsed with deionized water, and the reflectance measured. The films additionally were aged in an Atlas Sunchex weathering device (120 kJ of arc lamp exposure was applied at a mean wavelength of 385 nm). The additionally aged paint films were washed with the same four surfactant solutions, at varying concentrations, and the reflectance changes measured. Again, as the concentration of each surfactant approached its CMC, a marked increase in the amount of solubilized material was seen, and again, at about three times the CMC for each surfactant, the maximum amount of material was solubilized. Surprisingly, though, the additionally aged paint films seemed to retain more of the soiling material; that is, where the detergent solutions were sufficient to remove all of the residual soiling materials by themselves on the 40-year-old films, in the additionally aged samples this was not the case. Apparently, the nature of the soil-paint surface interaction had changed with the additional ageing.

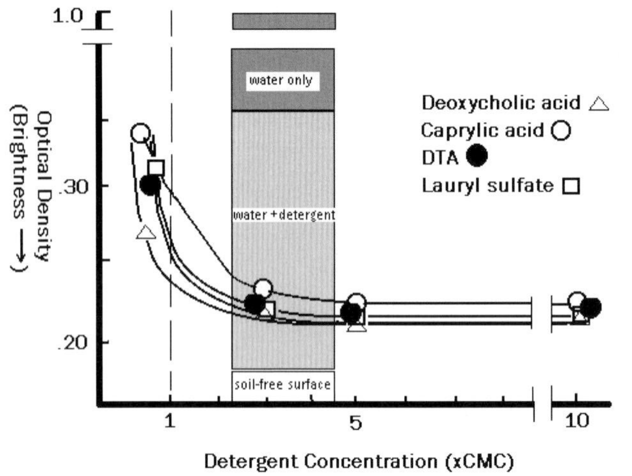

Figure 4.3 Desorption of soil from test paint film after additional ageing

One additional clue to the nature of the soil-paint interactions was obtained in a parallel study (Wolbers 1992) in which a series of chelators (citrate paired with three different counter-ions, and sodium EDTA) were tested at varying concentrations for their cleaning effect on the synthetically soiled 40-year-old paint films, and the soiled films additionally aged in the Sunchex unit (Figs 4.4 and 4.5). The additional ageing apparently produced a soil-paint interaction that responded better to chelation effects *after* additional ageing than had been the case before. In oil paint systems where the binding material is both prominent and substantially unweathered (relatively unoxidized), the solubilizing effect of a surfactant, slightly above its CMC, is probably going to be greatest. In terminology commonly adopted in paint film technology, such films would be considered to be at or below their CPC. The CPC, or critical pigment concentration, is the point at which, in a dried paint

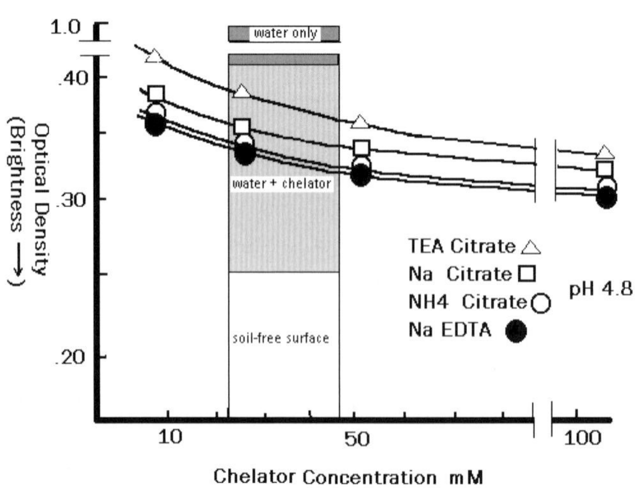

Figure 4.4 Desorption of soil from test paint film as a function of chelator concentration

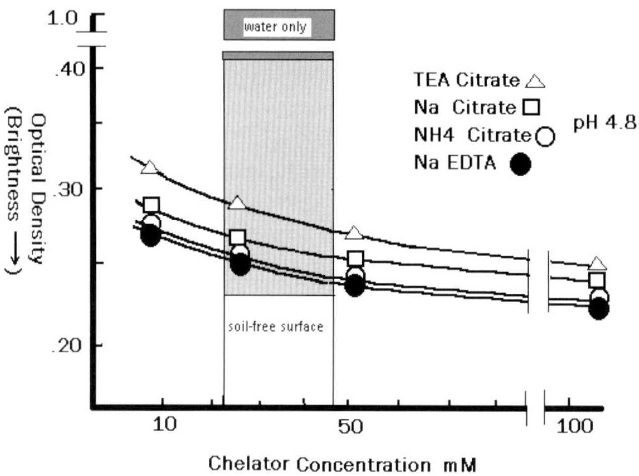

Figure 4.5 Desorption of soiling material as a function of chelator concentration after additional ageing

film, all the internal space between pigment particles are filled with binder. Below it, and a predominance of binder is present in a film; above it, and pigment particles are prominent, with increasing amounts of air voids, or binder-poor areas in the film as the CPC approaches 100%. If binding material is lost through weathering (or leaching), if a film is above its CPC, or if the binding material is substantially oxidized so that the paint surface is substantially more pigment-rich, or polar, or both, then ionic effects (chelation, pH, counter-ion) may be needed to aid in the solubilization of retained soiling materials. The laundry detergent model of surfactant/alkali/complex phosphate can be emulated to some degree on the paint film surfaces. Certainly a combination of surfactant and complexing agent (at an appropriate pH to minimize swelling in the paint film) can be an effective tool for soil removal on paint film substrates. But the *relative* effectiveness of either component (surfactant or complexing agent) may well be a function of the absolute paint film condition more than any other factor.

4.5 Adsorption of surfactants on soil and substrate surfaces

Wetting and spreading of water on a surface is the first step in the detergency process; but the adsorption of surfactant at the soil/water and/or substrate/water interface is also an important step in most descriptions of the detergency process. Fig. 4.6 gives adsorption curves at two different temperatures for dodecyl benzene sodium sulfonate on cotton (Fava & Eyring 1956). Both curves exhibit features common to these sorts of plots. They reflect a temperature dependency for such plots; for any given temperature, a unique adsorption profile or *isotherm* would result. Specifically, while adsorption generally increases initially with increasing amounts of surfactant, the amount adsorbed increases steeply at the CMC (point A on each curve), and reaches a maximum well above the CMC (point B on each curve), and then tends to level off with additional surfactant in the bulk solution. Clearly, at the CMC, surfactant is adsorbed on the substrate or soil surface in a micellular arrangement; this accounts for the particular increase at this point on the curves. The maximum adsorption peak may reflect the saturation of the surface in question by layers of micelles. The levelling off of adsorption may be due to rearrangement of surfactant from wholly micellular, to intermediate or different types of structures; whatever the absolute arrangement, the *rate* of adsorption tends to approach a maximum. The following equation describes the rate of adsorption, again measured isothermally (Wagner 1964):

$$\frac{d\phi}{dt} = -2k' \sinh b\phi \qquad [4.1]$$

where ϕ is defined as

$$\phi = \frac{a - a_f}{a_i - a_f} \qquad [4.2]$$

and a_i, a, and a_f are the amounts of surfactant adsorbed initially, at time t, and at infinity, respectively; b is a constant (1.26), and is temperature-independent; k' is a second constant that is temperature-dependent.

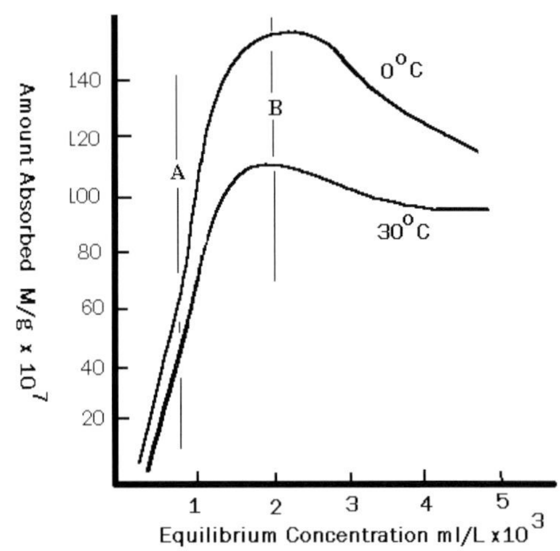

Figure 4.6 Surfactant adsorption versus equilibrium concentration at two different temperatures

Apart from temperature, adsorption can be affected by other solution conditions. Sodium sulfate has been shown (Wagner 1963) to increase the adsorption of certain surfactants (e.g., alkyl aryl sulfonates) on cotton; Ca^{+2} increased the adsorption of the surfactants, while tetrasodium pyrophosphate lowered the adsorption of the same surfactants, at low Ca^{+2} concentrations (presumably through the complexing of the Ca^{+2} ions) on the same substrate.

Although direct studies of the adsorption of surfactants on substrates and soils that relate to paint films and painted surfaces are few in number, these surfaces share a number of features in common with other so-called 'hard surface' materials. Hard surfaces might include metals, dishware, tiles, painted surfaces, etc. Bourne and Jennings (1963) present an excellent review of the kinetics of hard-surface cleaning. The cleaning of metals has been specifically reviewed by Saubestre (1975) and ceramics cleaning methods and material have been reviewed by Mizuno (1975). The substrate surface in most hard-surface cleaning situations is generally taken as much smaller, and less porous than on fabrics. The kinetic models developed for such surfaces allow for much less diffusion and capillarity in the substrate material than in models of fabric. Cox and Matson (1984) investigated the effect of nonionic surfactant structure on the removal of stearine wax, and powdered graphite from painted surfaces, vinyl floor tiles, and metal surfaces. They found that soil removal depended on the size of the hydrophobic portion of the surfactant molecule. The length of the polyoxyethylene chain for optimal soil removal was dependent on the overall amount of surfactant in solution. The optimal surfactant composition was a blend of C_6, C_8, and C_{10} alcohols that were oxyethylenated to 50% by weight. Interestingly, Cox and Matson also observed that the weight of the soil (stearine specifically) increased on immersion in solution of nonionics indicating that a cryoscopic effect had occurred; that is, that both water and surfactant had diffused into the soiling material before dissolution or solubilization had taken place. The rate of weight gain and soil removal increased with the decreasing size of the hydrophobic (hydrocarbon) portion of the surfactants.

4.6 Surfactant adsorption as a function of CMC, pH, and counter-ion concentration

On low-energy surfaces, such as oil paint films, adsorption can be linked directly to the size of the hydrocarbon moiety of the applied surfactant. Using radiolabelled detergents, the amount of surfactant adsorbed onto a test oil paint film (expressed as a percentage of the total amount of surfactant applied) under defined solution conditions (pH, 5 × CMC of each surfactant) was measured (Wolbers 1990). Fig. 4.7 is a plot of the results. The sodium salts of C_8, C_{10}, and C_{12} fatty acid soaps, and sodium deoxycholate, essentially yielded a plot for adsorption that decreased as CMC increased. In other words, as the hydrocarbon chain length or structure decreased in size, the adsorption also decreased. This should be explainable by the increased water solubility of the surfactants in this series as the CMC increased (and concomitantly there was a decrease in the solubility through adsorption and partitioning) on the oily surface of the paint film. When the test paint film was aged an additional 100 hours in an Atlas Weather-o-meter, the same sort of relationship was seen between CMC and adsorption on the test paint films, although the decrease with increasing CMC was less pronounced. Interestingly, when the substrate oil paint films were subjected to an elevated pH (and were therefore presumably more swollen), as shown in Fig. 4.8, the amounts of surfactant adsorbed were dramatically higher, although they showed the same decrease in adsorption with an increase in CMC, and after additional ageing adsorbed the highest amounts of

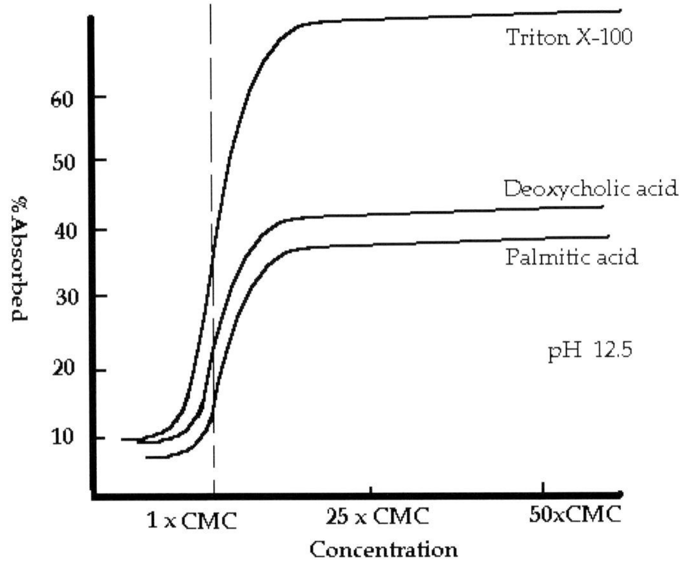

Figure 4.11 Surfactant absorbed versus concentration (in units of CMC) for Triton X-100, deoxycholic acid and palmitic acid

4.7 Detergent systems design

The implications for the design of a detergent system for soils on an oil paint film can be summarized as follows. Wetting and adsorption are requisite steps in the effective solubilization of most soils on painted surfaces. Adsorption of surfactant to the paint surface itself is problematic in a number of ways.

First, we run the risk of depleting the amount of surfactant in the bulk solution so that wetting and solubilization are inhibited. We can design around this by working at an excess of the surfactant in the bulk solution. At concentrations five times the CMC a sufficient excess of surfactant is present to solubilize most soils, but not be depleted immediately on contact. While elevated temperatures generally decrease adsorption and adsorption rate (equation 4.1), we cannot realistically carry out cleaning operations at elevated temperatures on painted fine art or decorative art surfaces. Certain counter-ions can enhance or retard adsorption – Na^+ and K^+ in particular are useful counter-ions where increased ionic strength may be needed or present in a detergent system, but increased adsorption would not be desirable (as might be the case with NH_4^+ or TEA^+). The pH will certainly affect the performance of ionic surfactants, but will also, as pointed out above, affect the rate of swelling and/or dissolution of oil paint films. The reasonable design of detergent systems for painted surfaces dictates that we look for materials and conditions that minimize the swelling and adsorption of surfactants on the paint surface, while at the same time maximize surfactant and water adsorption and penetration into soils (and any other complicating materials we wish to solubilize) likely to be present.

The second concern is for the efficient clearance of applied materials; the more adsorption is favoured on a surface, the harder it will be to remove effectively the applied detergent. Elevated pHs, the choice of less soluble counter-ions, and inappropriate excess of surfactant will only make clearance more difficult from oil-bound paint films. In this regard, the relationship between CMC and adsorption is especially important; for low-energy surfaces predominately hydrocarbon in nature, i.e., oil films, low CMC surfactants (lower than say 1 mM) may be inappropriate for a number of reasons. Their generally lower solubility in water makes their adsorption onto these surfaces all the more likely, and their clearance by rinsing with water (i.e. by dilution) not favourable. Ageing (natural or artificial) promotes changes in the surface of oil-bound paints; as these surfaces weather (oxidize, lose binder, etc.) they inevitably become more polar, and the soil–paint interactions must become more polar (hydrogen bonding, dipolar, ionic, interactions) as well. 'Builders' (complexing agents) such as tetrasodium pyrophosphate may become increasingly important for releasing soils from aged films, although as we shall see in Chapter 6, certain types of complexing agents may be more suitable for paint films than others in analogous cleaning applications.

Case History 4.1: Joan Brown, *Kitchen Still Life* (oil on canvas, 1964)

The painting was brought to the studio after a boiler 'puff back' in the owner's home deposited a substantial oily soot layer on the painting's surface. Some time had elapsed before the painting had been brought in, and the soot seemed to be tenaciously bound to the paint surface. Tests with water alone (deionized) only seemed to smudge the soot at best; hydrocarbon solvents could slowly lift the soot from the paint surface, but areas treated with solvent tended to dry, after the evaporation of solvent, to a rather matt surface. Saliva also only seemed to remove a portion of the soot or soiling material, and on drying, it too left a matt surface.

The following aqueous system was constructed to clean the painting surface:

water (deionized)	100 ml
Brij 700	4.5 g

were mixed together on a warm stirrer hot plate to dissolve the solid surfactant, the solution obtained was cooled and then

acetic acid (glacial)	0.5 ml

was added. The pH was adjusted with 1N NaOH to 6.0, then, the following added:

methyl cellulose (4000 cps)	1.5 g
Dowicide OBCP	0.05 g

Typically, the aqueous gel was applied to the painting surface with a small brush (00) over areas of a few square centimetres, allowed to remain for a moment, and then wiped away with a dry cotton swab along with the solubilized soot. The areas thus treated were rinsed with deionized water, and allowed to air dry.

Commentary

It should be clear from the detergency discussion above, that the oily 'soot' contaminating the oil painting surface is a material that can be solubilized with a detergent solution if certain precautions are taken to protect the very young oil film that it was adsorbed onto. Water is a poor solvent for drying oil films, especially a film as young as this one; lowering the pH with the sodium acetate/acetic acid buffer (6.0) helps to keep the oil film as unswollen as possible (remember, at pHs above neutral and especially above about 8.5, pronounced swelling occurs in oil systems; this pH sensitivity is only exacerbated on ageing and oxidation of the oil binder).

In the choice of a surfactant, a nonionic structure will work over a range of pHs, including the pH we want to use in this system (6.0) provided we can find a structure that is suitable to wet water onto the paint surface, and strongly adsorb onto and into the soot. It is clear from Cox and Matson that at high polyoxyethylene (POE) to hydrocarbon ratios, nonionic structures show improved adsorption into oily soils in hard-surface cleaning situations. Hsaio (see section 3.7) showed that the CMC for nonionics generally goes up as the overall weight percentage of polyoxyethylene goes up in the surfactant molecule. The author correlated CMC to adsorption on oil paints, and suggested that surfactant structures with CMCs of at least 1–2 mM be used for surface cleaning applications on oil paint films where water rinsibility is important. For these three reasons, the nonionic structure we should be looking for would necessarily have a relatively high POE-to-hydrocarbon ratio. Brij 700 (or 700s) is a logical choice because it has a very high POE-to-hydrocarbon ratio. Its structure is POE (100) stearyl ether (the 100 mole adduct of oxyethylene to stearyl alcohol). The CMC for this structure is about 1–2 mM, meaning that at least this amount is needed to reach the CMC (MW = 4585, so 2 mM = 0.92 g/100 ml). Since most surfactants maximally lower the surface tension of water at or slightly above this value, we can certainly assume that wetting should occur (the HLB of this surfactant is 18.8, also high enough to predict good wetting; see section 5.2.2). But remember that detergency *per se* often peaks at some excess of surfactant above the CMC. And also recall that the author observed that at only about three times the CMC the maximum soil was removed from a test oil film by a number of surfactants. The amount of Brij 700 prescribed in the recipe above is approximately five times the CMC (4.5 g/100 ml) to provide just the amount of excess surfactant needed for maximum detergency (but not too much in order to avoid being faced with the difficulties in clearing the material later on). Brij 700 is water rinsible (its CMC should indicate this), and water should be the rinsing agent of choice in this case. As a nonionic, the pH of the rinse water is a non-factor; but again, water is such a poor swelling agent for oil (hydrophobic) bound paints that we can expect that water alone should be the best rinsing material in this case for the applied cleaning materials. The use of Na^+ ions as part of the buffering system was a conscious choice of a counter-ion that minimizes the adsorption of surfactant onto the oil paint film, as an additional precaution in the overall system design. The methyl cellulose (4000 cps) was present to aid with thickening and soil suspension, and as a weak complexing agent for divalent metals which might be present. The Dowicide OBCP (o-benzyl-p-chlorophenol) was a preservative (neutral) that was added to confer increased 'shelf life' on the cleaning preparation.

Consider for a moment, as a counter example, if another surfactant were used in this same situation. Triton X-100 is the POE (9–10) octyl phenol. Its CMC is 0.23 mM; however, this low a CMC should preclude its use on a very young, hydrophobic oil film. It would be much more strongly adsorbed both into the soot *and* onto the oil paint film because of its much lower POE-to-hydrocarbon ratio than, for instance, Brij 700. Its HLB is 13.5, so it should predictably act as both wetting agent and detergent in this case (see section 5.2.2). It can certainly function as a surfactant over a range of pHs as a nonionic structure, but from the radiolabelled surfactant study carried out by the author, the adsorption of Triton X-100 on an oil paint film would only be exacerbated at pHs above 7.0; even at a pH of 6.0, as in the system above, it would probably be adsorbed onto a hydrophobic oil paint too strongly to be of practical importance. Very low CMC surfactants are generally sparingly soluble in water, and the more strongly adsorbed they are onto an oil film, the more difficult it is to imagine clearing them away with water alone. Triton X-100 is soluble in aliphatic/aromatic solvent blends in all proportions, so it is conceivable that we could rinse the Triton X-100 away with a solvent blend. But as was pointed out at the beginning of the case history, even relatively non-polar solvents left the paint film 'dry' looking or leached (through the loss of surface paint film constituents, e.g., metal soaps which are very soluble in even aliphatic hydrocarbon solvents), so it was not appropriate in this case.

On oil paint films or surfaces which are more polar, i.e., far more oxidized and weathered, it is easy to imagine that on an increasingly higher surface energy paint film, wetting with water would in general be easier, and that low CMC surfactants like Triton X-100 could be used to their best advantage. Again Triton X-100 has an HLB number of 13.5, and should act predictably as a (weak but effective) detergent. Its low POE-to-hydrocarbon ratio, and low CMC, should indicate that while it may not be as strongly adsorbed into oily soiling materials, it may more readily be adsorbed into more polar soils. On a weathered oil paint surface the types of soils, and soil interactions, tend to change with the change in surface polarity. Triton X-100 would be a good surfactant choice on an aged paint film on account of rinsing concerns; because of its low CMC it is soluble in aliphatic/hydrocarbon blends, and could be effectively rinsed away with these materials rather than with water, which might have more effect on an aged film (swelling) than it would as a general solvent on an unaged film.

Case History 4.2: Unattributed, Corner Cupboard (composite object, Pennsylvania 1830–1840)

Before surface cleaning was carried out, cross-sections were made from one or two sites on the presentation surfaces. The surface decoration appeared to be two layers of an oil-bound light pinkish or light red iron oxide coloured base paint (they were positive with Rhodamine B), over which a black patterning layer was applied (carbon black in oil, which was positive with Rhodamine B), and finally, a toned, transparent resin-oil coating. The resin-oil coating had collected a soiling layer, and carried traces of old wax and oil-containing polishing materials as well. The following were constructed to surface clean the cupboard:

water (deionized)	100 ml
triethanolamine	1.5 ml

The above materials were mixed together and the pH adjusted to 8.5 with 1M acetic acid, then the following were added:

Triton® XL80N	0.5 ml
hydroxypropylmethyl cellulose (4000 cps)	1.5 g

Typically the detergent gel preparation was applied with a cotton swab, rolled on the surface for a moment then wiped off the surface with a dry cotton swab. The area thus treated was rinsed with deionized water and, after it had air dried, rinsed a second time with a 3:1 mineral spirits to xylene solvent blend.

Commentary

The waxy soil accumulated on the resin-oil surface could be solubilized with a surfactant of an HLB (see section 5.2.2) starting at about 13 or higher. Anionics or nonionics would be the best choice on a degraded resin-oil surface; cationics (and positively charged amphoterics) would tend to precipitate on these weakly acidic (oppositely charged) surfaces, and be difficult to clear. Triton XL80N (a nonionic) has an HLB of 13.5, so it is just strong enough to be able to pick up the soiling materials present. Its CMC is 0.23 mM (MW = 624), so in the system above, there is a sufficient excess (about 35 times the CMC) of Triton XL80N available to us for detergency purposes. Adsorption on substrate surfaces is a critical issue for a number of reasons. Detergency depends on the adsorption of surfactant onto and into soiling materials; but minimal adsorption onto the substrate surface is desirable. The low CMC for Triton XL80N (<1mM) should indicate that it is a relatively hydrophobic structure, and probably sparingly water soluble. Low CMC surfactants tend to be harder to rinse from surfaces with water than surfactants with CMCs greater than 1–2 mM. Hydrophobic surfaces would tend to adsorb Triton XL80N strongly (fresh or relatively unoxidized resin, oil surfaces), and rinsing would be difficult. In this case, the resin-oil coating over the graining is fairly weathered (oxidized) so while it isn't likely that the Triton XL80N will be retained strongly on the surface, both a water rinse *and* a solvent rinse are included in the protocol, to ensure that it is cleared from the surface. The surface chemistry of the resin-oil is of special interest here. The weakly acidic groups that may be present on its surface as a result of ageing will probably have pK_as in the range of 5.5–7.0. At the stated pH (8.5) most of these will be ionized to some extent, and hydrated. On drying, the predominant counter-ion in this system (triethanolamine) will form ion pairs with the available acid groups, to form electrically neutral salts with these functional groups. The choice of counter-ion in this case is important; if NaOH or KOH were used to raise the pH in this system rather than triethanolamine (TEA), Na^+ and K^+ would be available as cations to form ion pairs (salts) with available acid groups on drying. These are rather hygroscopic ions, and would tend to remain so on the 'dried' surface (they might tend to blanch the surface, at high RHs). If no counter-ion were available (if deionized water itself were used to clean the surface of the coating), the acids would pair with a hydrogen ion (H^+) from water itself, and dry in the free acid form (–COOH). But this kind of surface would tend to be electrostatically charged readily and would, in time, tend to re-attract soils. A counter-ion (TEA) of relatively lower water solubility is provided in this cleaning system, to leave the surface electrically neutral, and less prone to form electrostatic charges. TEA is a buffer in this system as well; the amount called for in the recipe above is equal to 100 mM of TEA. At the stated pH (8.5) TEA can act as a buffer in this system (pK_b = 7.9).

4.8 Detergency in non-aqueous systems

While there is an abundance of literature on surfactants and surfactant properties in aqueous systems, published material on the use of surfactants in non-aqueous systems is considerably more limited. The dry cleaning industry is the chief consumer of this technology, and it is for this user that what literature has been produced is available (Wirtz 1977; Kroschwitz 1991c). Dry cleaning involves the use of predominantly perchlorethene (1,2-dichloroethene), or a limited range of other aliphatic and/or aromatic solvents, with small amounts of water emulsified in them with surfactants to clean otherwise water-sensitive materials and fibres. There are two advantages to note. The first is that the solvents used are of low enough surface tension that they easily wet and spread over many different fibre types, and dissolve oily soils directly into the solvent. They tend not to need the adjuvancy of a surfactant. The second advantage, as indicated above, is that of carrying out the solubilization of polar soils, soils that would essentially require water as a solvent, in a system that is not likely to swell certain polar substrates or fibre types. Both of these advantages can be of use to us in solving certain cleaning problems on painted surfaces.

Although we are not generally concerned with lowering surface tension in solvent systems, as we were in the detergency process in aqueous systems, the adsorption, formation of micellular structures, and the solubilization of soiling materials are still of importance in predominantly solvent-based systems. When surfactants are dissolved into solvents, at some critical concentration they spontaneously form micellular structures just as they might under aqueous conditions, and for the same reasons. Generally, to lower the surface activity of the polar portion of the surfactant structure, 'inverse' micelles form with the polar end in the interior of the micelle, and the hydrocarbon portion pointed outwards into the general or bulk solvent solution at the CMC. As in aqueous systems, the relative hydrocarbon-to-polar aspect of a given surfactant molecule is largely obtained through observation, not calculation; the additional point here is that the nature of the solvent or solvent blend, the temperature, and the amount of water adsorbed onto the polar end of the surfactant can also affect the absolute CMC value observed for a particular surfactant, and that CMC values for surfactants in specific solvent systems are, at best, difficult to find.

Typically, in dry cleaning preparations, about 1.5–4% by weight of the cleaning mixture is detergent and the remainder is solvent (Wentz 1987). Detergents are predominantly surfactant (90%) and water (5%), with the addition of small amounts of other compounds (whiteners, sizes, bleaches, etc.). The relationship of water to surfactant is of special note here. Detergents for dry cleaning applications are generally sold as preprepared dispersions in the same solvent as the bulk dry cleaning solvent. Typically, in these preparations, the surfactant is dissolved into the solvent first; at high enough concentrations, micelles of surfactant would likely be present in the bulk solvent. A small amount of water is added (slowly) to the surfactant-solvent solution and the first molecules of water to go into the micellular containing solution are strongly adsorbed onto the polar end of the surfactant – so strongly, in fact, that its specific volume is considerably reduced from that observed for bulk water itself. These first few water molecules that go onto the surfactant are considered to be waters of hydration; water molecules tightly coordinated about the polar end of the surfactant at the centre of the micelle. Additional water added to this system would behave much more like free water, or water in a separate phase. If an ionic surfactant structure is present, this additional water then can act as a medium to dissolve the ionic moieties present, i.e., it allows both surfactant and counter-ion to behave as free ions in solution. At very low amounts of additional water, then, the ionic strength at the core of these micelles would be tremendously high until considerable amounts of water were added to dilute substantially the ionic concentration.

It has been debated strongly whether these small amounts of water associated with the inverse micelles of surfactant-in-solvent are technically microemulsions (see section 5.7 below) (Shinoda & Friberg 1975). At very low concentrations of water, either the coordination about the polar end of the surfactant, or the high ion concentration, would so lower the vapour pressure of the water present that it would be hard to imagine much free water acting as a separate phase material. So technically, at very low water concentrations, these preparations probably cannot be considered emulsions *per se*. It has been observed that with Aerosol OT, for instance, approximately 50 molecules of water can be added per molecule of surfactant before a phase separation can be detected (Lin 1978). Considering that a single Na^+ ion can require 30 molecules of water to dissolve fully, the observed value of water on Aerosol OT fits with the amount of water that might be coordinated about the polar end(s) of this surfactant (as the dioctylester of sodium sulfosuccinate), and the single sodium ion present in this surfactant.

Certain surfactants with a high enough hydrophile-lipophile balance in their structure (polar-to-hydrocarbon ratio) can form these stable micellular arrangements with solvents and small amounts of water, if when hydrated and/or ionized, they are not so polar that they become entirely insoluble in the solvent. The best dry cleaning surfactants behave in this manner, and for our purposes, so too will these structures when we make surfactant-in-solvent preparations. The solubilization of polar materials in these micelles of water and surfactant is linearly related to the amount of additional water (beyond that needed for hydration and ionization) added to the system, and the *relative* solubility of polar soils in this additional water.

Two other added concerns in dry cleaning preparations are, first, the loss of water (through partitioning) onto polar fibre types. In other words, we may start with a certain amount of bound water, but some water may be lost on application to fibres or substrates which can adsorb it from the micelles (which then become hydrated themselves). This loss of water can result in an overall decreased solubilization effect for polar soils, and if bound water is completely lost, *no* solubilization might occur. The second concern is (and this is similar to aqueous solutions of detergents) soil redeposition. In aqueous systems, colloids, polymers and the like are used to prevent soil redeposition by helping to suspend solubilized materials, so they can be removed from substrate surfaces. Up until recently, it has been difficult to imagine the range of polymer structures soluble in the solvents used in dry cleaning applications, which might work in this capacity.

On fine art and decorative painted surfaces, there are instances when we need to solubilize polar soils from surfaces that are certainly water sensitive, and surfactants in non-aqueous solvent systems may be of use for these purposes. It is certainly the case that with varnish or clear coatings that are prone to oxidation, while the bulk of the coating material may be soluble in a convenient range of solvents (solubility parameter range), excessively weathered portions of the coating may be so polar (especially if they are concentrated in the surface of the coating) that they preclude wetting, swelling, or dissolution of the bulk material in a convenient solvent system. Again, surfactant-in-solvent systems may be of use in solubilizing these types of materials if certain precautions are taken. In aqueous detergent systems, three or so theoretical models were advanced above (all of which might be correct under certain circumstances) for the adsorption of surfactant onto a soil, and the mechanism of its dissolution. It seems just as likely (or unlikely, in some cases), that a process akin to 'rolling up' may occur, for instance, in surfactant and solvent systems, as they do in aqueous detergent preparations. Binding materials in coatings and paints which can be swollen effectively with certain solvents (in lower surface tension solvents than might be required to dissolve them outright), can be dispersed in these lower surface tension solvents if their surface energies can be lowered sufficiently with the addition of a surfactant to that of the dispersing solvent. In other words, a surfactant might orient itself to surround and disperse a relatively polar polymer or macromolecule in a non-polar solvent, if the surfactant is chosen carefully to balance hydrophobe to solvent and polar aspect to polymer.

The practical problem of using surfactant-in-solvent systems is twofold. First, as was indicated above, the CMC for a surfactant in a particular solvent is sometimes hard to obtain. What experimental data is available seems to be obtained through dye-inclusion (visible light scattering) types of measurements (as micelles form at the CMC, dyes are concentrated into them and begin to absorb at different wavelengths, or to scatter light more effectively, etc.). Electrical measurements (conductivity) are difficult or impossible in solvent media; so too are viscosity measurements, in certain cases. In summary, the CMC data needed to ascertain how much of a surfactant to put into solution in a given solvent, to reach or slightly surpass the CMC, may not be easily obtained or available. Generally, this problem is handled by adding an excess of surfactant to the solvent system, but while this may work in certain other applications (dry cleaning, for instance), on painted surfaces, excesses of surfactants usually result in removal problems at the rinse or clearance stage of application. The second concern, especially with large amounts of materials to solubilize (paint films, retouching paints, coatings, etc. – i.e., more than might be present in a simple soiling layer), is that redeposition, i.e. the lack of 'suspension' of the solubilized materials, is a critical problem. Acrylic polymers, clays, and 'functionalized' colloids (clays that have been modified to be less polar) have all been used by the author as suspension aids in these types of preparation.

An example of a solvent-detergent system for soil removal from a paint surface, where both of these concerns are addressed, may be considered. A polyionic material such as polyacrylic acid can be dissolved in even relatively non-polar solvents, if it is complexed with a basic aliphatic amine (say dodecyl amine) with a high enough substitution. Generally, at ratios of about 100 acid monomer units for each amine complexed or associated with the polymer, the entire polyacrylate/dodecylamine complex can be dissolved into solvents as non-polar as mineral spirits or petroleum ether. Water, of course, is required in this system to complex the amine with the polyacid (since the transfer of a hydrogen ion is needed for the association or complexing of acid and base). Typically, the amine and polyacrylic acid are mixed together to form a uniform paste, the paste is then dispersed in the solvent, and the water is added incrementally until acid and base combine, and the complex dissolves in the solvent to form a clear, single phase, viscous gel. The water in this system resides at the acid/base ion pair, and occasionally, at free acid groups at unsubstituted monomer units down the length of the polymer as coordinated waters of hydration. Assuming a regular substitution down the length of the polymer, the dodecylamine complexed with the polyacrylic acid forms in essence a large nonionic structure in the solvent capable of solubilizing polar soils. The polymeric form of this nonionic structure essentially has an aggregation number of 1, since it can accommodate a large amount of polar material on (and about) its structure. There certainly is an excess of dodecylamine in this system. The CMC for dodecylamine in mineral spirits is not known, but since all of the amine is substituted onto the polymer, no excess is really free or available in the bulk solution to be a problem for clearance. The substituted polymer is, in effect, its own suspension aid, due to its enormous size (the polyacrylic acids used for such applications are on the order of 30–40 kilodaltons in molecular weight). Additionally, oily soils are directly soluble in the solvent. The removal or clearance of the substituted polymer is by dilution (rinses) in the solvent alone.

Case History 4.3: Unattributed, Massachusetts Hinged Writing Desk (composite object, 1750–1780)

The case piece was brought to the studio for examination and minor surface restoration work prior to its exhibition. Years of accumulated waxy polish application had not only occluded the finish surface (see Fig. 4.3.1), but had seemed to entrain a substantial amount of soiling material on the clear coated surfaces (see Fig. 4.3.2). It was decided that the surface should be cleaned, but that no actual finish materials should be removed (or added) to the presentation surfaces of the piece prior to exhibition. The following were formulated for the cleaning:

Armeen 12D	20 ml
Carbopol 934	2 g

These were mixed together to form a lump-free paste, and then the following was added:

mineral spirits	100 ml

The above ingredients mix to form a milky dispersion, then the following was added dropwise while stirring the mixture with a high torque stirrer:

water (deionized)	1.5 ml

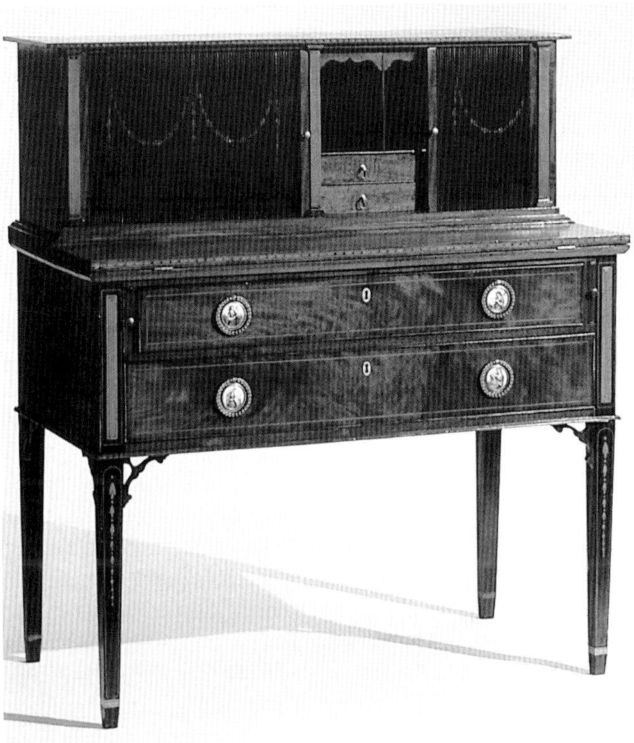

Figure 4.3.1 Unattributed, Massachusetts Hinged Writing Desk (composite object, 1750–1780) (see colour plates)

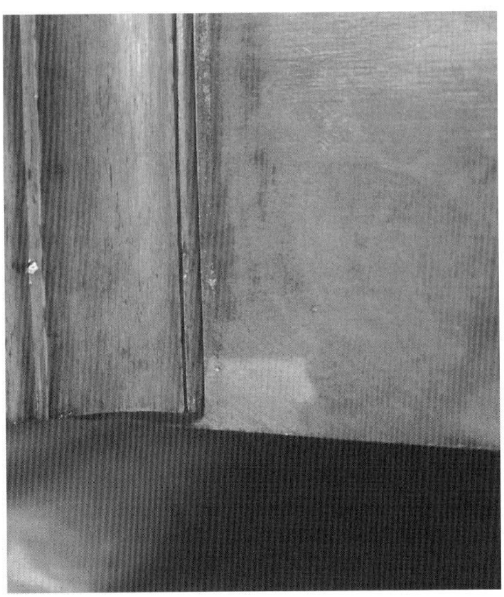

Figure 4.3.2 Unattributed, Massachusetts Hinged Writing Desk, soiling material on clear coated surfaces (see colour plates)

Typically, the solvent-surfactant gel produced was applied to the clear coated surfaces of the desk with a cotton swab; the gel was rolled on the surface for a moment, and then the bulk of the gel was wiped away on a clean dry swab. The area thus treated was rinsed with mineral spirits to clear any residual amount of gel and waxy soil from the clear coating surface.

Commentary

This solvent-surfactant gel is a good example of a (polymeric) surfactant-in-solvent system with water present in a coordinated way, rather than as in a separate phase, as it might be in a microemulsion or macroemulsion system. At the weights given, there are about 6.6×10^{-4} moles of polyacrylic acid present (MW of Carbopol 934 = 30K), and 1.08 moles of dodecylamine (MW of Armeen 12D = 184) blended together initially. Now each acrylic acid monomer unit on the polymer can conceivably complex with one dodecylamine molecule. If each acrylic unit has a MW of 72, there are about 416 monomer units, on average, in each polyacrylic acid molecule so the dodecylamine-to-polymer ratio is about 4:1. This means that for every 100 or so monomer units there is a dodecylamine molecule substituted on the polymer. The amount of water in this system is rather low, about 0.8 molar, or close to a 1:1 molar ratio of water to dodecylamine; the amount of water could probably be increased by about two to three times before it would start to be included, not as bound water of hydration but as a separate emulsified phase. As a separate phase the water could conceivably affect the oil-resin coating surface, and dissolve polar materials in the surface coating – or be dissolved itself in the coating to 'blanch' it. But in a bound form, essentially as part of the surfactant molecule (the polyacid/amine complex in this case), it can facilitate the solubilization of polar soils without free water being present. The waxy accumulated 'polish' residues in this case are soluble directly in the mineral spirits, so the combination is an effective cleaner for this type of soiled surface. Since the polyacid/amine complex is soluble in mineral spirits, it can be (diluted) rinsed away in the same solvent as well.

Case History 4.4: William Naismith, *Pastoral Landscape* (oil on canvas, nineteenth century)

The canvas had sustained three small tears at various points on the composition; these had been badly mended and retouched in oil paints that were now a poor match for the surrounding colours. The landscape had a decidedly dry and leathery look overall to the surface; it had accumulated a substantial soiling layer, and appeared to carry two clear coatings on its surface which had darkened and discoloured considerably with age (see Fig. 4.4.1). From cross-sections (Fig. 4.4.2 in visible light and Fig. 4.4.3 in UV light), it was verified that there were two coatings present, neither of which appeared to be original. Both coatings seemed to include a high oil content (they were positive with Rhodamine B), along with natural resin materials. The paints were apparently oil bound (they were positive with Rhodamine B), as was the off-white coloured ground beneath. Interestingly, both a slight uptake of a protein stain (fluorescamine), and a positive staining for a carbohydrate moiety (triphenyl tetrazolium chloride) were seen in the original paint layers in the cross-sections, suggesting a binding system that was certainly a drying oil, but with a small amount of a dispersed aqueous material in it (not illustrated here). Solvent tests on the painting indicated that very polar solvents or solvent blends were required to solubilize the coating layers (ethanol, for instance, seemed to dissolve the uppermost coating slowly and methanol, at best, only appeared to swell the older coating on the

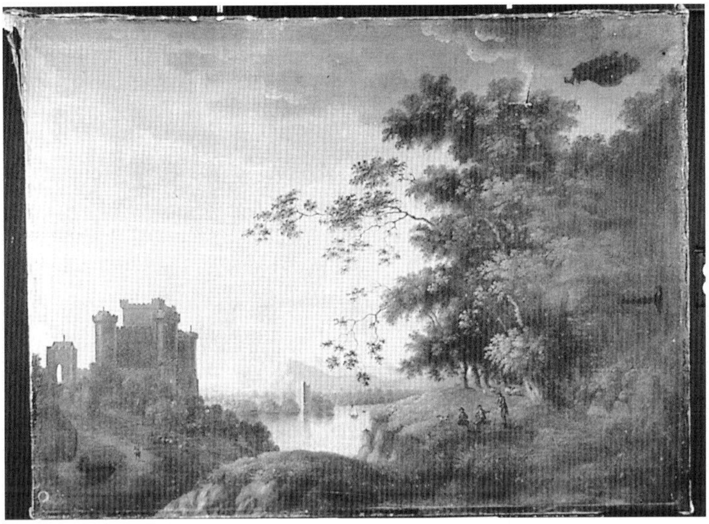

Figure 4.4.1 William Naismith, *Pastoral Landscape* (oil on canvas, nineteenth century), before cleaning (see colour plates)

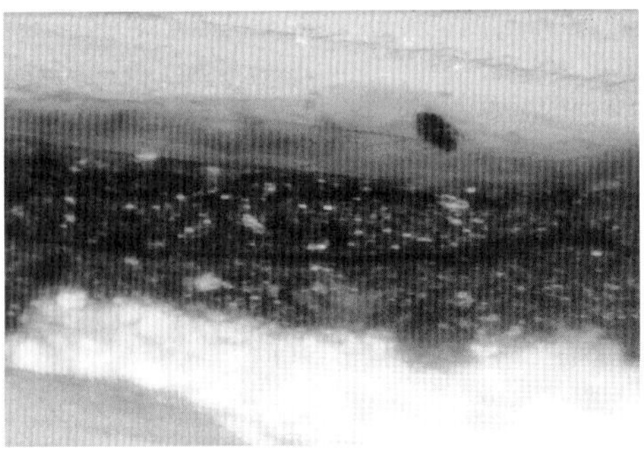

Figure 4.4.2 (see colour plates)

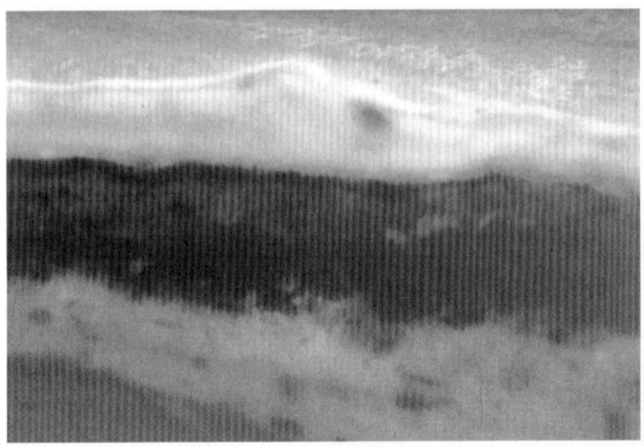

Figure 4.4.3 (see colour plates)

surface). A solvent-surfactant system (gel) was formulated that seemed effective at solubilizing the uppermost coating. Once it had been removed, the older varnish or coating layer responded to an aqueous detergent system, which featured a chelating or complexing material in its formula. Initially then, the first coating was removed with:

Ethomeen C-25	20 ml
Carbopol 934	2 g

which were mixed together to form a lump-free paste, and then the following were added:

ethanol	80 ml
xylene	20 ml

The above ingredients were mixed to form a milky dispersion, then the following was added dropwise while stirring the mixture with a high torque stirrer:

water (deionized)	12 ml

Typically, the solvent-surfactant gel produced was applied to the uppermost coating with a cotton swab; the gel was rolled on the surface for a moment, and then the bulk of the gel was wiped away on a clean dry swab. The area thus treated was rinsed with isopropanol:mineral spirits (1:1) to clear any residual amount of gel. The older coating on the painting surface was removed with the following preparation:

water (deionized)	100 ml
HSRE (free acid)	2 g

Triethanolamine was added dropwise until the pH was raised in the solution to 6.0, and then the following was added:

Tetronic 908	5 ml
methyl cellulose (4000 cps)	1.5 g

The above mixture was stirred until a clear gel was produced.

Typically, the gel was applied to the paint surface with a small brush (00), stirred for a moment on the surface, and was then removed on a dry cotton swab, along with the dissolved older surface coating. The area thus treated was rinsed with deionized water and left to air dry.

Commentary

The substantial amount of oil added to the uppermost coating, along with its considerable ageing (oxidation), and the overall soil accumulation on it surface suggested in this case a solvent-surfactant system. The coating barely dissolved in ethanol, mainly because of the cross-linked oil in it. Instead of attempting to solubilize it fully in a polar solvent or solvent blend, a surfactant coupled to a less polar solvent (or blend) might disperse the oily component more effectively. In other words, rather than dissolving problematic materials through matching solubility parameter of solvent to potential solute, it might be easier (and more beneficial for the painting) to lower the solute surface tension sufficiently to disperse it with a surfactant in a less polar solvent. Now this coating probably contained a range of resin structures in a variety of oxidation states; the solvent blend used (80:20 ethanol:xylene) was still fairly polar – by itself it would not have dissolved the coating rapidly – but with the addition of the surfactant (here, the Carbopol/Ethomeen C-25 complex) the oily component could be dispersed in a solvent blend of at least this polarity. Again, the construction of the surfactant-solvent gel is critical to the situation. At the amounts given, 20ml Ethomeen C-25 (a POE (15) cocoalkylamine, MW approximately 850), equal to 0.2 moles, and 6.0×10^{-4} M of Carbopol 934 (2g) are used in this system. Assuming that there are about 416 monomer units of acrylic acid (0.24M) on a single polymer chain of Carbopol, the substitution rate of Ethomeen C-25 to Carbopol is about 1:1 in this formula i.e., for each polymer chain, a single nonionic 'tail' has been added. This 'tail' represents the polar end of the complex Carbopol/Ethomeen C-25 structure, and the acrylic polymer is the less polar, 'lipophile' portion of the molecule. The nonionic 'tail' can adsorb a certain amount of water, coordinated around the ethereal oxygens of the ethoxylate (POE) chain (at least 2–3 water molecules/etherial oxygen). This water is bound to the polar end of the complex surfactant (polymer/ Ethomeen) structure and behaves differently than if it were 'free' (miscible with the surrounding solvents) or in a separate phase entirely. The overall solubility parameter of this surfactant-solvent system is still largely that of ethanol:xylene (80:20), and yet, with the surfactant and water in place, very polar soils and coating constituents can be solubilized in this mixture. The polymeric nature to the Carbopol/Ethomeen C-25 complex is also its own suspension aid. Rinsing is effected with a less polar solvent blend than the ethanol:xylene mixture (isopropanol/mineral spirits); we can rinse the complex away in any solvent polar enough to retain the Carbopol/Ethomeen C-25 complex in solution. The ethoxylated 'tail' to the polymer allows us to rinse with solvent polarities much less than would be required for the polymer by itself (Carbopol, as a polyacrylic acid, could conceivably be soluble in a range of polar solvents, from ethanol to water).

The second stage in cleaning, with the HEDTA and Tetronic 908, is of interest. The older coating was probably so degraded (i.e. oxidized) that it would be water soluble were it not for metal ions contributed from the paint layers themselves, and the polar constituents in the oil paint films which might also be incorporated into the coating on application. HEDTA is a chelator (see section 6.1.4 below) strong enough to complex Pb^{+2} ion from a range of weakly acidic binding or coating materials. At a pH of 6.0, it can function as a chelator, and the oil film beneath the older coating will still be minimally swollen at this pH. A surfactant of high HLB (24) was chosen in this case (Tetronic 908, an unusual nonionic 'block' polymer structure consisting of a short chain propoxylate polymer linked to an ethoxylate polymer chain), mainly to help solubilize the material released by the chelator; as the chelator would complex $Pb^{+2,}$ for instance, the Tetronic could then be available to help solubilize the oily and resinous materials freed from the metal ions.

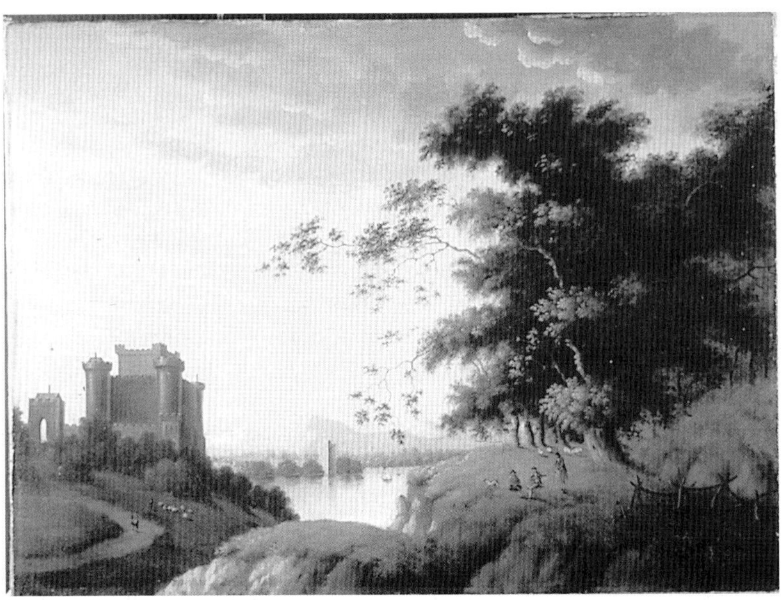

Figure 4.4.4 After cleaning (see colour plates)

Case History 4.5: Frederic Remington, *In Defense of the Barricade* (oil on canvas, 1889)

The painting was from a period in Remington's life when he was producing a myriad of black and white images for magazine illustrations of the 'Old West'. At some point in the painting's history (well after the artist's death), a clear coating (a natural resin with a bright yellowish autofluorescence in near UV) had been applied to the paint surface. At some subsequent point, possibly in the 1940s, a highly chromatic palette of oil paints was applied to the painting to 'colourize' it, i.e., make it appear as if it were originally intended or constructed as an easel painting and not an illustration. More recently, the surface of the painting was coated with an acrylic clear coating that seemed to resist resolubilization even in a moderately polar range of solvents (acetone, propan-2-ol). Other materials or conditions tested (more polar solvents, alkaline preparations etc.), only seemed to undercut the overpaint and dissolve the original oil paints more quickly. The cleaning task was to remove the acrylic coating and the oil overpaints, and, if possible, recover the coated surface to the black and white painting beneath as intact as possible. The following surfactant-solvent gel was prepared to remove the overpaint:

Ethomeen C-25	20 ml
Carbopol 934	2 g

These were mixed together to form a lump-free paste, and then the following was added:

N-Pyrrole	100 ml

The above ingredients were mixed to form a milky dispersion, then the following was added dropwise while stirring the mixture with a high torque stirrer:

water (deionized)	12 ml

Typically, the solvent-surfactant gel produced was applied to the overpainted areas of the painting with a cotton swab; the gel was rolled on the surface for a moment, and then the bulk of the gel and solubilized overpaint material was wiped away on a clean dry swab. The area thus treated was rinsed with isopropanol: mineral spirits (1:1) to clear any residual amount of gel and solubilized acrylic and oil overpaint from the (still natural resin coated) painting surface beneath.

Commentary

The construction of the surfactant-solvent gel in this case is similar to that described above in Case History 4.4. The amounts of polyacrylic acid, water and Ethomeen C-25 all are chosen to build specifically a hydrated nonionic complex of polymer and Ethomeen in the general solvent N Pyrrole (1-methyl-2-pyrrolidinone). This solvent is particularly effective in swelling and solubilizing cross-linked acrylic polymers. The oil overpaints were coated with a now intermixed layer of acrylic resin on their surface; its cross-linking only added to the difficulty observed in solubilizing the oil overpaints directly. The N- Pyrrole was viscous enough (15–20 Kcps) in this gel form that it could remain on the overpaint surface for a few moments and be restricted from penetrating to the underlying materials. Once the acrylic was substantially solubilized by the N- Pyrrole, the 1940s overpaints, swollen by the solvent as well, could be rinsed away with a relatively non-polar solvent blend (isopropanol: mineral spirits).

Case History 4.6: Unattributed, Tilt-top Tea Table (composite object, Philadelphia c.1765)

A 'piecrust' tilt-top tea table (*c.*1765), originally purchased by Henry Francis du Pont before 1950, was normally on display in the Blackwell Parlor of the Winterthur Museum, and represented the best of Philadelphia Chippendale or Rococo furniture from that period. The table's finish had become disturbingly gray and turbid (see Fig. 4.6.1). Colour slides from about 1960 indicated that at that time, the base of the table had a dark, alligatored finish. The top had a complete, though worn, coating of what was considered at the time to be shellac.

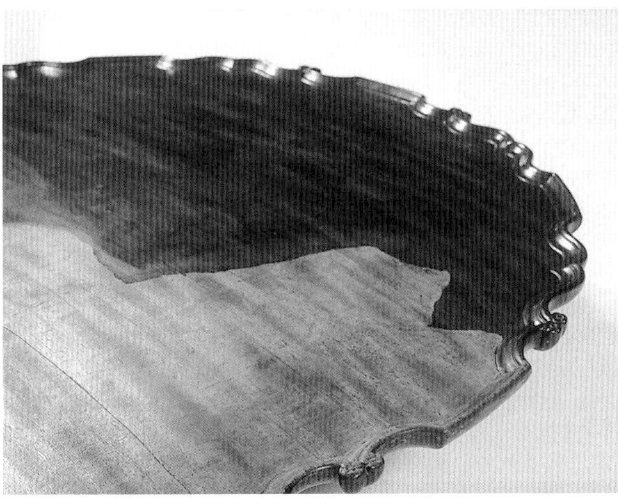

Figure 4.6.1 Unattributed, Tilt-top Tea Table (composite object, Philadelphia *c.*1765) (see colour plates)

A brief treatment report from 1974 stated that the old finish on the table top was removed because of severe water damage to the shellac finish. It did not note the cleaning materials used to remove the coating, but suggested that a solvent system such as ethyl alcohol had been used. The table top was then recoated with six coats of Zar brand polyurethane. The gray or turbid quality now visible seemed to have developed since the 1974 treatment. Other treatments included the report of one in June of 1981 which indicated that the finish on the base of the table was removed to allow for a study of the carving. It was then recoated with a thin coat of lemon shellac followed by a waxing (see Fig. 4.6.2). In the 1981 report, the polyurethane coating of the table top was noted as having already developed a hazy or gray appearance. It also appeared to have a toned or *faux* graining layer streaked on under the

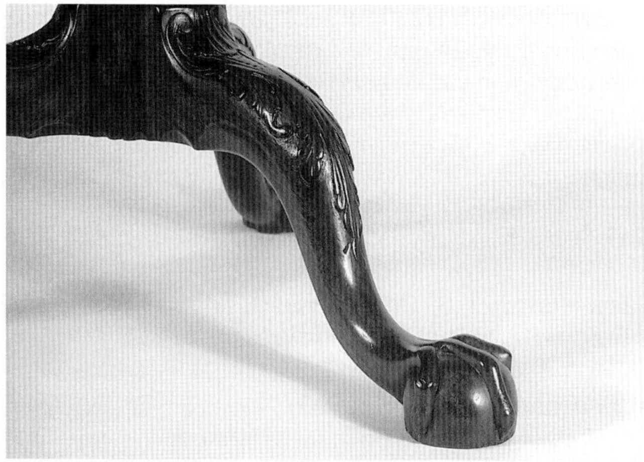

Figure 4.6.2
(see colour plates)

polyurethane. In cross-sections from the table top, it was clear that a still-continuous oil-resin coating was discernible on and in the wood substrate, below the polyurethane layer. The oil resin appeared to be quite old, if not original to the table. As such, it would provide saturation and colour to the surface which would have been lost to the solvent or mechanical reduction normally required to remove polyurethanes. Small areas were tested with solvent mixtures of wide-ranging solubility parameters and were examined for efficacy in preferentially removing the polyurethane and oil 'toning' layers. Of all the materials tested, only aromatic solvents, e.g. xylene and toluene, produced even a slight swelling of the polyurethane layer. Proprietary paint strippers comprised of methylene chloride and methanol in gelled carriers removed the polyurethane and oil-staining layers. However, they also invaded and solvated the underlying oleo resinous materials at a rapid rate. The result was an exposed and raw-looking wood substrate surface. The goal of the cleaning strategy was to remove the greying polyurethane coat and oil-toning layer beneath. The oleo-resinous materials below were to be left as undisturbed as possible to recapture the best possible surface for the underlying wood, i.e., its 'patina'. The polyurethane was removed with the following surfactant-solvent system:

Ethomeen C-25	8 ml
Carbopol 940	1.5 g

These were mixed together to form a lump-free paste, and then the following was added:

Acetone	200 ml
benzyl alcohol	50 ml

The above ingredients mix to form a milky dispersion, then the following was added dropwise while stirring the mixture with a high torque stirrer:

water (deionized)	25 ml

Typically, the solvent-surfactant gel produced was applied to the polyurethane coating with a cotton swab; the gel was rolled on the surface for a moment, and then the bulk of the gel was wiped away on a clean dry swab, along with the swollen and/or solubilized polyurethane. The area thus treated was rinsed with acetone:mineral spirits (1:1) to clear any residual amount of gel and solubilized polyurethane from the table top surface. After the polyurethane was removed, substantial amounts of the oil 'toning' layer were still present on the table top surface. The following aqueous mixture was applied as a second stage in cleaning the surface:

water (deionized)	100 ml
Trizma-HCl, pH 8.4	0.6 g
Triton X-100	1 ml
Lipase (Type VII, Sigma)	1 g

Typically the enzyme-detergent solution was applied to the table top with a small synthetic bristle brush (00) (see Fig. 4.6.3), was stirred for a moment and then removed with a dry cotton swab, along with any dissolved oil 'toning' material. The area thus treated was rinsed with deionized water, and finally mineral spirits (see Fig. 4.6.4).

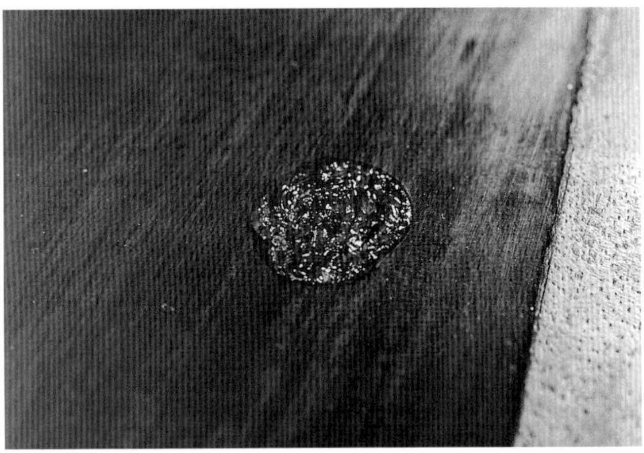

Figure 4.6.3
(see colour plates)

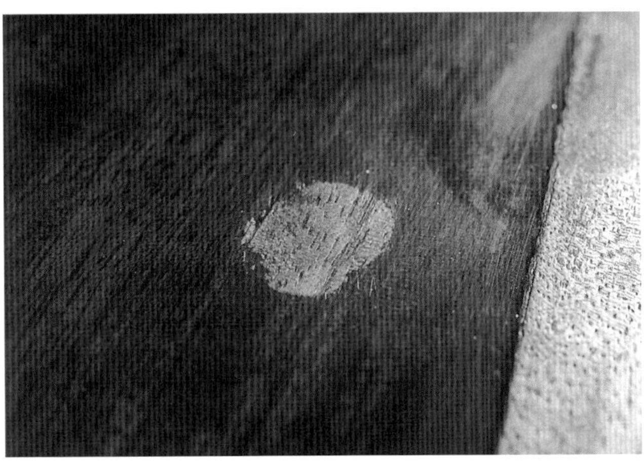

Figure 4.6.4
(see colour plates)

Commentary

The particular solvent blend specified in the initial step in this case history should be polar enough to swell a cross-linked polyurethane (at a molar ratio of 10:1:2; acetone:benzyl alcohol:water). The selection of an aromatic and a polar solvent in particular at this molar ratio (10:1) should predictably have some solvency effect on this and similar isocyanate, glycerol, and mono-glyceride derived structures. Depending on just how much cross-linking has occurred in this polymeric system (cross-linking in this case is through the 'drying' or addition together of unsaturated fatty acid groups esterified down the length of the polymer chain), the rate of dissolution should be increased if the surface tension of the bulk polymer can be lowered to match that of the solvent blend surrounding it by a surfactant. Again, a surfactant-solvent system has been prepared consisting of a polyacrylic acid and an ethoxylated amine derivative (Carbopol and Ethomeen C-25) dissolved into the specified solvent blend in a hydrated form. Fortunately, in this case, a 'mistake' was made in the application of an oil 'toning' layer immediately beneath the polyurethane. Unpolymerized oily material from the underlying toning or graining layer probably intermixed with the polyurethane to a limited degree (as it was applied just before the polyurethane). The presence of added unpolymerized oil in the urethane inhibited its cross-linking, allowing it to remain (for a bit longer than usual) soluble (or at least dispersible) in the surfactant-solvent system used in the initial step in this treatment. The residual oily material from the 'toning' layer that remained on the oil-resin varnish surface of the table top could be solubilized in an aqueous system; if the pH were not too high (8.5), and the surfactant not too high in HLB number (Triton X-100, 13.5), the oily toning material could be dispersed in a solvent (water) and under conditions (pH, surfactant strength) that would minimally affect the original oil-resin coating. Whether the added hydrolyzing and solubilization effect of the lipase was needed or really augmented the surfactant and water activity alone can, in this case, be debated since the enzyme activity would be generally suppressed by the high concentration of Triton X-100 used here.

5

Emulsions

5.1 Emulsions: definition

An emulsion is usually defined as a dispersion of two mutually immiscible or insoluble liquids (Osipow 1962: 295). Emulsions usually contain an emulsifying agent (surfactant) that helps to stabilize the dispersion of the two insoluble liquids. Normally, when an excess of one of the immiscible liquids is present, the other liquid is said to be the *dispersed* or *discontinuous phase* material. The liquid in excess is usually referred to as the *dispersing* or *continuous phase* material. For convenience, the easiest model of such immiscible liquids is a combination of oil and water. Neither liquid can interact well with the other; water is only capable of forming hydrogen or dipolar types of interactions with itself and other molecules. Oils, on the other hand, are essentially hydrocarbons and are only capable of forming London or Van der Waals type of interactions. When brought together in a dispersion of one in the other, oil and water don't easily mix. A considerable amount of interfacial tension exists between the two materials because of the lack of secondary bonding or attractive forces between the two. Regardless of how much mechanical agitation might be exerted on the two materials to physically distribute one material in the other, no amount of energy through mechanical means can overcome the inherent instability in mixing these two types of material. A molecule like a surfactant can help to reduce the considerable amount of interfacial tension between the two materials by establishing weak secondary interactions simultaneously with both liquids. The oil and water analogy is so convenient, that the oil-in-water (O/W) or water-in-oil (W/O) shorthand notations are now recognized as general designations or representations for all immiscible liquids (i.e., solvents, melted waxes and water) brought together in emulsion types of arrangements (Osipow 1962: 296).

Figs 5.1 and 5.2 may help to illustrate the two basic types of emulsion (O/W or W/O) structures and the position of the surfactant or emulsifying agent in both. One

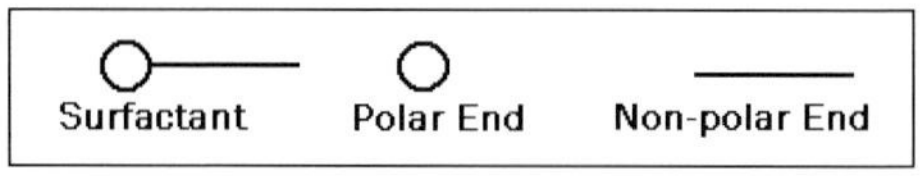

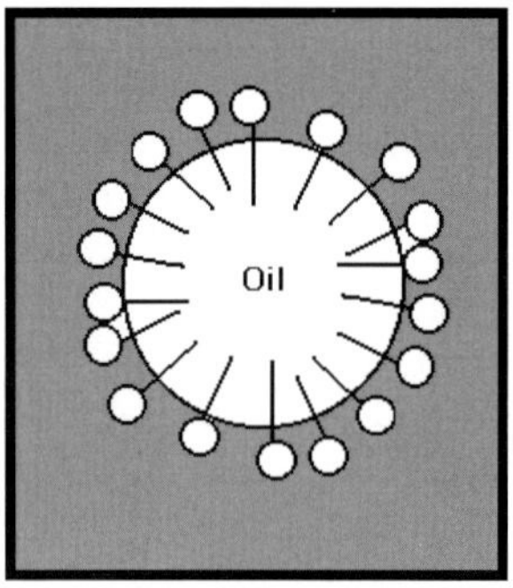

O/W Type of Emulsion

Figure 5.1

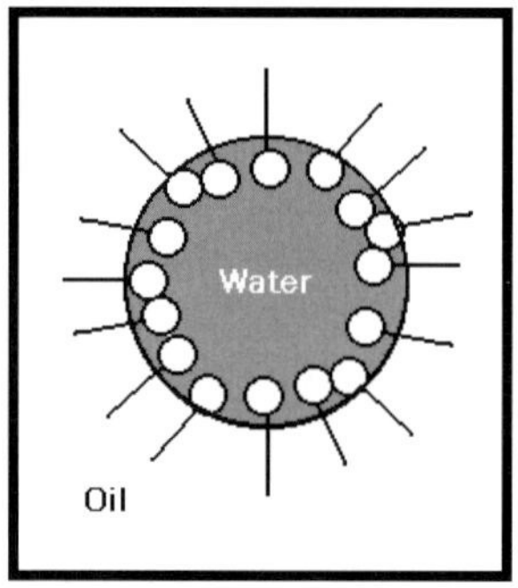

W/O Type of Emulsion

Figure 5.2

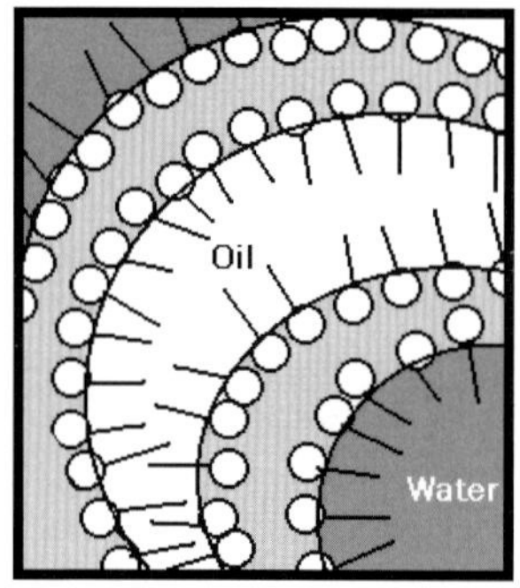

Inversion or Dual Emulsion

Figure 5.3

other possibility that should be mentioned for a type of dispersion is a so-called *dual emulsion*, or *inversion emulsion*. Still using the oil and water model; when the proportions of oil and water are nearly equal, the dispersion of one material in the other cannot be categorized as either the W/O or O/W type, but takes on a decidedly lamellar type of arrangement. Neither material is clearly the dispersing or dispersed phase material, as in Fig. 5.3. These lamellar types of emulsions have special properties and applications specific to them which will be discussed shortly. But to begin with, since surfactants are so central to the stable construction of emulsions of whatever form, estimating accurately their lipophilic and hydrophilic tendencies or abilities will be of immediate practical benefit.

5.2 Hydrophile-lipophile balance (HLB) number

The HLB system is a numerical scale developed within the detergent industry to help describe a surfactant's relative ability both to form and to stabilize emulsion systems (Griffin 1949: 311). The scale runs from 0 to 40; the lower the number on this scale, the weaker a given surfactant's ability to emulsify oil in water. The higher numbers concomitantly designate surfactants with the strongest ability to form stable oil in water emulsions. Empirically, the HLB number for a given surfactant could be determined by mixing a set amount of a given surfactant with standard volumes of mineral oil and water. The surfactant/oil/water mixture could be shaken, and the emulsion thus produced could be timed for how long it remained stable (time for separation into oil and water phases again). As an example, lauryl sulfate can produce a very stable and long-lived emulsion between mineral oil and water; its HLB designation has been determined experimentally to be, not surprisingly, at the high end of the HLB scale (40). Lecithin (phosphatidyl choline), on the other hand, is a naturally occurring emulsifier and wetting agent found in egg white; if lecithin were to be mixed and shaken with mineral oil and water, the emulsion produced would be short-lived and would separate in minutes. Its HLB number is quite low (about 4). While it may not be immediately obvious, the usefulness of the HLB scale lies in its ability to assign *relative* numerical values to a variety of surfactant structures. At the last count, there were something like 30,000 trade-named surfactants on the market in North America alone, and at least as many in Europe (*McCutcheon's* 1991). While undoubtedly some of these materials are similar in chemical structure, comparing one surfactant to another, and more importantly, interchanging one surfactant functionally for another, might be a difficult task without comparing HLB numbers for each. Regardless of structural differences that may exist between surfactants, if both materials carry the same HLB designation, they exhibit the same relative degrees of hydrophilic and lipophilic tendencies, and they may often be used interchangeably in the same or similar applications or functions. The magnitude of the HLB number describes a fundamental surfactant property, but it would be wise to note here that, at least empirically, the HLB number is based on the relative affinity of a surfactant for a low melting point paraffinic compound like mineral oil and water. High HLB numbered surfactants exhibit both strong lipophilic and hydrophilic tendencies in their structure; they are usually characterized by a strongly hydrophilic group or groups at one end of the surfactant molecule (carboxylate, sulfate, sulfonate, amine) and a lipophilic structure at the other (optimum: a linear C_{12} hydrocarbon). Low HLB surfactants, on the other hand, can be characterized by structures which have predominantly either hydrophilic *or* lipophilic tendencies. Polysaccharides, for instance, can exhibit weak surfactant properties and can experimentally yield low HLB numbers; these structures are predominately hydrophilic in character with very few, if any, lipophilic groups on them. Likewise, some waxy esters (of C_{20} or greater hydrocarbons) would also yield low HLB numbers, although these structures would be predominately hydrocarbon in nature. There is an interesting correlation between HLB number and CMCs for surfactants; usually low CMC structures (< 1 mM) are predominately lipophilic in structure, and exhibit low HLB numbers. High CMC surfactants (> 20 mM) are predominately hydrophilic in structure, and also exhibit low HLBs. Mid-range CMC surfactants (2 – 20 mM) tend to have the highest HLBs. Low HLB surfactants can therefore often be characterized as 'out of balance; in one direction or the other (either towards the hydrophilic or the lipophilic), while high HLB surfactants have strong polarities in both directions.

5.2.1 HLB from group number

The HLB numbers for many commercially available surfactants can be found in such standard sources as *McCutcheon's Emulsifiers and Detergents* (1991) or directly from the manufacturers of these materials. When the HLB number is not available (or has yet to be determined for a new structure, for instance), an approximation of the value can be mathematically calculated using standard values associated with specific functional groups. Table 5.1 overleaf presents a selected list of functional groups. Assuming a basic C_{12} linear alkyl structure, the values given reflect the number that would be contributed (added or subtracted) to the overall HLB number of a surfactant that contained any of these additional groups.

Sodium lauryl sulfate, as a linear C_{12} alkyl sulfate, could be assigned an HLB number of 38.7 (the single sulfate group, and no additional carbons beyond the

Table 5.1 Group numbers of selected functional groups (Griffin 1949: 331)

		Group number
Hydrophilic groups	$—SO_4^{\ -}Na^+$	38.7
	$—COO^-K^+$	21.1
	$—COO^-Na^+$	19.1
	N (tertiary amine)	9.4
	Ester (sorbitan ring)	6.8
	Ester (free)	2.4
	—COOH	2.1
	—OH (free)	1.9
	—O—	1.3
	Hydroxyl (sorbitan ring)	0.5
Lipophilic groups	$—CH_2–$	−0.475
	$—CH_3$	−0.475
	==C==	−0.475
	==CH—	−0.475
Derived groups	$—(CH_2—CH_2—0)$	0.33
	$—(CH_2\text{-}CH_2\text{-}CH_2—O)\text{-}$	−0.15

basic 12, would yield a calculated value of 38.7, and this, of course, is close to the experimental value of 40). As an additional example, calculating the HLB number for sodium deoxycholate (a common bile acid or 'soap' associated with lipid transport in the bloodstream and gut, $C_{24}H_{39}O_4Na$) from group numbers would work as follows:

2	==C==	2 × (−0.475)	=	−0.95
8	==CH—	8 × (−0.475)	=	−3.8
3	$—CH_3$	1 × (−0.475)	=	−0.475
10	$—CH_2–$	0 × (−0.475)	=	0
2	—OH(free)	2 × (1.9)	=	3.8
1	$—COO^-Na^+$	1 × (19.1)	=	19.1
				17.65

Note: the 10 methylene carbons, and 2 of the methyl carbons would, in this case, be considered the initial 'C_{12}' unit; the additional methyl group, the OHs, etc. would then be totalled to arrive at the net HLB number for this structure. Generally then, sodium deoxycholate as a surfactant can be given an approximate HLB number of 17.6, which would put it near the middle of the HLB scale.

The predicted HLB numbers from group numbers can often correlate well with the numbers determined experimentally, especially for certain structures (anionic or cationic linear alkyl materials).

Again, there is a high degree of correlation to observed HLBs when structures are essentially linear alkyl hydrocarbon chains substituted with single (and simple) hydrophilic groups. For ethylene glycol, propylene glycol (and polymers of these functional groups), or more complex hydrophilic groups (polyols like sorbitan, for instance), wide deviations can occur between group number HLBs and observed or

Table 5.2 Comparison of selected surfactant HLBs derived experimentally and through group number (Davies 1957)

Surfactant	HLB (experimental)	HLB (group number)
Na lauryl sulfate	40	38.5
K oleate	20	18.2
Na oleate	18	16.2
Tween 80 (POE 20 sorbitan mono-oleate)	15	17.5
POE 10 sorbitan mono-oleate	13.5	13.2
Tween 81 (POE 5 sorbitan mono-oleate)	10	12.5
Tween 61 (POE 4 sorbitan monostearate)	9.6	14.1
Sorbitan mono-laurate	8.6	13.8
PEG 100 laurate	7.4	33
POE 2 sorbitan mono-oleate	7	12.8
Triglycerol monostearate	7	2.0
Sorbitan mono-oleate	7	10.9
Sorbitan mono-palmitate	6.7	11.9
Sorbitan mono-stearate	5.9	14.8
Span 80 (sorbitol mono-oleate)	4.3	10.9
Propylene glycol mono-laurate	4.5	1.7
Sorbitan distearate	3.5	13
Glycerol monostearate	3.8	1.28
Propylene glycol monostearate	3.5	0.8
Sorbitan tristearate	2.1	11.2
Cetyl alcohol	1	1.9
Oleic acid	1	(0)
Sorbitan tetrastearate	0.5	9.5

experimental HLBs. PEG 100 laurate is a good example; by group number the HLB is predicted to be 33 while experimentally the observed HLB is only 7.4. Wide deviations also occur when the hydrophilic group is centrally located in a molecule rather than on one end of a hydrocarbon chain; when multiple substitutions of hydrocarbon chains are present and when branching of hydrocarbon chains occurs. In the series or sorbitan mono-, di-, tri-, and tetrastearates, the HLB numbers should decrease as more hydrocarbon chains are substituted onto the sorbitan ring (the hydrophilic group). While the HLBs do decrease in order of substitution, the magnitude of the HLBs predicted vary greatly from (they are much higher than) the experimentally observed values.

The HLBs of structures that contain ethoxylated (polymers of glycol), propoxylated (polymers of propylene glycol), and polyhydric hydrophilic groups are better estimated using the following formula (Osipow 1962: 313):

$$\text{HLB} = \frac{E + P}{5} \qquad [5.1]$$

where E is the weight per cent of the structure that is ethoxylate, and P is the weight per cent that is polyhydric in the overall molecule. Again, take for example, the series sorbitan mono-, di-, tri-, and tetra stearate (see Table 5.3 overleaf).

Table 5.3 Experimental versus calculated HLBs (Griffin 1949: 331)

	Experimental HLB	Calculated HLB
Sorbitan mono-stearate	8.6	7.7
Sorbitan distearate	3.5	4.8
Sorbitan tristearate	2.1	3.5
Sorbitan tetrastearate	0.5	2.7

(Example: the molecular weight of sorbitan mono-stearate is 374; the molecular weight of the sorbitan portion of the molecule is 145; the weight % of polyhydric structure in the molecule is therefore 38.7%; the sum divided by 5 is 7.7).

It should be noted from the formula (equation 5.1) that, since the weight per cent of either (or both) the ethoxylate and/or polyhydric content of a given structure cannot exceed 100, the highest HLB value possible for these types of hydrophile-containing surfactants is 20.

HLB numbers for anionics and cationics can vary significantly according to the ion paired with a weakly acidic or basic hydophilic group. Consider the HLBs determined experimentally for these oleates (Table 5.4).

Table 5.4 HLB of various oleates (Griffin 1949: 320)

	HLB
Triethanolamine^{+} oleate	12
K^{+} oleate	20
Na^{+} oleate	18
Oleic acid	1

With weakly acidic or basic structures, counter-ions tend to exert a greater net influence over the observed HLBs; triethanolamine, as an alcoholic amine, lowers the HLB of the oleate anion because of the increased association of this counter-ion with the oleate ion in solution when it is protonated, when compared to the Na^{+} or K^{+} salts. Free oleic acid has such a high pK_a (4.5), and the free acid is virtually insoluble in water at or below this pH.

5.2.2 HLB numbers used to define functional uses

Whether the data is derived mathematically, or experimentally, HLB numbers can often provide a useful reference point for the functional uses for surfactants. Table 5.5 lists the HLB number ranges traditionally associated with, or used to define, certain uses for surfactants.

Table 5.5 implies that, at, or above the specified HLB range, certain uses are associated with, or possible for, a given surfactant structure. Because of the relatively high surface tension of water, very little chemical 'work' needs to be done by a surfactant to stabilize the surface to a water droplet in a hydrophobic environment, and effectively create a stable dispersion of it in an oily phase. Hence, very low HLB surfactants (4 – 6) are associated with the effective dispersion of water-in-oil (W/O) type preparations. The ranges defined in Table 5.5 are only the minimum HLBs required for the end use specified – higher HLBs would also work for a given

Table 5.5 HLB numbers and functional uses for surfactants (Griffin 1949: 320)

HLB range	Use
4– 6	W/O emulsifiers
7– 9	Wetting agents
8– 18	O/W emulsifiers
13– 15	Detergents
15– 18	Solubilizing

application. To 'wet' water onto a hydrophobic surface requires more chemical work for a surfactant, and this is reflected in the higher HLB (7–9) range designated for wetting agents. Low surface tension materials are actually harder to disperse in water than water in oil, and higher HLB surfactants (8–18) are required to make these kinds of stable arrangements. It may be somewhat arbitrary to distinguish 'detergency' from 'solubilization', but detergency is usually taken to refer to the dispersion of soiling materials in particular (carbon, iron oxide, etc.), and solubilization usually refers to dispersing wider ranges of non-water soluble materials (resins, etc.). Surfactants with HLBs in the 13–18 range or greater are sufficiently strong to disperse a range of solid hydrophobic materials. In the present context, a surfactant with an HLB of 18 will just barely be able to carry this out; as the HLB increases though, so too would a given surfactant's ability to disperse a hydrophobic material. Practically speaking, it is in the range of HLBs from 18 to 40 that we begin to select for surfactant structures for cleaning and solubilizing effects – the higher HLB number surfactant we choose, the stronger the solubilizing effect on hydrophobic materials (i.e., the stronger the ability to overcome strong interfacial tension). By analogy, when we select or blend solvents to help dissolve a varnish, say on a painting surface, we consider more and more polar solvents or solvent blends until we find a polarity that dissolves a resinous material and (hopefully) minimally swells underlying oil-bound materials. The HLB scale, in effect, defines a strength or affinity scale for surfactants towards hydrophobes; but it is a *relative* scale, given the fact that it is based, by definition, on the emulsification of a *particular* lipophilic material, mineral oil, in water. While HLB numbers will help in defining and describing a surfactant's ability to solubilize certain materials, it falls short in those cases where materials are not similar to paraffinic hydrocarbons such as mineral oil.

5.2.3 HLBs and surfactant mixtures

Surfactants are often blended for a variety of reasons: cost effectiveness, synergistic effects of combining more than one structure, etc. When two or more surfactants are blended together, the net HLB of the combined surfactants is derived by the following formula (Osipow 1962: 313):

$$\mathrm{HLB}_{\mathrm{mix}} = \Sigma\,(\mathrm{HLB}_{\mathrm{A}})\,(\mathrm{W}_{\mathrm{A}}) + (\mathrm{HLB}_{\mathrm{B}})(\mathrm{W}_{\mathrm{B}}) + \ldots + (\mathrm{HLB}_{n})\,(\mathrm{W}_{n}) \quad [5.2]$$

where W_n is the individual fractional weight per cent of the total amount of surfactants used, and HLB_n are the individual HLB numbers of each surfactant. As an example, two surfactants of HLB 20 and 40 respectively are blended together.

If 20% of surfactant A were used, and 80% of B, the net HLB for the mixture would be:

$$HLB_{mix} = (20)(0.2) + (40)(0.8) = 36$$

This ability to derive a single net HLB from combinations of individual surfactant HLBs has enormous practical implications. A simple binary mixture of an HLB 40 surfactant and an HLB 20 surfactant could conceivably be used to make surfactant mixtures that span the entire range of HLBs from 20 to 40, by simply varying the proportions of each to obtain the desired net HLB. For example: a single ionic surfactant (HLB 40, say lauryl sulfate) could be easily blended with a nonionic (HLB 13.5, say, Triton X-100), with no compatibility problems (as might occur if cationics and anionics were mixed). By varying the proportions of each, any HLB between 13.5 and 40 can be generated. This saves time in estimating and formulating a tailored HLB surfactant system for a desired cleaning effect; it also limits the number of surfactants practically needed on hand in the studio.

5.3 Macroemulsions

Under normal conditions, the HLB number of a surfactant can be used as a good predictor of whether or not a stable emulsion of one non-miscible liquid or phase will be made in an excess of another continuous phase liquid. In these types of macroemulsions, swollen micelles containing the dispersed phase material are present in more or less spherically shaped macromolecular complexes surrounded by a layer of surfactant. The absolute size of these swollen micelles can vary depending on a number of solution factors including temperature, ionic strength, surfactant type, counter-ion type, amount of surfactant, amount of dispersed material, etc. The size of micellular structures can also be affected by the degree of mechanical agitation used to create the dispersion of one material into the continuous phase of another. Micellular size can often be estimated by the appearance of the emulsion.

As micellular diameters approach the magnitude of the wavelength of visible light (0.5 μm), light is increasingly more efficiently scattered from the micellular surfaces, and the emulsion begins to take on a more opaque visual aspect.

Emulsion stability may be theoretically predicted by HLB number, but stability per se is a relative notion. In time, all stabilized emulsions break or separate into individually distinct phases, again due to a variety of forces. With ionic surfactants, a large measure of added stability is derived from the arrangement of the surfactant on the micellular surface. With either positively charged (cationic) or negatively charged (anionic) hydrophilic groups oriented outwardly towards the continuous

Table 5.6 Micelle size versus appearance (Kroschwitz 1999)

Size range (diameter)	Appearance
Larger than 1 μm	Milky white
1 to 0.1 μm	Blue-white emulsion
0.1 to 0.005 μm	Translucent (greyish)
< 0.005 μm	Transparent

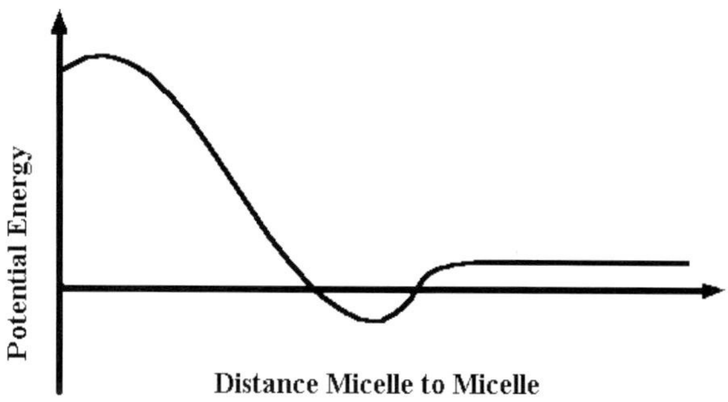

Figure 5.4 Potential energy micelle to micelle

water phase in an O/W type of emulsion, there is a strong charge-charge repulsive force between micellular surfaces. These repulsive forces tend to keep micelles separated. A typical potential energy diagram for an anionically stabilized emulsion might look something like the diagram in Fig. 5.4 (Kruyt 1952). As the distance from micelle to micelle decreases, the energy needed to bring them together first diminishes slightly, then increases dramatically (as charge-charge repulsions dominate), and then tends to decrease slightly (or is offset) when recombination of dispersed phase material occurs (with new Van der Waals forces created as they join together). *Flocculation* and *coalescence* are the technical terms for this coming together and readsorption or recombination of dispersed phase material respectively.

Part of the energy required to overcome the potential energy 'hill' of charge-charge repulsions can be provided mechanically. By simply physically stirring the emulsion we can break micelles and allow separate phases to reform. As they come in contact with, or are forced onto surfaces, micelles will break. Gravity itself acts on micelles on standing; they impinge on one another, and by their own weight, recombine. This latter case can be used to illustrate the forces at work helping to stabilize emulsions, as well as give us important clues about how we can extend the stability of these types of preparations. The sedimentation force, or the force bringing together dispersed micelles under the influence of gravity, can be described generally by the Stokes equation (Osipow 1962: 315):

$$\gamma = \frac{\frac{4}{3}\pi r^3 g(d_1 - d_2)}{6\pi\eta r} \qquad [5.3]$$

where d_1 is the density of the dispersed phase material, d_2 is the density of the continuous phase material, g is the gravitational force, and η is the viscosity of the continuous phase material. It should be noted that when there is a great deal of difference between the densities of the continuous phase material and the dispersed material (dispersed > than continuous), then the viscosity of the continuous phase is small, or when micelles are large, the sedimentation force is greatest.

Once brought together, or flocculated, by whatever force or means (mechanical, gravitational), the actual rate of combining one micelle with another, or coalescence, can be expressed by the following equation (Davies 1957):

$$\text{rate of coalescence} = A_1 e^{-\theta E_h/RT} \qquad [5.4]$$

where A_1 is a constant that includes the dispersed phase volume and the viscosity of water; E_h is the total energy required to readsorb the surfactant into the continuous phase material again; θ is the interfacial area lost on combination of the two micelles; R the gas constant; and T the temperature in kelvin.

If equations 5.3 and 5.4 describe the situation generally where, on standing, micelles recombine or coalesce, eventually breaking prepared emulsions, then several strategies are immediately apparent from these equations for increased emulsion stabilization:

1. The viscosity of the continuous phase material can be increased.
2. Make the readsorption of surfactant difficult in the continuous phase material; and/or use high concentrations of surfactant.
3. Decrease micelle size.
4. Work at higher temperatures.
5. Keep densities of dispersed material as close as possible to that of the continuous phase material.
6. Go to higher HLB number surfactants or mixtures.
7. Make sure that the concentration of counter-ions is kept low, and a proper pH is maintained, so that ionic surfactants are kept fully charged.

Strategy 1 is simply a consequence of both the Stokes equation and the rate of coalescence equation as stated above; raising the viscosity of the continuous phase (with the addition of, say, methyl cellulose, in an O/W emulsion), will have the effect of lowering the sedimentation rate. It also slows diffusion of micelles, and makes recombination difficult as well. Strategy 2 reflects the fact that at high concentrations of surfactant in the continuous phase, readsorption of more is made difficult, thereby favouring (if only slightly) the surfactants remaining at the micelle surface. But there is another important consequence of this strategy (which will be discussed below) and that is the relative solubility of a given surfactant in either continuous or dispersed phase (or neither!) is temperature-dependent (see section 5.4). Strategies 2 and 4 are similar in this regard; for every surfactant, there is a temperature where the solubility of the surfactant is less favoured in one phase or the other. By working at this temperature, we can make it harder to readsorb, in this case, the stabilizing surfactant into the continuous phase, and thereby favour the maintenance of the micellular structure. What this means on a practical level is that a surfactant should be selected that is more likely to be soluble in the dispersed phase material at room temperature than it is in the continuous phase. Decreasing micelle size (Strategy 3) will keep these structures more finely divided, and given enough surfactant to stabilize the increased micellular surface area as micelle diameter goes down, this should also work to add stability to emulsion preparations.

Strategy 5 is easy to imagine when we are dealing with O/W types of emulsions: most non-miscible oils, solvents, and other hydrocarbons we are likely to disperse in water are less dense than water and again, as a consequence of the Stokes equation, the sedimentation force should be minimal in most cases. This is usually *not* the case when we are dealing with W/O types of dispersions, given the higher density of water compared to these other common non-miscible materials.

Strategy 6 is a restatement of the operational or functional definition of the HLB scale; any surfactant with an HLB above a certain point (4–6 for W/O, and 8–18 for

O/W) will suffice theoretically to create a stable emulsion. Recall that the higher the HLB, the stronger the tendency in both hydrophilic and lipophilic directions, and the stronger the balance between the two forces. For the painting conservator this is problematic; the higher the HLB, the more stabilizing effect on an emulsion, but the stronger the solubilization effect on oily materials. High HLB surfactants are good at solubilizing oily materials, but the job of the painting conservator is to preserve the integrity of oil-bound paints, while at the same time separating weakly absorbed oily or hydrocarbon materials from these surfaces. It is best to start with a surfactant with a sufficiently high HLB to create a given emulsion type, and then use one (or all) of the other strategies listed above to extend its stability and usefulness.

Strategy 7 should be obvious, but any excess of counter-ions will tend to remove the charge from ionic hydrophilic groups and negate the strong charge-charge repulsive force possible with these functional groups. Likewise, metals that might complex with anionics, in particular, should be avoided or complexed with chelates if possible. Ionics are pH-sensitive, so the proper pH to maintain charged hydrophilic groups will also be important.

5.4 Phase inversion temperature (PIT)

As stated above, there is a relationship between macroemulsion stability and temperature. For example, consider the dispersion of mineral oil in water (O/W). A considerable surface tension exists at room temperature at the interface of oil and water, and it is only through the intermediary of a surfactant that these materials can be brought together in a stable dispersed arrangement. As the temperature is increased, the interfacial tension between the two phases decreases, though. In fact, if the temperature is raised high enough, the interfacial tension can be reduced to zero, and the micelles of dispersed oil would disappear completely. The milky O/W dispersion would become nearly transparent at this point. If the temperature were raised still higher, micelles of water in oil would tend to appear, and the once continuous phase water would become the dispersed material.

The temperature at which this change-over in phases occurs is called, not surprisingly, the phase inversion temperature (PIT) for a surfactant, and it is a characteristic feature of most surfactant structures (Shinoda & Arai 1964). As the temperature is raised, the interaction between water and the hydrophilic group on a surfactant decreases. As this happens, the surfactant exhibits more and more of a lipophilic character. When the temperature is reached when hydrophilic and lipophilic tendencies are exactly balanced, *three* phases exist simultaneously; the water and oil phases, and a third phase of essentially surfactant only. Depending on the size of the hydrocarbon portion of the surfactant molecule, this surfactant phase can either be a liquid (for lower molecular weight hydrocarbons) or a liquid crystal (for higher molecular weight hydrocarbons). In either case, at the PIT for a surfactant, the appearance of the initial emulsion changes from milky to transparent because the three phases (surfactant, water, oil) are essentially lamellar in arrangement; they transmit light at visible wavelengths, rather than scatter it as more conventional micelles spheres might.

5.5 Cloud point

As an additional note for temperature effects and surfactant behaviour, nonionics in particular exhibit what have been referred to as 'cloud points' when the temperature is increased around them (Osipow 1962: 221). Similarly to the discussion of PITs and surfactants, as the temperature is increased around a surfactant, the interaction (the solubility) of the hydrophilic portion of the surfactant structure with the surrounding water is decreased. If the temperature is raised sufficiently high to eliminate most, if not all, the hydrophile-water interaction, nonionics in particular will form turbid, cloudy solutions. These, in effect, are self-emulsified phases of the nonionic surfactant beginning to form and scatter light. The cloud point for Triton X-100 is 65°C; compare this value to its PIT, which actually falls nearly in the same range of about 60–65°C.

5.6 A ternary system: xylene/water/Triton X-100

Consider the ternary system of xylene, water and Triton X-100 as an example of an emulsion system (Friberg & Larsson 1963). The HLB of Triton X-100 is 13.5, so it should be able to form both W/O and O/W emulsions. Triton X-100 is a nonionic structure (the 9–10 ethoxylate of nonyl phenol), so it is generally unaffected by pH and counter-ion concentrations. If equal amounts of xylene and water (say 50 ml of each) were mixed in a separatory funnel and shaken, they would immediately separate into distinct solvent and water phases. The water, as the more dense material, would form a lower phase and the xylene would form an upper phase. Now if a small volume of Triton X-100 (e.g. 0.5 ml of the surfactant) were introduced into the funnel, and the mixture again shaken and allowed to stand, two apparent phases would again form. The bottom phase would be milky-white, and would be an emulsion of xylene-in-water; the upper phase would be slightly turbid (nearly transparent), and would be an emulsion of water in xylene (although as we will see, a very special kind of emulsion called a *microemulsion* of the water in xylene, see section 5.7 below).

You will recall that Triton X-100 has a high enough HLB theoretically to form either emulsion (W/O or O/W), and it does. The surfactant has a relative solubility in either phase, and is capable of taking in some small volume of water-into-xylene or xylene-into-water, depending on how it partitions itself (at room temperature) between the two phases. Actually, at room temperature, Triton X-100 tends to favour the formation of xylene micelles in water, so a good deal of the Triton X-100 will end up in the water phase despite its rather low overall solubility in water when compared to xylene. If more Triton X-100 (up to about 10–11 ml of the surfactant) were introduced in the funnel, and it was again shaken and allowed to stand, a larger lower phase might form (again milky-white in appearance), but the overall mixture would take longer to separate into distinctly separate phases. At concentrations of Triton X-100 above 12–13% (of the overall mixture), and less than about 20%, Triton X-100 would start to form a separate (lamellar) phase of liquid crystal surfactant, and the mixture would take on a decidedly thick gel-like, and increasingly transparent, aspect.

To help visualize what is happening in this water-surfactant-xylene system, we need a phase diagram to relate different compositional amounts of the three components to the structures they are likely to form. Figure 5.5 illustrates this type of phase diagram. At or close to the PIT for Triton X-100, four structures are possible, depending on the exact proportions of each of the three materials present. The area designated *A* represents proportions of xylene/water/Triton X-100 that would tend to form traditional spherical micellular structures of xylene-in-water. Area *B* (shaded black for convenience), represents proportions of xylene, water, and Triton X-100 that too would give rise to lamellar arrangement of the three materials (these preparations would be very thick, and nearly transparent), and where all three materials would form distinctly separate phases. Areas *C* and *D* represent proportions of the three components that form, respectively, water-in-xylene, and xylene-in-water *microemulsions* (these will be discussed at length in section 5.7).

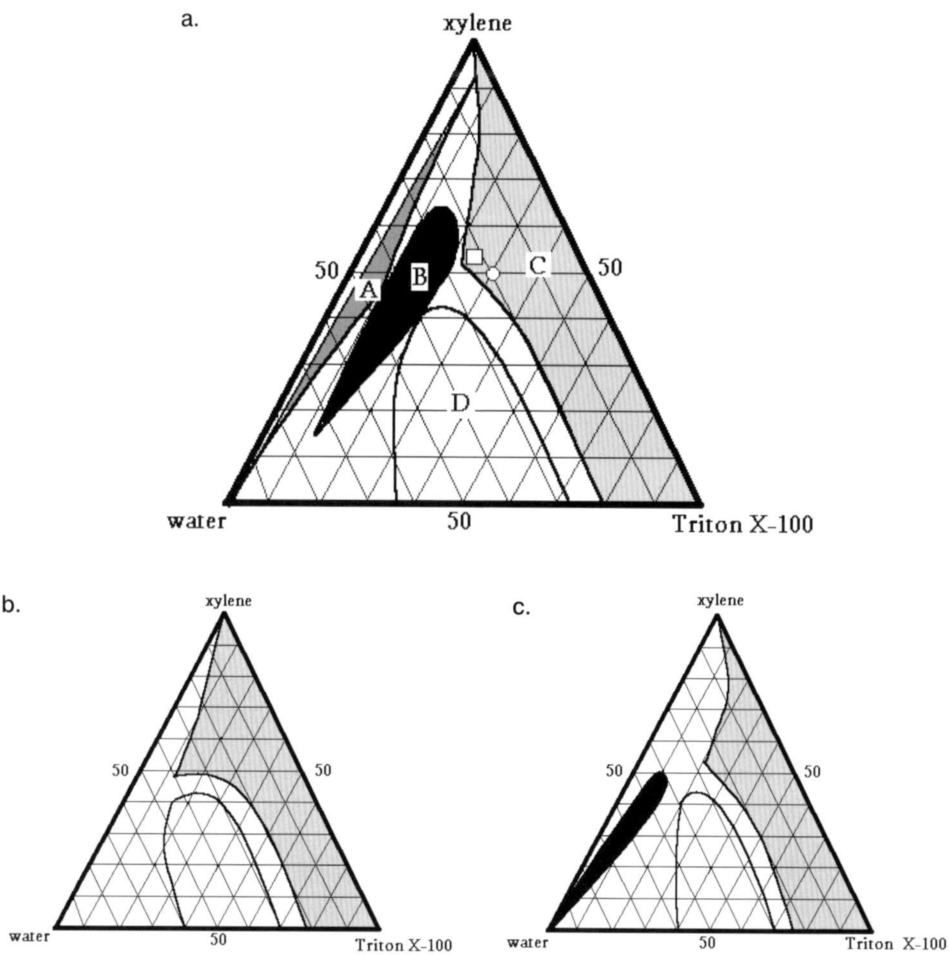

Figure 5.5 Structure vs composition for the ternary system of water/Triton X-100/xylene at three different temperatures

Figure 5.5 is essentially an iso-thermal equilibrium diagram in that it shows the structures likely to be present, at a given proportion of surfactant/water/xylene, at the stated temperature (in this case, the PIT for Triton X-100, i.e. 37–40°C). At higher or lower temperatures than the PIT, the phase diagram for Triton X-100 would change (or if another solvent other than xylene were to be used; or if there were other conditions or materials present in the water, etc.). For instance, if the temperature were dropped much lower than the PIT, the three-phase area *B* would tend to shift towards the water corner of the diagram (Fig. 5.5a). In other words at below the PIT, the three-phase structure would only form at high concentrations of water, and low concentrations of xylene and surfactant. Conversely, at temperatures well above the PIT, the three-phase system would not form at all, but simply be absorbed into the xylene microemulsion area *C* (Fig. 5.5b). At high temperatures virtually no water as a separate phase might be present; only that strongly absorbed water that might remain directly on the surfactant's hydrophilic group might be present.

The practical aspect of Figure 5.5 is in its rendering of structure versus composition. There are practical benefits, for instance, from mixtures that lie in the three-phase region of the diagram. These compositions are very thick, gel-like, nearly transparent, and tend to be very stable preparations. Without any additional polymeric thickener, these kinds of preparations can reach very high viscosities. The phase diagram also tells us exactly how much of a dispersed material we are likely to hold in a continuous phase material when we set about constructing these types of preparations. Consider in Figure 5.5 that, predictably, we can expect to hold or disperse at most about 25% water in xylene and Triton X-100 (the square point in Fig. 5.5a which corresponds to an approximate composition of 53% xylene, 22% Triton X-100, 25% water). This would yield a water-in-xylene microemulsion (in all likelihood) of very good stability. It would allow us to solubilize very polar materials (materials that might be water soluble only), and deliver the water in a solvent-continuous phase that might be safer for (i.e. less likely to swell or dissolve) a surface than if water alone were used to carry out the same operation. The removal of airborne particulates from water-sensitive surfaces or films (water-gilding, distemper paints, gouaches, etc.) illustrates this situation; the problem is to solubilize polar materials without bringing free water or aqueous systems to these kinds of surfaces.

Case History 5.1: Unattributed, Polychrome Trade Sign, Bust of George Washington (composite object, late nineteenth century)

A polychrome bust of George Washington on permanent display over the main entrance to the Winterthur Museum came to the studio ostensibly for cleaning. Originally, in the late 1880s, the bust served as the business symbol for the Philadelphia Hose Company and was acquired in the 1950s for the H. F. du Pont collection. At that time, it was reduced in size, but it retained an original semi-circular format. After installation at the Winterthur Museum, the surface of the bust darkened substantially (see Fig. 5.1.1). Additionally, a local or incipient cleavage problem developed in the paint on Washington's face. The cleavage was 'set down' during a 1975 restoration program when the entire figure was 'cleaned and retouched'. But by the mid-1980s, the bust had again taken on a very darkened appearance and was brought to the studio for re-examination. In the course of this it was noted that certain elements were painted over what appeared to be a bituminous black material.

Cross-sections confirmed the layered sequence of the decorative materials: the carved wooden substrate was covered initially with what appeared by its colour and autofluorescence to be a bituminous material. This initial priming layer was presumably intended to be a form of weatherproofing prior to the application of the presentation decorative paints. The only area devoid of the bituminous priming material seemed to be a field of white paint surrounding the central carved bust relief. The white paint was composed of a 'whitewash' type of preparation (estimated by polarized light microscopy and microchemical tests to be $CaCO_3$, with a small amount of a proteinaceous constituent as a binder indicated by staining with Lissamine Rhodamine sulfonyl chloride). Most of the remaining decorative elements tested positive for an oil binder (with Rhodamine B), and had basic lead carbonate as the chief pigmenting material (by polarized light examination of a dispersed sample, and a positive micro-chemical test with potassium iodide). Areas covered with a metallic bronze powder (staff points and tassels on a garland of carved flags surrounding the central bust) tested positive for resinous binder (with antimony pentachloride). Asphalt and bituminous materials can retard drying in oil films, and have been noted to cause discolouration in other fine art objects.

As a result of the underlying priming layer of a bituminous material, the decorative materials on this polychrome surface were quite sensitive to even moderately polar solvents such as xylene, acetone, propan-1-ol, and diacetone alcohol. A marked heat sensitivity with deformation occurring at about 55°C was also noted for the paint films. The microscopic cross-sections stained with antimony pentachloride suggested that the asphalt material had diffused a substantial distance into the subsequently applied oil-bound design materials. It could have accounted for the increased solvent and heat sensitivity observed on the polychromy. The surface discolouration, however, which had prompted the polychrome sign being brought to the studio for re-examination, seemed only 'skin deep' in cross-section. The darkening effect was

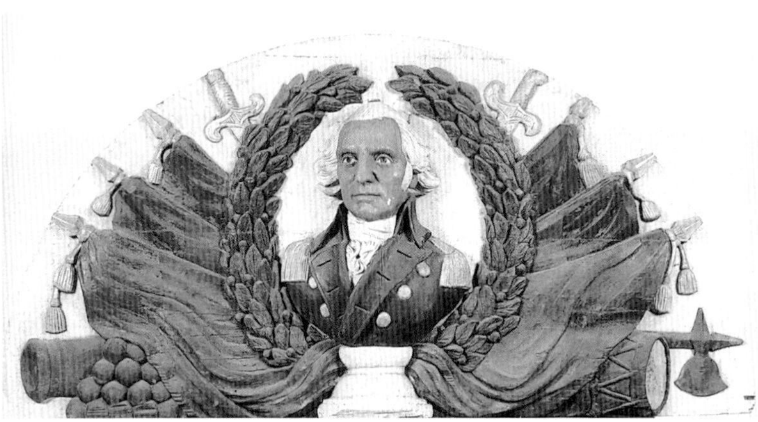

Figure 5.1.1 Unattributed, Polychrome Trade Sign, Bust of George Washington (composite object, late nineteenth century) (see colour plates)

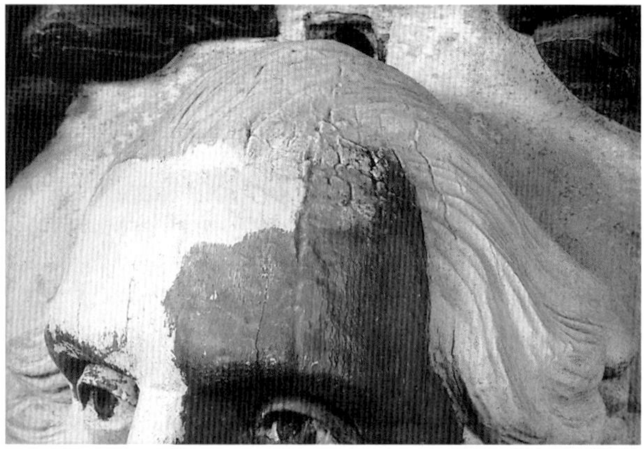

Figure 5.1.2
(see colour plates)

more than likely due to a substantial and tenaciously bound grime layer rather than the bituminous adulteration of the paint (see Fig. 5.1.2). It was also clear from the cross-sections that the surface of the paint had been exposed to the air some time before an initial natural resin coating had been applied. The surface looked undifferentiated in normal light, but under long-wave UV, it was brightly fluorescent, suggesting a residual resin content to the surface of the paint. Grime, which was clearly deposited directly on the paint surface, had been covered over with the natural resin coating, and had been bound there by it. Initially, the focus of the cleaning was simply to address the ever-darkening surface of the paint, especially in the area of the face of George Washington.

It was clear from the cross-sections that the darkening was also due, in part, to a poorly executed restoration and repainting carried out during the 1975 treatment. Fortunately, this repaint could be removed with aromatic solvents. The more problematic aspect to the cleaning was a soiled and residual varnish-laden surface beneath the repainting. Polar solvents would certainly take up the resin coating, but at the expense of swelling sensitive underlying paints and, in any case, the recovered surface still tenaciously retained the soiling material. However, an emulsion system of some sort could address both needs: a water phase might be tailored to deal with the general soiling material, and a non-water miscible solvent phase could help solvate the residual resin varnish material. The following emulsion was constructed to remove both residual resin and soiling material (see Fig. 5.1.3):

xylene	50 ml
water (deionized)	30 ml
Triton X-100	20 ml
Triethanolamine	1 ml

pH adjusted to 8.5 with 1N HCl.

The thick, clear, gel-like emulsion was made as follows. The Triton X-100 was dissolved in the xylene, and set aside while the triethanolamine was dissolved in the water and the pH adjusted to 8.5 with 1N HCl. The water phase and the xylene phase were combined in a screwcap jar and shaken vigorously until the emulsion was formed. Typically, the emulsion was applied with a small brush (00), stirred for a

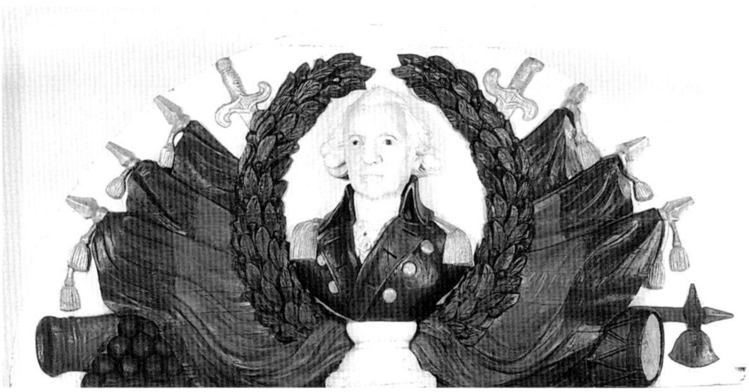

Figure 5.1.3
(see colour plates)

moment on the soiled paint surface, and then removed on a dry cotton swab, along with the solubilized grime and residual resin varnish. The area thus treated was rinsed with xylene and allowed to evaporate to dryness.

Commentary

The rationale for using an emulsion of one form or another is based on the observation that two very different types of materials have to be solubilized nearly simultaneously to effect any kind of even cleaning of the oil painted surfaces of the polychrome sign. The original oil paints seem to have collected a soiling layer, and it became tenaciously bound to the paint surfaces, undoubtedly because of the high proportion of lead white in the fleshtone colours of the bust. The surface of lead white containing oil films tends to have an appreciable Pb^{+2} concentration on ageing which helps to 'lock on' weakly acidic organic materials by forming insoluble salts or complexes. Superimposed on this bound soiling layer was a natural resin varnish that had become more polar with time. In the previous cleaning attempt neither material was satisfactorily removed. With solvents polar enough to be effective at removing the resin, because of the overall sensitivity of the oil film (due to the bitumen) to solvent swelling and abrasion, the resin-soil mix was undercut by dissolving the paint itself, rather than being solubilized directly. Solvent blends would not help with solubilizing the bound soil, and solvents too polar would damage the underlying paint film. But a combination of an aqueous system, and a relatively non-polar (and non-miscible) solvent might just solubilize the combination of both resin and soil.

The conditions in the aqueous phase were relatively straightforward. The pH was raised slightly to solubilize weakly acidic soiling materials; in this case the buffer chosen was triethanolamine (TEA) because its pK_b (8.0) is close to the desired pH of 8.5. The amount of TEA, 1 ml in 30 ml water (0.5M), was chosen so that an excess of TEA was present in the system beyond what might be needed as a general buffer (about 0.05M of a buffer would normally suffice for aqueous surface cleaning on soiled paint films). TEA would serve as both buffer and weak chelating agent (TEA has a log K of about 4 for Pb^{+2} ion). Xylene was used to remove the 1975 retouching, and generally, it seemed not to swell the original oil paint surface. An emulsion of xylene and water could be constructed with Triton X-100; its HLB number is 13.5, so it could theoretically produce a stable emulsion of either the W/O or O/W types – in this case it didn't matter which type was used since substantial amounts of both phases would be required to solubilize the soil-resin mixture on the paint surface. If we look back to Figure 5.5, we see that any of the ternary xylene/water/Triton X-100 mixtures that lie within the black area B would produce a stable emulsion of the three components with the added advantage of being thick (gel-like) and transparent in application. Figure 5.5 also hints at how to rinse the emulsion away after application. Xylene and Triton X-100 are virtually miscible in all proportions: xylene would be far more effective at rinsing Triton X-100 (the only really non-volatile component of the cleaning system to remain on the treated surface), than water. Finally, Triton X-100, as a nonionic, will not be affected by pH or high ionic strength conditions; the increased amount of TEA (or pH) will not affect the stability of the emulsion, as might be the case with an ionic surfactant.

5.7 Microemulsions

As stated in section 5.3, the size of micelles dispersed in a continuous phase material could be characterized by the visual appearance of the emulsion. When the diameter of dispersed micelles drops below certain levels, emulsions tend to appear translucent (0.005–0.1 μm), or even clear (< 0.005 μm). Technically, while there has been a great deal of debate about the exact structures that may be formed in microemulsions, the size of the structures clearly fall below the 0.1 mm diameter range. On first approach, then, the definition of a microemulsion is simply based on the relative size of the dispersed structures likely to be formed, and appearance (transparency). To understand the debate, though, we might consider the formation of a traditional W/O type of macroemulsion. The most common route to forming stable, finely divided macroemulsions of the W/O type has been through the creation of a microemulsion of water in solvent first, and *not* through the direct mechanical dispersion of water in the oil.

Suppose we want to form a stable, finely divided macroemulsion consisting of a water phase dispersed in a hydrocarbon-like mineral oil using a traditional soap like oleic acid as the surfactant. As we have seen above (Table 5.4), the HLB of oleic acid varies tremendously as a function of the counter-ion paired with it. The HLB of sodium oleate though is 18 – certainly high enough to form a stable emulsion of the W/O type. While water or soaps such as sodium oleate individually are generally not appreciably soluble in solvents like higher order linear alcohols (C_5 or higher), when combined together, especially in certain ratios, they become instantly soluble. This solubility in large part has a great deal to do with the counter-ion (Na^+) that is paired with the oleic acid; as the sodium salt, six molecules of water can pack around the sodium ion. In the case of potassium or ammoniate as counter-ions, three water molecules can additionally be added to the structure. At a molar ratio of about 1:6, then, sodium oleate and water can combine and be soluble in the alcohol. As a hydrated structure, sodium oleate is soluble in the alcohol and behaves simply as a general solute, giving a transparent solution capable of further dilution in the solvent. As it turns out, if we were to plot the amount of water that can be dissolved in the alcohol by sodium oleate, we would find that it is related to the ratio of sodium oleate to alcohol.

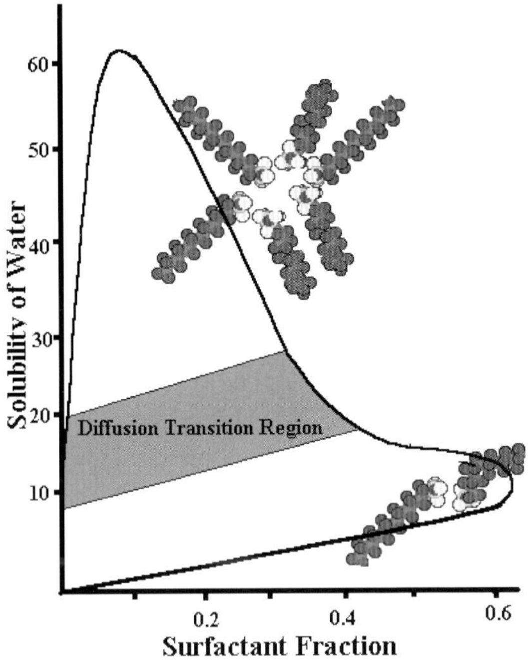

Figure 5.6 Concentration of water in an alcohol/sodium oleate system both in non-micellular and micellular arrangements at low and high concentrations of water respectively.

Figure 5.6 suggests that at low concentrations of water (< 20% of the overall composition), the water that can be dissolved in the alcohol by the surfactant may simply be in the form of individual hydrated soap molecules; beyond 20% by weight, an excess of water, beyond that which might be predicted by the sodium ion hydration alone, seems to be capable of being dissolved efficiently (and spontaneously). It is not clear whether micellular or 'sub-micellular' arrangements of the soap and water are forming, but whatever macromolecular structures are forming, it is clear that (1) they are spontaneously formed (thermodynamically stable) and (2) even at these relatively higher amounts of water, these preparations behave as if they were still a solution of the alcohol (solvent) with a solute of one form or another dissolved in it. Consider the importance of this; at a concentration of water of 55% of the overall composition, and a ratio of about 2:1 alcohol to soap, this particular ratio of water/soap/alcohol would behave as if it were still an alcoholic solution and would remain transparent even though the water would, at that point, represent the greatest single component in the system! And as an alcoholic solution, any hydrocarbon oil (like mineral oil) that was miscible with the alcohol could be mixed with it forming, in essence, a water-in-oil preparation. As more and more oil was added however, the solubility of the water would again diminish and start to form a separate, more traditional macroemulsion of the W/O type of arrangement.

These water/surfactant/alcohol preparations (the alcohol is sometimes referred to as a *co-surfactant*) are a convenient route to the production of finely divided macroemulsions of water in oil. By producing the microemulsion first (the solution-like dispersion of water in solvent), and then carefully and slowly diluting it with a hydrocarbon (oil), a very finely divided macroemulsion of the W/O can be produced with a minimum of mechanical energy. Anionics and cationics with co-surfactants of alcohols and amines respectively have been a useful route to macroemulsion preparation. Nonionics have also been used in an analogous manner to surfactants/co-surfactants for W/O preparations as well. Again, looking back at Figure 5.5 above; with Triton X-100, regions C and D represent proportions of xylene/water/surfactant that would theoretically form microemulsions (with solution-like properties) of the W/O and the O/W types respectively.

The importance of creating W/O types of emulsions cannot be overstated in a practical sense. By dispersing water in a stable way in a hydrocarbon-continuous phase, we can bring the chemistry of water to bear on surfaces that might otherwise be quite water-sensitive. Consider a casein bound paint layer that may contain basic lead carbonate as the primary inorganic pigment. Soiling layers on such a film might be complicated by appreciable Pb^{+2} and Ca^{+2} ion concentrations, contributed by the pigment and the binding materials, respectively. Salts of lead and/or calcium could form in time on the paint surface with weakly acidic soiling components, giving rise to a very insoluble greyish film or grime layer. Water, surfactants, chelators, and other aqueous cleaning tools or methods could certainly be employed to solubilize these soiling materials, but it would be difficult to envisage bringing an aqueous system *unrestricted* to such a surface without some effect on the paint layer beneath. On the other hand, if the aqueous materials were delivered to the water-sensitive paint surface in a dispersed form, where the paint would largely be exposed to a hydrocarbon-continuous phase (a poor solubilizer for most of the paint layer materials, including pigments and binder), then far less swelling, extraction, or abrasion by the aqueous system could be expected to occur.

Case History 5.2: Unattributed, Gilded Frame (composite object, nineteenth century)

The gilded frame belonged to a landscape by the American artist, John La Farge. The frame was constructed from a high relief wooden moulding that carried 'compo' raised relief garland and border elements. The frame was substantially oil-gilded on what appeared to be a yellow bole/gesso preparatory surface on the relief areas, but certain elements (the frame inner border, for instance), were apparently water-gilded over a greyish bole and burnished to a high degree of polish (see Fig. 5.2.1). Adding to the complicated decorative nature of the frame was a yellow ochre paint that was applied to the sides of the frame on all four edges, and appeared original to the frame decoration. The yellow ochre paint showed a marked water sensitivity, as did the highly burnished water-gilded elements (see Fig. 5.2.2). The oil-gilded areas were cleaned with an aqueous preparation that featured a slightly acidic pH, a weak chelator, and a nonionic surfactant system:

water (deionized)	100 ml
KH_2PO_4	1.36 g
diammonium citrate	1.1 g

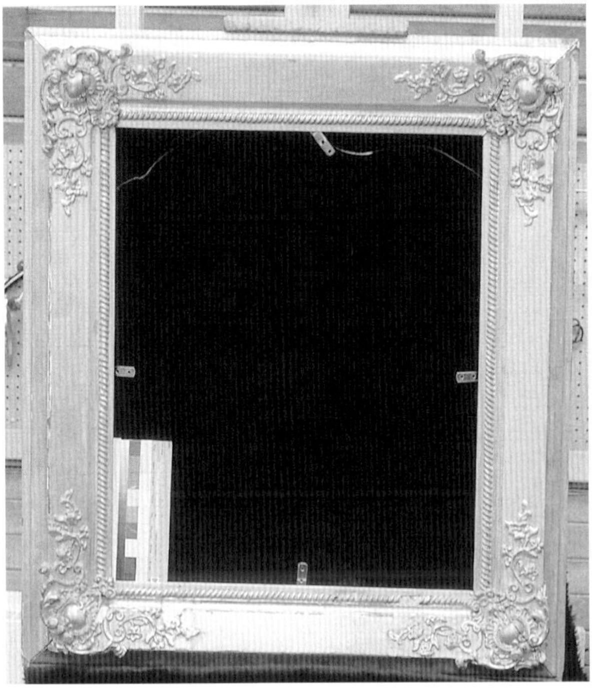

Figure 5.2.1 Unattributed, Gilded Frame (composite object, nineteenth century), after cleaning (see colour plates)

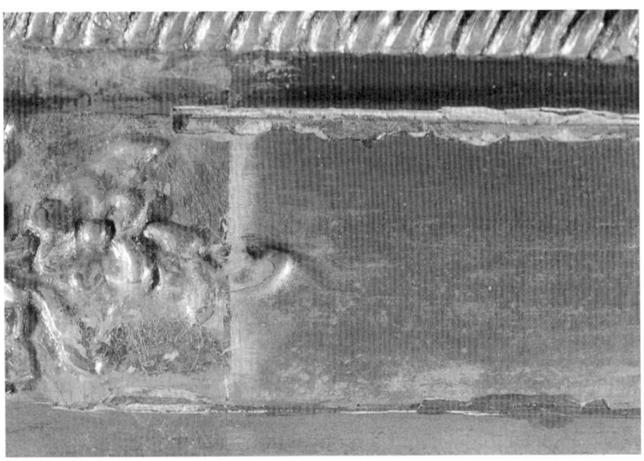

Figure 5.2.2
(see colour plates)

The pH was adjusted to 6.0 with 0.1M NaOH before the addition of:

Triton X-100	0.5 ml
methyl cellulose (4000 cps)	1.5 g

Typically, the aqueous gel was applied with a small brush (00) stirred for a moment on the gilded surface, and wiped away with a dry cotton swab along with the solubilized soiling materials. The areas thus treated were allowed to dry, rinsed with xylene, and then allowed to evaporate to dryness. The water-sensitive gilded/painted areas were cleaned with the following:

A	water (deionized)	100 ml
	KH_2PO_4	1.36 g
	diammonium citrate	1.1 g

The pH was adjusted to 6.0 with 0.1M NaOH,

B	xylene	60 ml
	Triton X-100	30 ml

An emulsion was prepared from solutions A and B as follows: 25 ml of solution A was slowly added with constant stirring on a magnetic stirrer to solution B to form a translucent microemulsion preparation. Typically, the microemulsion was applied with a small brush (00) stirred for a moment on the water-gilded surface, and wiped away with a dry cotton swab along with the solubilized soiling materials. The areas thus treated were allowed to dry, rinsed with xylene, and then allowed to evaporate to dryness.

Commentary

The cleaning mixture used on the oil-gilded surfaces was basically designed for minimum swelling of the oil binder beneath the metal leaf. The slightly acidic pH (6.0), the buffer used (KH_2PO_4; 100 mM), the chelator (citrate; 50 mM), and the nonionic surfactant (Triton X-100 HLB 13.5, CMC 0.23 mM) were all chosen as materials or conditions that would minimally swell the oil binder, and yet still solubilize the anticipated soiling materials safely from the metal leaf surface. Note that the choice of counter-ion varies (K^+, NH_4^+, Na^+), so that no one ion predominates and that, specifically, Na^+ as the only counter-ion is stringently avoided in this case. This aqueous mixture would be used on the water-gilded areas as well (to save time and effort), but with the added precaution of using it in a dispersed form in xylene, as a microemulsion preparation. If we look back at Figure 5.5 for the ternary system of xylene/water/Triton X-100, we should, at the proportions of A mixed into B in step two above (60 ml xylene/25 ml A/30 ml Triton X-100), favour the formation of a water in a xylene microemulsion (52.1% xylene/21.8% water/26.1% Triton X-100). We can expose the water-gilded surface to this amount of water (21.8%) without appreciably undercutting it to dissolve the glue beneath. We need to bring the water in a dispersed form to the surface but it is just as important to bring the pH, chelator, and surfactant Triton X-100 to this surface (as they were to the oil-gilded surfaces) to remove the soiling materials effectively. There must be an upper limit to the amount of dissolved salts that we could expect to carry in this limited dispersed aqueous phase (after all, each dissolved Na^+ ion, for instance, requires 16 water molecules surrounding it to stay in solution), so care has been taken in this formulation specifically not to choose Na^+ for the counter-ion to the citrate; $H_2PO_4^-$, or OH^- ions are required.

Case History 5.3: Elmer Garnsey, Architectural Decorative Paint (early twentieth century)

Corridors adjacent to the main rotunda in a state capitol building had originally been decorated with distemper paints over prepared plaster wall surfaces. Large rectangular fields of light gray and tan, linear border elements, and *trompe l'oeil* garlands lining the larger fields were painted by Garnsey to complement decorative motifs that were begun in the rotunda ceiling. The requirement for cleaning was to remove a soiling layer that disfigured the corridor decorative paints, especially at those heights where passers-by might easily reach up and touch the wall. A highly viscous preparation was needed to work well on the vertical surfaces. The nature of the soiling material was oily human sebum. The overriding concern though was for the safety of the water-sensitive decorative paints. Free solvents did very little to remove the soiling material, while aqueous systems alone would release the grime but also immediately solubilize the paints underneath. The following emulsion-gel was made:

A	mineral spirits	100 ml
	Carbopol 954	2 g
	Ethomeen C-12	25 ml
	water (deionized)	1.5 ml
B	mineral spirits	50 ml
	Brij 35	5 g
C	water (deionized)	50 ml
	triethanolamine	1 ml

with the pH adjusted to 8.5 with 1M HCl.

The emulsion was constructed as follows: Brij 35 was dissolved in the mineral spirits with stirring and gentle warming on a hot plate (B). In a wide mouth jar that was tightly capped, 5 ml of (C) was shaken into (B) and allowed to stand for half an hour. The upper phase material was drawn off and added to the mineral spirits gel (A) by slowly folding the upper-phase emulsion into the solvent gel with a minimum of mechanical agitation. (A) is made by combining the Ethomeen and Carbopol into a uniform paste, adding the mineral spirits, and then adding the water slowly (dropwise) with constant stirring until a clear gel is formed. Typically, the emulsion-gel was applied with a small brush (00) stirred for a moment on the painted surface, and wiped away with a dry cotton swab, along with the solubilized soiling materials. The areas thus treated were allowed to dry, rinsed with mineral spirits, and then allowed to evaporate to dryness.

Commentary

Macroemulsion stability can be largely enhanced by increasing the viscosity of the continuous-phase material. A very thick solvent gel (20 kcps) preparation is made with the Carbopol/Ethomeen/mineral spirits system and 'folded' into what is essentially a W/O macroemulsion made separately to facilitate its construction (by hand 'shaking' in this case), and ease of dilution into the pre-made solvent gel. It

6.1.1 Structure and function of chelates

For the sake of clarity, it will help if we begin with a few definitions. In the present context we shall let the letter *M* stand for a metal atom, and M^{+n} for the cation of a metal (in a valence state of n). A metal atom (depending on the particular metal) can form bonds to, or *coordinate* with, up to 4–6 electron donor atoms around it, if the donating groups are spaced at just the right points geometrically about it. The *coordination number* of a metal *M* then can be defined as the number of potential binding sites about a given metal atom or centre (Martell & Calvin 1952). Actually, the number of bonded groups can be higher than the coordination number may suggest, if the metal is ionized (so that other anions can be held by it), and will also be a function of the valence state of the metal cation (M^{+n}). Usually, the electron-donating atoms or groups are given the designation *L* (for *ligand*), and are most often N, O, or S containing functional groups (although P, As, and Se can and will occur in some of the chelate structures) (Martell & Calvin 1952: 524). When a metal cation such as Cu^{+2} is dissolved in water, for instance, it 'coordinates' or forms a shell of water molecules about it (six in all) as one of the unbonded electrons on the oxygen atom from each water molecule that surrounds it is shared with the metal. In this instance, each individual water molecule functions as an individual ligand, and water is referred to as a *monodentate* ligand. As was stated above, most metals can coordinate between 4–6 ligands about them. Na^+, K^+, ions are exceptional in that they are unusually large in size, and can accommodate or coordinate more ligands about them. In water, Na^+ can coordinate up to 16 water molecules about it efficiently and K^+ can coordinate 10. This helps to explain why these metal ions in particular tend to form extremely water-soluble salts with various anionic materials, and why they dissolve so completely and readily in aqueous solutions.

Chelates are molecules that are usually *bi-, tri-, or polydentate* structures; they contain two, three, or more functional groups in the same molecule that can coordinate or bond to a metal (Martell & Calvin 1952: 524). In Figure 6.1, 2,4-pentanedione (a water-soluble molecule) could be considered a *bidentate* type of structure; both ketonyl oxygens on it are spaced at just the right distance and can donate or share an unbonded electron with Cu^{+2}, so that the molecule as a whole can be held or complexed by the metal ion. 2,4-pentanedione tends to displace the monodentate water molecules initially bound to the Cu^{+2} ions in solution, mainly for thermodynamic reasons; the release of the smaller, individual water molecules tends to increase the entropy in the solution as a whole, as more water molecules are returned to the aqueous solution. In this illustration, two 2,4-pentanedione molecules are coordinated about the Cu^{+2} ion; if the coordination number of a metal atom is greater than the number of ligand or donor groups on the chelate, additional chelate molecules of the same or different type can be arranged around it. Combinations of chelates are, therefore, possible about some metals, and it is also

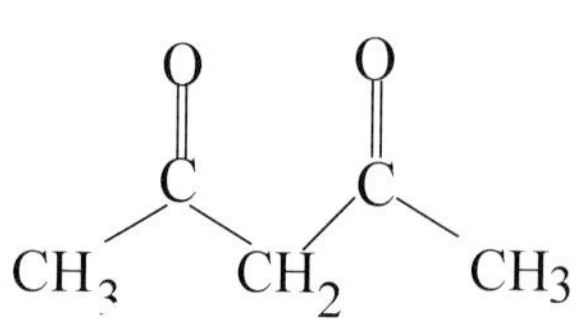

Figure 6.1 2,4-pentanedione

possible that chelates with a large number of ligand or donor groups can also bind more than one metal atom at a time.

6.1.2 Metal-chelate formation equilibria

Chelate ligands can be neutral or ionic in character. When anionic groups or ligands are present, exceptionally strong interactions between metal cations and chelate anionic functional groups can exist. However, these forces can be modified by the ionic environment around the metal-chelate complex. Concentrations of competing counter-ions, or changes in the pH of the solution (the hydrogen ion concentration itself) can act to strengthen or weaken (even eliminate) this type of interaction. In Figure 6.2 the structure of the citrate ion is given (Kroschwitz 1999: 766). The citrate molecule contains three carboxylic acid groups and a secondary alcohol on a three carbon backbone. The pK_as of the three acid groups vary slightly: 3.13, 4.76 and 6.40 (Dean 1985: Table 5–8). In an aqueous solution, citric acid could be considered a mono-, di-, or even tridentate structure, depending on the pH of the solution. At a pH of say 5.5 (or greater), both of the acid groups on the first and third carbons of the backbone are fully ionized and capable of forming ionic associations with cations in solution. Cu^{+2} ions for instance, as divalent cations, can be held or chelated by these two oppositely charged and strongly attractive groups on the citrate molecule. Actually, the alcohol group on the second carbon can also participate in attracting and holding the metal ion, by donating one of the unbonded electrons on the oxygen atom in that functional group to the metal, creating an additional third bond or force between them. Even with the Cu^{+2} ion bound by the citrate molecule in this manner, the complex remains water soluble; the oxygen-containing functional groups on the citrate molecule (those that are not bound directly to the metal) are still capable of interacting with the surrounding water molecules, enabling the bound Cu^{+2}-citrate complex to stay in solution. If the pH of the solution around the citrate molecule were to be as high as 6.4 or greater, the third carboxylic acid group (on the second carbon atom of the backbone) would be substantially or completely ionized, and much more strongly bound or attracted to the surrounding water. This would add to the overall ability or likelihood of the Cu^{+2}-citrate complex staying solubilized in water, but it would also further stabilize the Cu^{+2}-citrate complex itself (that is, add to the strength of the chelation effect) by making the alcohol group on the second carbon more tightly bound to the Cu^{+2} atom (by virtue of the increased electron-withdrawing effect of the additionally ionized third acid group). At very high pHs, the chelation effect would rapidly diminish. Increasing concentrations of OH^- ions would compete with the carboxylate anions on the citrate molecule for the Cu^{+2}, and eventually replace them, binding to the Cu^{+2} ion instead of the citrate, if the pH

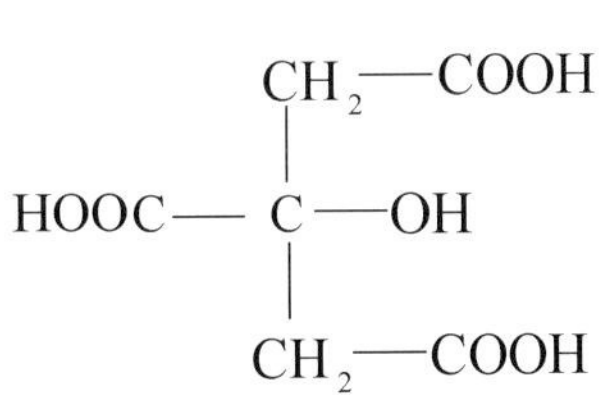

Figure 6.2 Citric acid

were high enough. If the pH of the surrounding solution were to fall, on the other hand, to say 4.0 or lower, H^+ ions would neutralize the charge on two of the three carboxylate groups, taking away much of the citrate's ability to bind the Cu^{+2} ion, and decreasing the overall stability of the metal-citrate complex. At pHs substantially below 3.1, no ionic interaction between chelate and metal are possible, as the increased H^+ ions would neutralize the charge on the remaining carboxylate group. Metal complexing with Cu^{+2} may occur at this point, but it would be through the extremely weak interactions exerted by the neutral oxygen-containing functional groups on the citric acid molecule.

6.1.3 Metal-chelate reaction kinetics

The Cu^{+2}-citrate complex example cited above can be used to illustrate another general property of chelating materials; specifically, the kinetics of the ligand-metal interactions. For bi-, tri-, or polydentate chelators, this process is usually step-wise. The formation of one ligand-metal bond makes it a bit easier to establish the second, and the second a third, and so on. The formation of each ligand-metal bond can be thought of as an individual reaction with a specific stability constant associated with it. The overall stability constant for the binding of the metal would therefore be the product of the individual stability constants for each individual ligand-metal bonds in water (Martell & Calvin 1952: 525):

$$K_{\mathrm{overall}} = K_1 \cdot K_2 \cdot K_3 \ldots K_n \qquad [6.1]$$

$$\mathrm{M} + \mathrm{L} \Leftrightarrow \mathrm{ML} \qquad K_1 = \frac{[\mathrm{ML}]}{[\mathrm{M}][\mathrm{L}]} \qquad [6.2]$$

$$\mathrm{ML} + \mathrm{L} \Leftrightarrow \mathrm{ML}_2 \qquad K_2 = \frac{[\mathrm{ML}_2]}{[\mathrm{ML}][\mathrm{L}]} \qquad [6.3]$$

$$\mathrm{ML}_2 + \mathrm{L} \Leftrightarrow \mathrm{ML}_3 \qquad K_3 = \frac{[\mathrm{ML}_3]}{[\mathrm{ML}_2][\mathrm{L}]} \qquad [6.4]$$

$$\mathrm{M} + n\mathrm{L} \Leftrightarrow \mathrm{ML}_n \qquad K_n = \frac{[\mathrm{ML}_n]}{[\mathrm{M}][\mathrm{L}]^n} \qquad [6.5]$$

where n usually = 4–6.

For the example of the Cu^{+2}-citrate complex cited above, at a pH of 5.5 (where two of the three carboxylic acid groups on the citrate molecule are ionized and capable of binding the Cu^{+2} ion), the stability constant, K, in water for the Cu^{+2}-citrate complex formed would be about 2.2×10^4 (Dean 1985: Table 5–15). For convenience, we shall also express this number as log K as well, which would be equal approximately to 4.35. The practical significance of the value of K (or log K) is that the larger it is, the more the metal-chelate complex is formed in preference to the individual metal cations and citrate anions remaining separately in solution. Another way of stating this would be to say that as K (or log K) gets larger, the more predictably *stable* the metal-chelate complex formed in water is (at least at this pH). Remember, the stability constant for the metal-chelate complex is the product of the individual stability constants for each of the ligand groups to bind the metal ion (in this case, $K_1 \cdot K_2$). For chelators that contain ionizable *acid* groups as ligands, such as citrate, which may participate in (and be affected by changes in pH) the overall complete reaction of metal binding may actually be further written as a combination of two separate reactions; the acid dissociation reaction, and the metal chelate formation reaction (where H_2L represents the protonated citrate molecule, with at least two ionizable ligand acid groups on it which can participate in binding or complexing a metal). The overall reaction would be:

$$M^{+2} + H_2L \Leftrightarrow ML + 2H^+ \qquad K' = \frac{[ML][H^+]^2}{[M^{+2}][H_2L]} \qquad [6.6]$$

where the acid dissociation reaction alone is

$$H_2L \Leftrightarrow L^{-2} + 2H^+ \qquad K_a = \frac{[L^{-2}][H^+]^2}{[H_2L]} \qquad [6.7]$$

and the metal complexing reaction alone would be again

$$M^{+2} + L^{-2} \Leftrightarrow ML \qquad K = \frac{[ML]}{[M^{+2}][L^{-2}]} \qquad [6.8]$$

where K is the metal-chelate formation constant, K_a is the acid dissociation constant, and K' would simply be the product of $K \cdot K_a$. Equation 6.6 is essentially a mathematical statement of the relationship between pH and the degree of complexing of metal to chelate; as the pH goes down (H^+ ion concentration increases), the amount of complex formed decreases. The free metal M^{+2} ion concentration in solution, as well as the protonated form of the chelate would increase, and K' would diminish. In other words, as the pH goes down, the equilibrium in equation 6.6 would tend to be pushed to the right.

6.1.4 Metal-chelate stability constants

Many K values for various chelators have been calculated experimentally using a variety of techniques (conductance, polarimetry, redox potential measurements, etc.), determined under specific experimental conditions (i.e., extremely dilute concentrations of metal ion and/or chelate, standard temperature, pressures, ionic strengths, etc.). Some of these values can be found in such standard chemical reference texts as *Lange's Handbook of Chemistry* (Dean 1985) or the *Handbook of Chemistry and Physics* (Lide 1992). While the K values thus derived are only really applicable under similar conditions to those under which they were experimentally determined, it is possible to estimate these values from more accessible data. One source for these values is solubility data itself; at molar concentrations of metal-chelate complexes, the stability constant can be derived directly from solubility product (K_{sp}) data:

$$M + nL \Leftrightarrow ML_n \qquad K_n = \frac{[ML_n]}{[M][L]^n} \qquad [6.9]$$

$$K = K_n = \frac{1}{K_{sp}} \qquad [6.10]$$

$$\log K = \log 1 - \log K_{sp} \qquad [6.11]$$

$$\log K = (0) - \log K_{sp} \qquad [6.12]$$

The –log K_{sp} or the pK_{sp} values for many compounds can be found in the same standard chemical reference texts as noted above (and see Table 6.1 below) (Dean 1985).

For citrate to bind Cu^{+2} (at a pH of about 5.5, where at least two of the carboxylate groups are available to bind the metal cation), K_1 for the first acid group to establish a bond to the metal ion would be 3.9×10 (or log K_1 would be 1.6). The second acid group would establish an overall bond much more tenacious; K_2 would be equal to 5.6×10^2 (or log K_2 would be 2.75). Again, the overall K would be the product of $K_1 \cdot K_2$ (or log K_1 + log K_2); 2.2×10^4 (or log $K = 4.35$). These values change dramatically as a function of pH, however, as was stated above, at pHs above 6.4 all three of the carboxylic acid groups on the citrate molecule are ionized. When this happens, the Cu^{+}-citrate complex is bound with even more force, is much more stable, and this added stability is reflected in a much higher value for K, 1.58×10^{14} (or log K = 14.2). And recall from above, at a pH of around 4.0, when citrate has essentially only one ionized carboxylate group to bind to Cu^{+2}, the stability constant would be equal to 3.9×10 (or log K would be 1.6).

Table 6.1 gives a listing of the logs of formation constants for a variety of metal ions and common chelators. It should be immediately apparent that, from the values shown in Table 6.1, a wide range exists in the degree of affinity of binding for

Table 6.1 Log K of formation constants for organic ligands and certain metals (Dean 1985: Table 5–15)

	EDTA	HEDTA	Citrate	Acetate	Glycine
Al	16.11	–	7.0	–	–
Ba	7.78	5.54	2.98	0.41	0.77
Ca	11.0	8.43	4.68	0.6	1.38
Cd	16.4	13.3	3.98	1.5	4.74
Co(II)	16.31	14.4	4.8	1.5	5.23
Cr(III)	13.6	–	–	1.8	–
Cu(II)	18.7	17.4	6.1	2.16	8.6
Fe(II)	14.33	11.6	3.08	3.2	4.3
Hg(II)	21.8	20.1	–	–	10.3
Mg	8.64	5.78	3.29	0.8	3.44
Ni	18.56	17.0	5.11	1.12	6.18
Pb	18.3	15.5	6.5	2.52	5.47
Zn	16.4	14.5	4.7	1.5	5.52

different metals with some individual chelators, and concomitantly, that for the same metal ion, different chelators can have widely differing affinities for the same metal. When we compare, for instance, the stability constant for EDTA (ethylenediaminetetraacetic acid, Fig. 6.3) and Cu^{+2} with that of citrate and Cu^{+2}, there is a huge difference (18.8 and 4.35, respectively). Both chelators are structurally similar in that they contain ionizable carboxylate groups, as well as other electron-donating functional groups, as ligands capable of binding metal oxo cations. From Figure 6.3, a representation of the EDTA molecule, it should be apparent that EDTA contains essentially six potential sites for binding metals; the two tertiary amines, and the four terminal carboxylate groups. As with citrate, the complexing of EDTA with metals is pH-dependent. One added dimension to the metal-complexing phenomenon in EDTA is the *spatial* arrangement of the specific ligands within the molecule. The molecular geometry is just right to 'wrap around' many metal ions, reaching conveniently all six possible coordination sites on metals capable of forming that many bonds. The added stability of coordinating at that many points about some metal atoms is reflected in the higher stability constants across the board for many metal ions, when compared to citrate. Citrate binds many metal ions with about the same affinity; when we scan down the list of the logs of formation constants, the values for most are close in magnitude (with some exceptions, of course, they all fall in the range of about 3–6). When we look at the same list of metal ions complexed with EDTA, the log K values tend to vary much more (from a high of 21.8 for Hg(II) to a low of 7.8 for Ba(II)). If the metal ions listed in Table 6.1 were essentially listed in increasing ionic radius in aqueous solution, a trend that might seem to emerge would be an inverse relationship between size of ion and log K. Ni(II) has an atomic radius of 0.072nm; Ca(II) on the other hand, has a radius of 0.099 nm in solution. At least some of the large disparity in the log K values for these two metal ions with EDTA may be accounted for by size considerations.

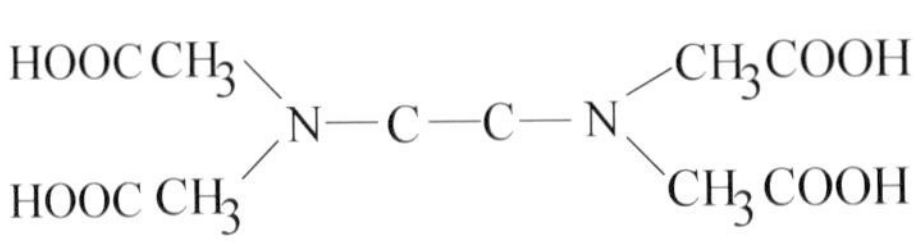

Figure 6.3 Structure of EDTA

The specific size of the bound metal ion may not exert a great deal of influence over the magnitude of the stability constant in complexes of metals with citrate, because citrate (as a tridentate chelator) only partially 'covers' the coordination sphere around most metal ions. With EDTA however, all six possible coordination points (on metals that can form that many interactions) are bound to EDTA, forming a kind of molecular 'pocket' that completely wraps around some metals. The smaller the metal ion, the more easily and securely it fits in the EDTA 'pocket', and the higher the log K value might be. With a metal ion like Ca(II) however, the EDTA 'pocket' can barely stretch to reach all of the requisite coordination points about the ion because of its size, and it is bound much less strongly (has a much lower log K) than Ni(II).

6.2 Metal displacement equilibria

The example above of the relative difference in binding affinity between EDTA and the Ni(II) and Ca(II) cations can serve to illustrate an important use for chelators; the selective binding or replacement of one metal over another. Consider the following general reaction:

$$ML + M' \Leftrightarrow M'L + M \qquad [6.13]$$

The equilibrium constant, $K_{e,}$ for this reaction would then be

$$K_e = \frac{[M][M'L]}{[ML][M']} = \frac{K'}{K} \qquad [6.14]$$

where K and K' are the individual stability constants for ML and M′L respectively. In other words for the exchange of M for M′ to take place on the chelator, K' has to be larger than K. When the difference in magnitude is about 10^4 (or the difference in log K is 4 or greater) we can expect at least 99% complete displacement to occur. In the example of Ni(II) and Ca(II), the log K of EDTA-Ni(II) is 18.56, and the log K of EDTA-Ca(II) is 11.0. From the enormous difference in log K values we can predict that, if both ions were in solution in equimolar amounts and available for binding, the Ni(II) would essentially be completely complexed to EDTA first. Once all the NI(II) was bound, any additional EDTA in solution would be available to complex the remaining Ca(II).

One practical application of this ion exchange phenomenon is the 'softening' of hard water, i.e., the removal and replacement of specific metal ions from tap water. The Na^+ salts of many chelators tend to have very low stability constants – i.e. they are very water soluble – and in the presence of appreciable concentrations of metals such as Fe(II) and Pb(II), will pick up and bind these other metals preferentially over Na^+. This exchange can be predicted by the large stability constants of these complexing agents, for these metals, when compared to their stability constants with Na^+. As a new metal-chelate complex is formed, a Na^+ is released into solution. 'Softening' water in this way – exchanging a much more soluble ion for a less soluble, more tightly bound ion – has the net effect of removing metals that would otherwise interfere with, or complex to, materials like soaps, that need to remain free anions in solution in order to work efficiently as cleaning agents. In terms of practical cleaning situations, we often start with the Na, K, or NH_4 salt of a chelator in a formulation, since these are such soluble counter-ions to pair with most chelators, making them all the more rapidly water dissociable or soluble in use.

6.3 Estimation of ion concentrations on paint films

Even the simplest model for an oil paint film would undoubtedly include a number of constituents, and allow for a variety of possible arrangements, for the materials likely to be present. A drying-oil binder would be present in substantial amounts, along with some sort of colourant or colourants (either pigments or dyes). In addition, dispersal or grinding aids for the pigmenting materials in the binder might be present, along with driers, fillers, flow or viscosity-controlling agents, and extenders. Theoretically, whenever water is brought to a material that is potentially ionizable, some dissolution will take place, and the potential degree of dissolution is expressed in the form of the solubility product of that material. If we consider for the moment even a short list of common pigments found in paints, as just one component in a paint film (Table 6.2), it is clear that, while quite a range of pK_{sp}s exist, all of the listed materials would potentially contribute to the total ionic concentration present on a wetted paint film that might include them as colourants.

Table 6.2 Some selected solubility product data (Dean 1985: Table 5–6)

Pigment	Chemical formula	pK_{sp}	K_{sp}	
Cadmium red	CdS	26.1	8.0×10^{-27}	
Lead white	$PbCO_3 \cdot Pb(OH)_2$	13.13	7.4×10^{-14}	(CO_3)
		14.93	1.2×10^{-15}	(OH)
Prussian blue	$Fe_4[Fe(CN)_6]_3$	40.52	3.3×10^{-41}	
Vermilion	HgS	52.4	4×10^{-53}	
Chalk	$CaCO_3$	8.35	4.5×10^{-9}	
Verdigris	$Cu(CH_3COO)_2 \cdot Cu(OH)_2$	3.2	1.58×10^{-3}	(CH_3COO)
		19.66	2.2×10^{-20}	(OH)
Chrome yellow	$PbCrO_4$	12.55	2.8×10^{-13}	
Orpiment	As_2S_3	21.68	2.1×10^{-22}	

In the simplest sense, if we were presented with, say, a verdigris/oil paint film, we could surmise the type of metal ion likely to be present – Cu^{+2}; that various salt forms of Cu^{+2} might be likely to have formed on its surface (given the predominance of a copper-containing pigment in the paint film); and an upper limit to the Cu^{+2} concentration (from the K_{sp} data and the amount of pigment per unit volume of the paint film). It is probably more practical, given the mixing of most artists' paints (that is, more than one pigment may be used to create a colour), and the variability of condition in terms of weathering, other additives, etc. to the film, to expect that more than one metal ion type would be present on any real paint surface. The metal ions present, though, might be characterized by several means. Here, two electrical methods will be suggested: ORP (oxidation/reduction potential) and/or direct conductivity measurements. Using an ion specific electrode (ORP) one could measure, fairly precisely, the oxidation-reduction potential(s) of any dissolved materials in an aqueous solution on the surface of a paint film. The magnitude of potential(s) measured would give an indication of at least some of the specific metal ions present, and again we could surmise the likely pigments that would have yielded these metal ions up, and, from K_{sp} data, set upper limits to the metal ion concentrations likely to be contributed by those pigments.

Another electrical means of estimating the ionic concentration on a paint surface might be to measure the conductance of an aqueous solution wetted onto it. The conductance of a wetted paint surface (measured in Siemens/cm, or fractions thereof, as mS/cm, etc.) can be directly related to a specific (molar) Na^+ ion concentration. This concentration might be used to extrapolate the total possible

Table 6.3 Measured conductivities of selected pigments (Lewis 1995)

Pigment	Conductivity ($\mu S/m \times 10^3$)	Equivalent NaCl conc. (mg/l)	Equivalent Na^+ conc. (mM)	Equivalent specific ion (M^{+n}) conc. (mM)
Titanium white	20	100	1.7	0.4 Ti(IV)
Bone black	100	500	8.5	...
Cadmium red	50	250	4.2	2.1 Cd(II)
Alizarin crimson	155	775	13.2	13.2 Na
Lead white	20	100	1.7	0.8 Pb(II)
Cerulean blue	30	150	2.5	1.2 Co(II)
Yellow ochre	130	650	11	5.5 Fe(II)
Phthalocyanine blue	440	2200	37.4	18.6 Cu(II)
Prussian blue	30	150	2.5	1 Fe(II,III)

Pigment Source: Leeben Color/Fezandie and Sperrle, Div of Tricon Colors Inc., Elmwood Park NJ 07407. The conductivities were measured on aqueous preparations of the pigments (1:2 w/v), in deionized water. All pigment/water pastes were agitated in a roller mill 24 hrs prior to measurement, in the presence of a neutral polymer (Aquazol 500).

monovalent ion concentration present, or taken as half that value, the total *divalent* ion concentration. The data in Table 6.3 are presented to help illustrate the magnitude of the conductivities observed with even a short list of common pigments when bound into a test or model, neutral polymeric film.

The overall ionic contribution to a wetted paint film surface may come from a variety of sources. The pigments used to formulate paints themselves are certainly not pure – that is, they may contain substantial amounts of soluble metal salts, other than the specified colourant itself, as residual materials from its manufacture or processing. Additionally, other sources for metals might include: driers, dispersal aids (as metal soaps or surfactants), and grime or soiling layers themselves, which may exhibit intrinsically a substantial metal ion concentration. Because there may be a variety of metals ions present on a wetted surface, it might be more practical to simply extrapolate an upper limit to the total divalent ion concentration for a given paint film surface from a limited number of simple surface conductance measurements, and thereby allow the choice and amount of chelator to be determined by estimate rather than absolute measurement. However the value is determined, the amount and type of metal ions present will, in effect, directly determine the choice and amount of chelator. Since binding of metal ion to a chelator is essentially a stoichiometric relationship – in most cases one chelator molecule will bind a single metal ion to form the metal chelator complex – then the amount of chelator needed will be an equimolar amount to the amount of metal ion present.

From Table 6.3 it should be clear that, even in a paint film of pure phthalocyanine blue, the conductance data indicates that, at most, an 18.6 mM amount of Cu^{+2} might be present on the surface of such a film on wetting, and/or extraction. A concomitant amount of citrate – say, a 20 mM solution in citrate – would be more than enough of that particular chelator to complex the Cu^{+2} likely to be present. Nominally, a 50 mM target amount of a chelator has been advanced by the author as more than sufficient in most surface cleaning (soil removal) applications to compensate for the total likely amount of all divalent metal (or metals) that might be found on the 'average' oil-containing paint film, even with a substantial soiling layer.

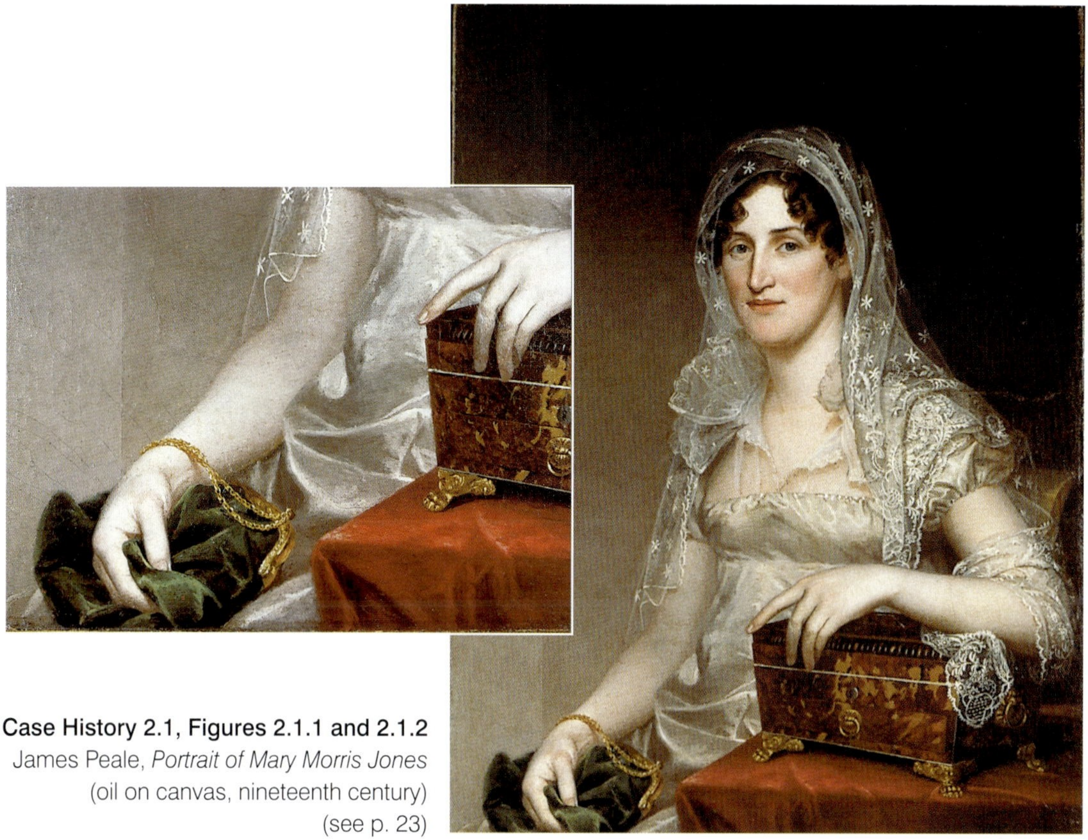

Case History 2.1, Figures 2.1.1 and 2.1.2
James Peale, *Portrait of Mary Morris Jones*
(oil on canvas, nineteenth century)
(see p. 23)

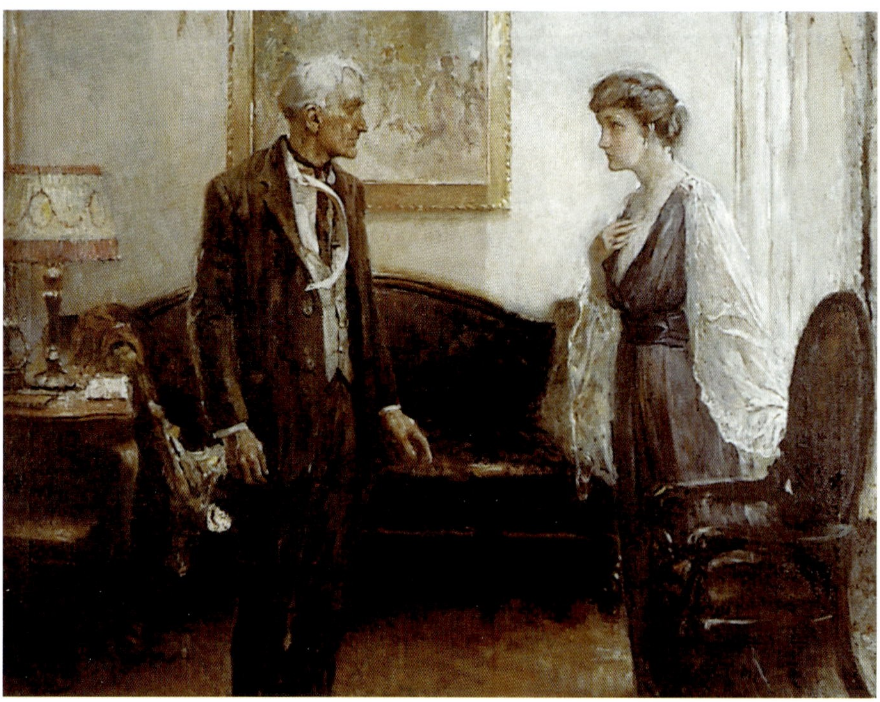

Case History 2.2, Figure 2.2.1 F. Schoonover, *The Prodigal Father* (oil on canvas, 1932) (see p. 26)

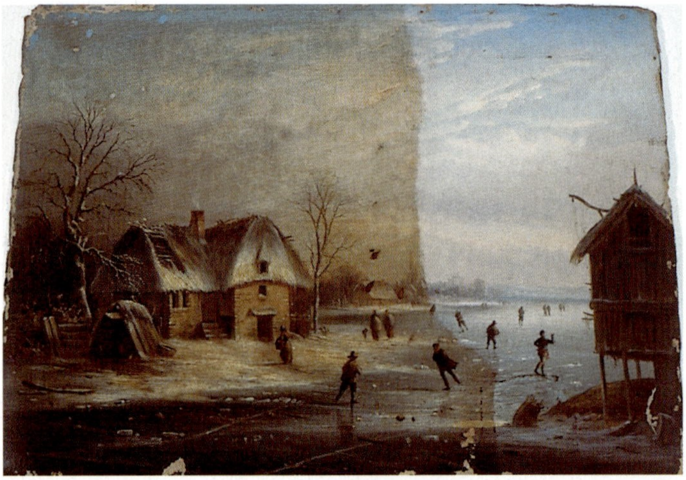

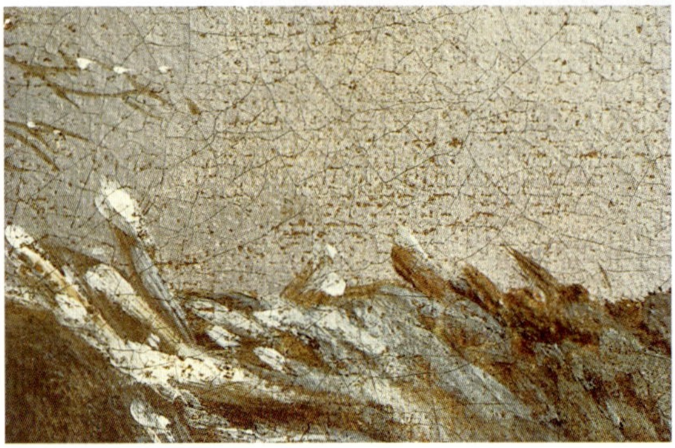

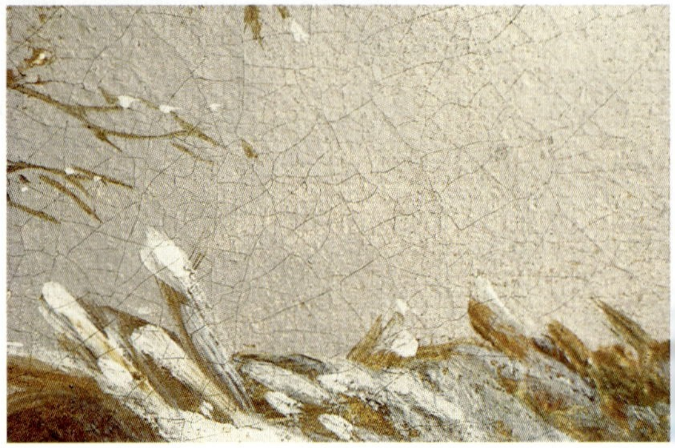

Case History 3.1, Figures 3.1.1, 3.1.2 and 3.1.3 E. Von Liebrach, *Winterscape: Skating on the Pond* (oil on canvas, nineteenth century) (see pp. 40, 41, 42)

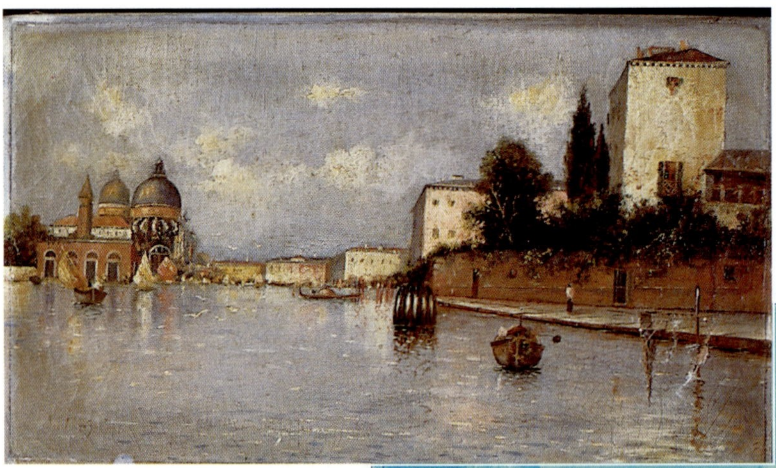

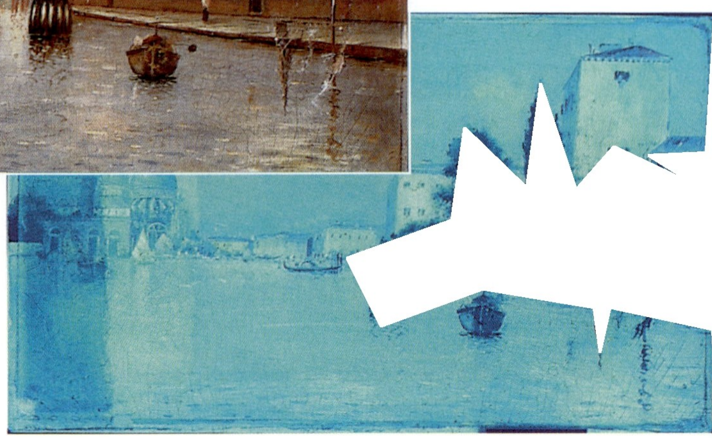

Case History 3.2, Figures 3.2.1 and 3.2.2 Unattributed, *Venetian Canal Scene* (oil on canvas, nineteenth century) (see p. 44)

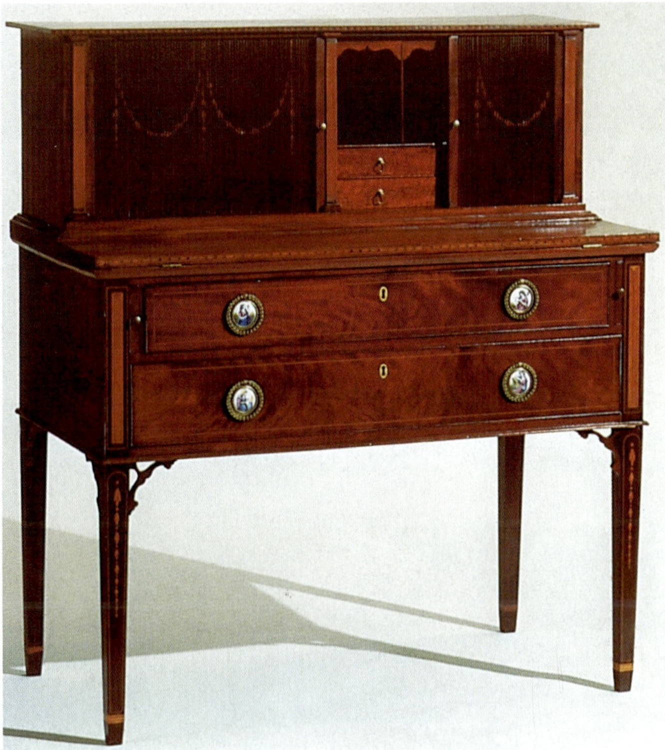

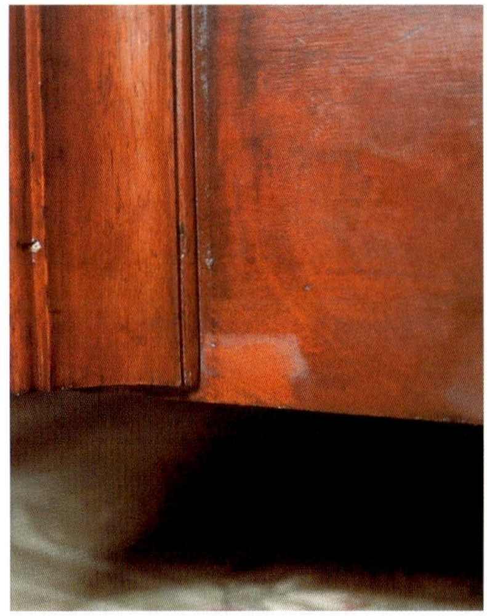

Case History 4.3, Figures 4.3.1 and 4.3.2 Unattributed, Massachusetts Hinged Writing Desk (composite object, 1750–1780) (see p. 75)

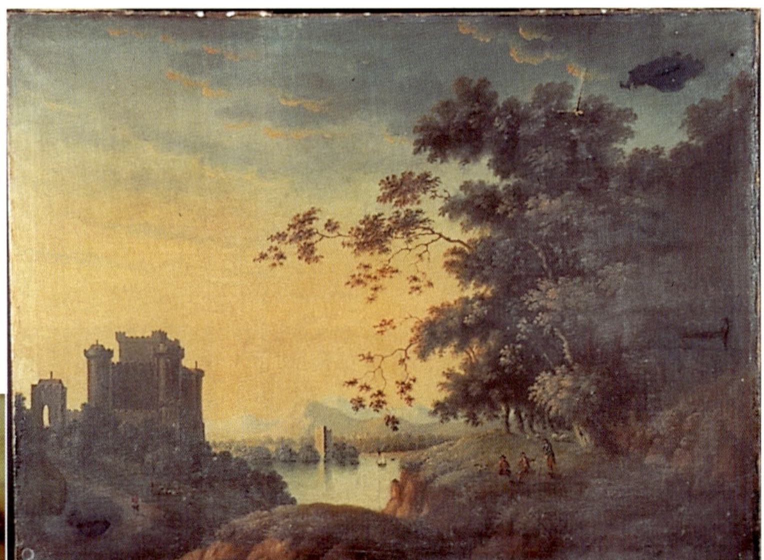

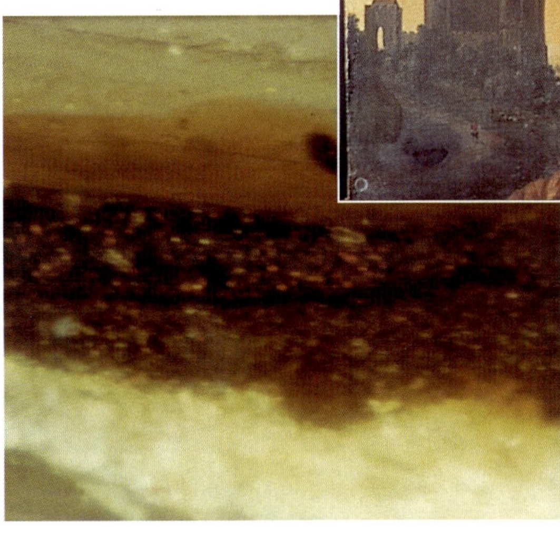

Case History 4.4, Figures 4.4.1 and 4.4.2 William Naismith, *Pastoral Landscape* (oil on canvas, nineteenth century), before cleaning (see p. 77)

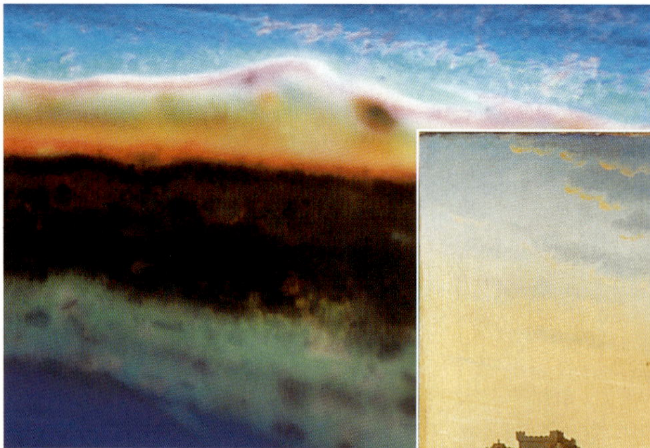

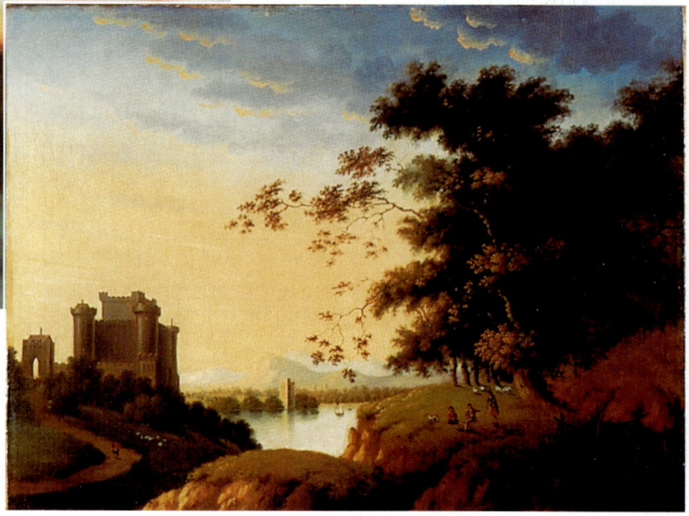

Case History 4.4, Figures 4.4.3 and 4.4.4 William Naismith, *Pastoral Landscape* (oil on canvas, nineteenth century), after cleaning (see pp. 77, 79)

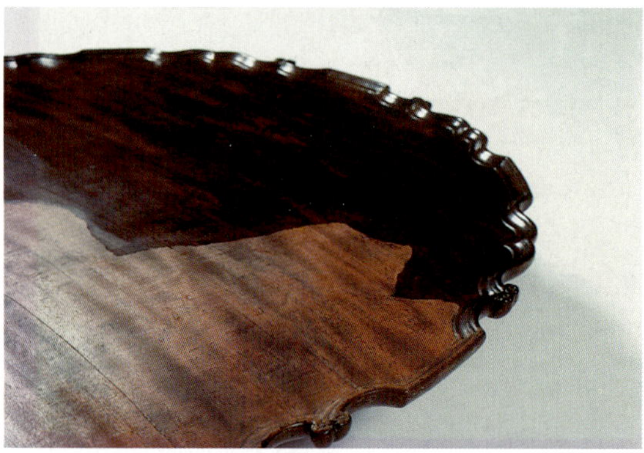

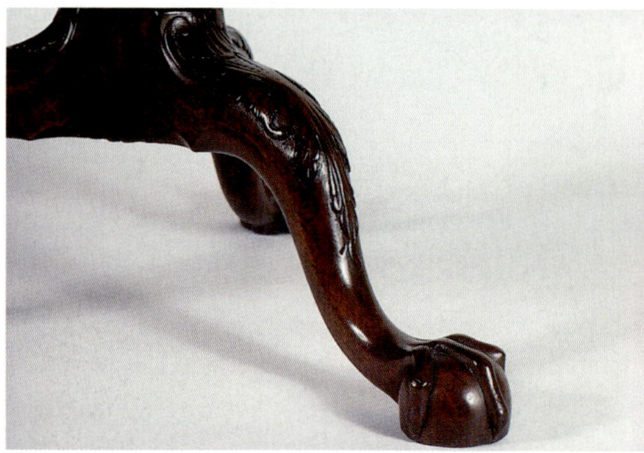

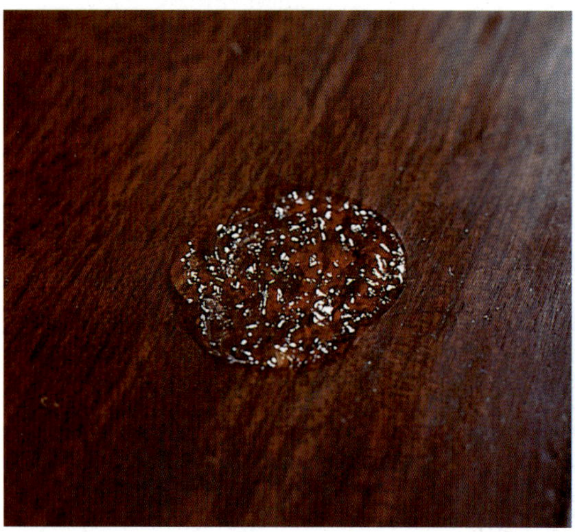

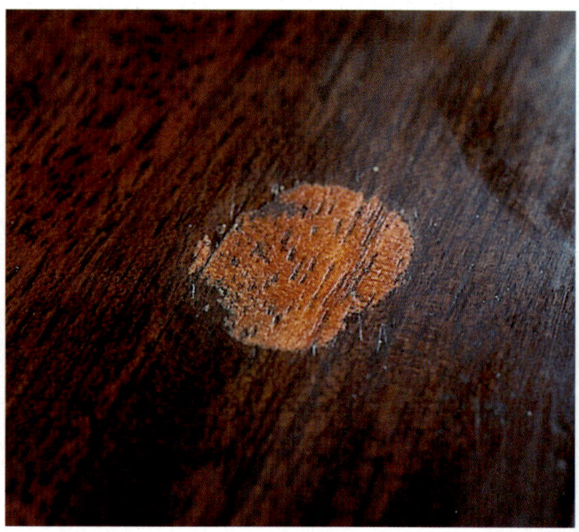

Case History 4.6, Figures 4.6.1, 4.6.2, 4.6.3 and 4.6.4 Unattributed, Tilt-top Tea Table (composite object, Philadelphia *c.*1765) (see pp. 81, 82, 83)

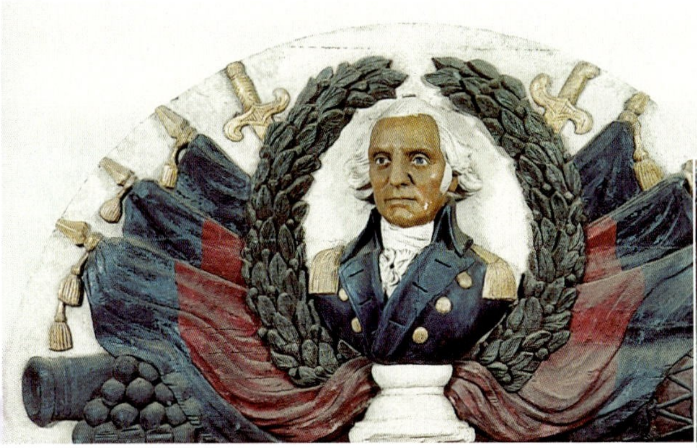
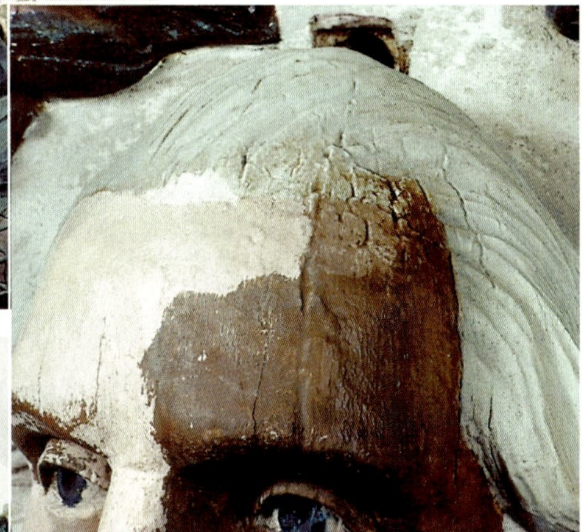
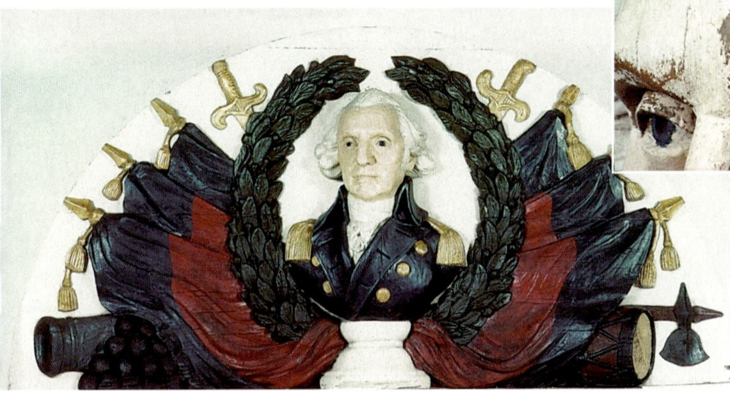

Case History 5.1, Figures 5.1.1, 5.1.2 and 5.1.3 Unattributed, Polychrome Trade Sign, Bust of George Washington (composite object, late nineteenth century) (see pp. 99, 100, 101)

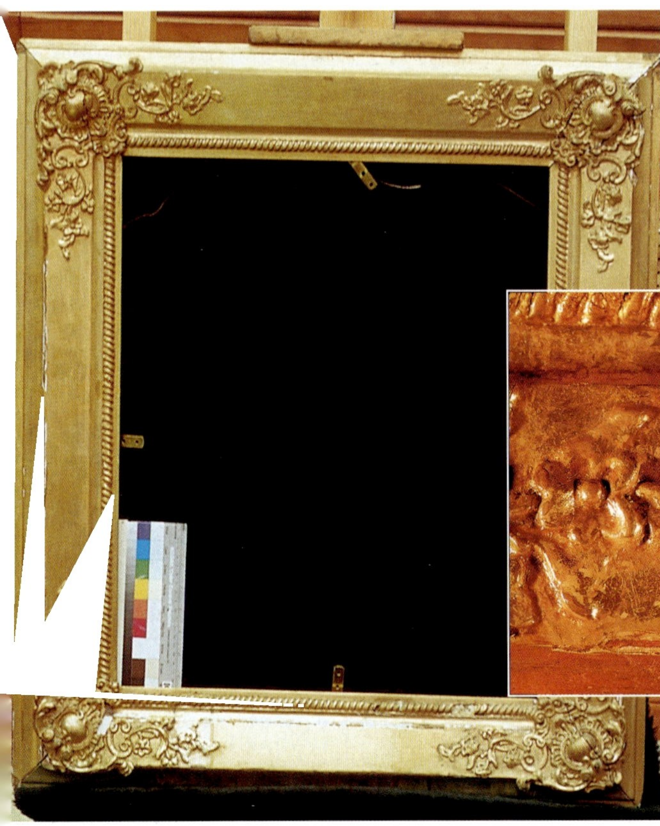
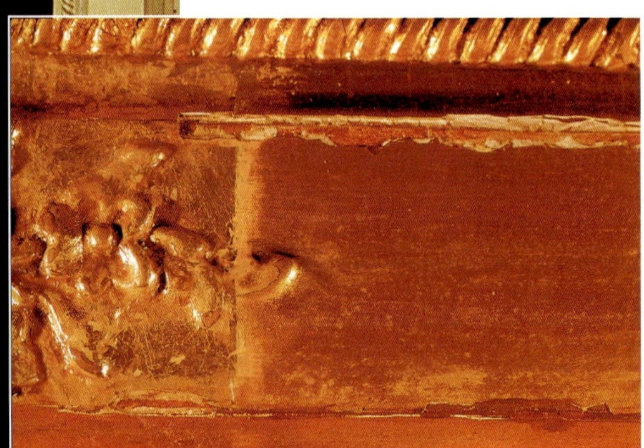

Case History 5.2, Figures 5.2.1 and 5.2.2 Unattributed, Gilded Frame (composite object, nineteenth century), after cleaning (see p. 105)

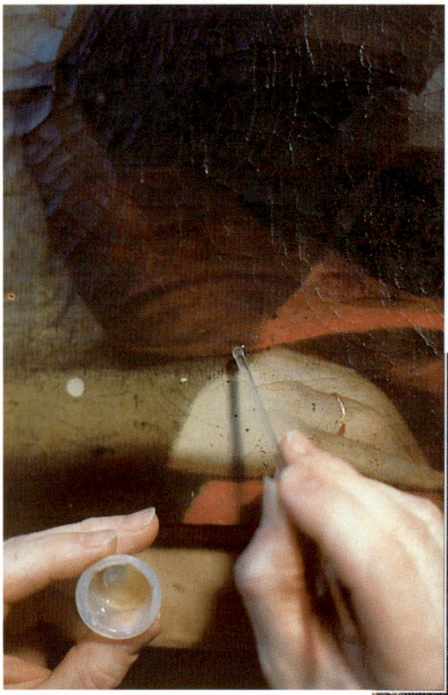

Case History 7.1, Figures 7.1.1, 7.1.2, 7.1.3 and 7.1.4
Jacob Eichholtz, *Portrait of Anne Ross Hopkins* (oil on canvas, nineteenth century) (see pp. 139, 141, 142)

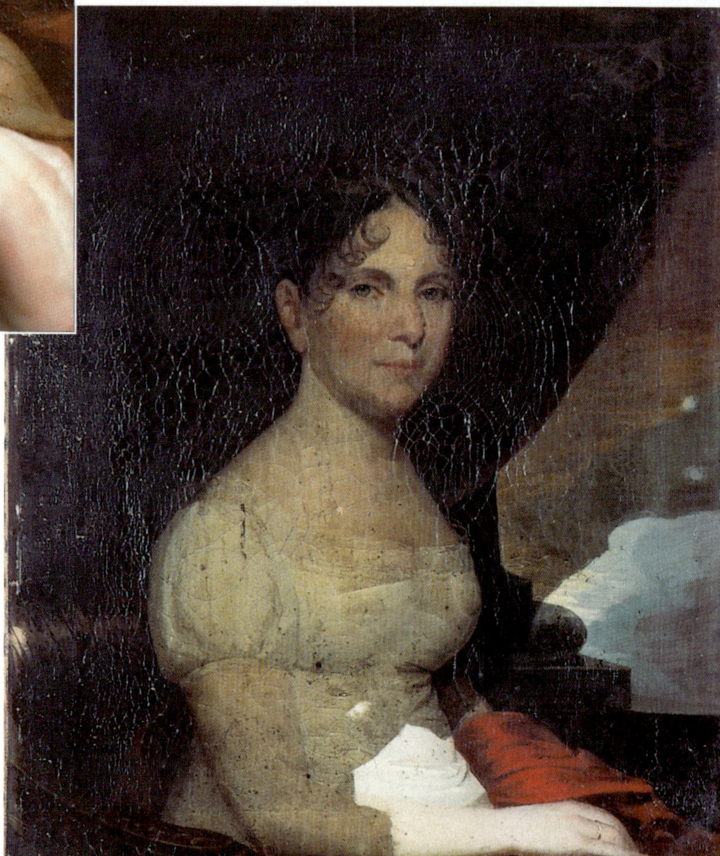

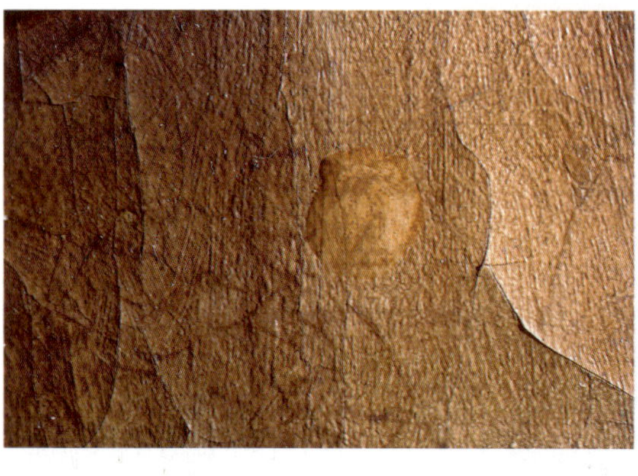

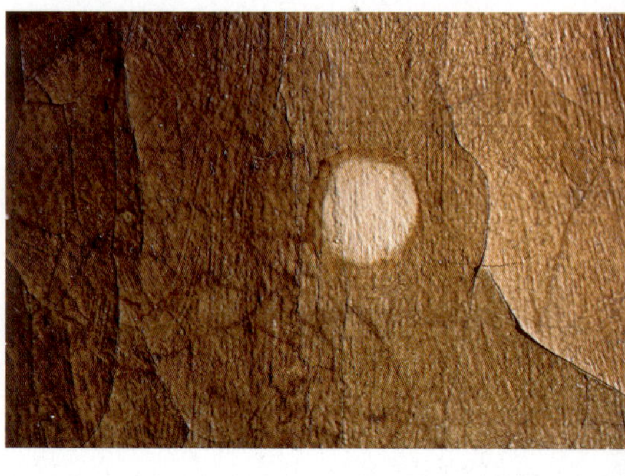

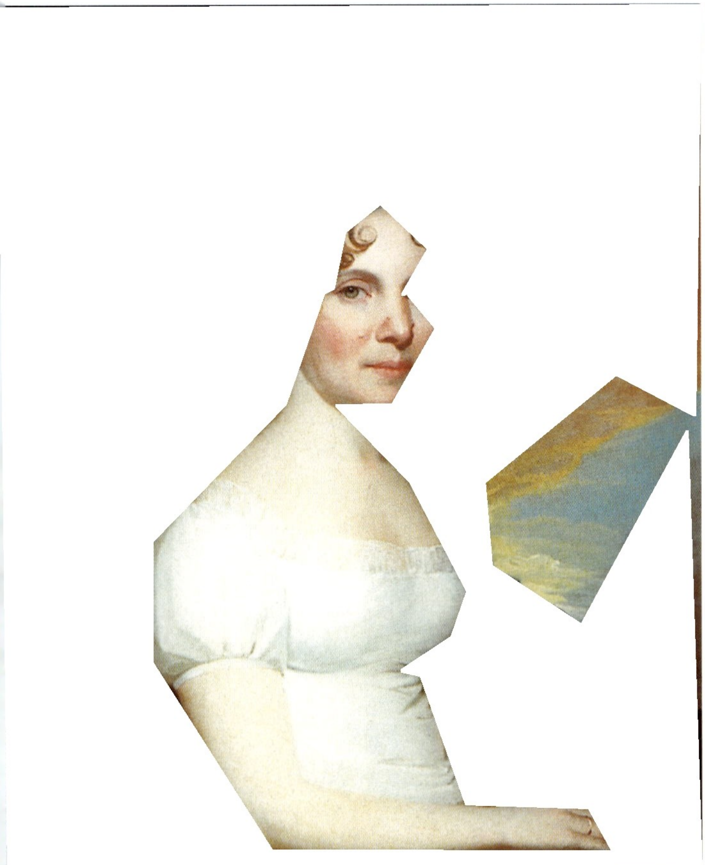

Case History 7.1, Figure 7.1.5
Jacob Eichholtz, *Portrait of Anne Ross Hopkins* (oil on canvas, nineteenth century) (see p. 142)

Case History 7.3, Figures 7.3.1 and 7.3.2
Unattributed, *In situ* view of wallpaper at Corbett-Sharp House, Odessa, Delaware (paper, early nineteenth century) (see p. 147)

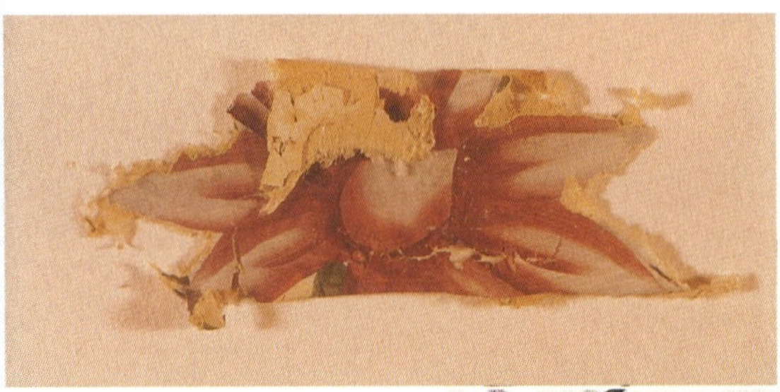

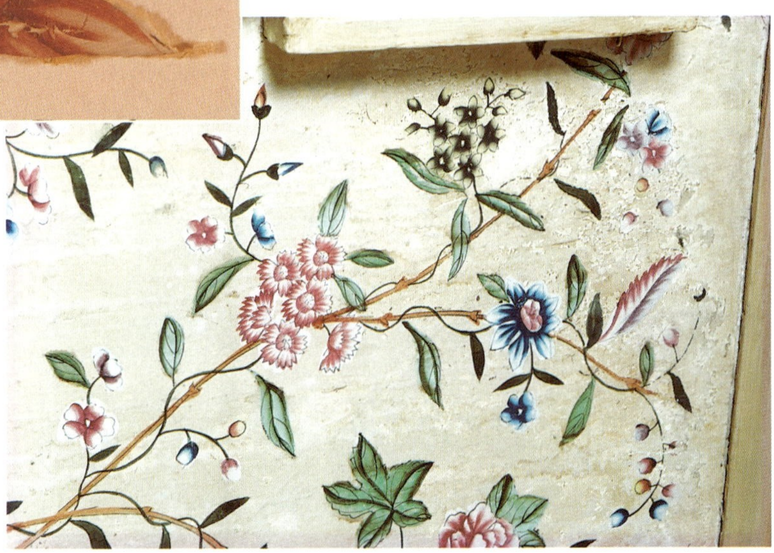

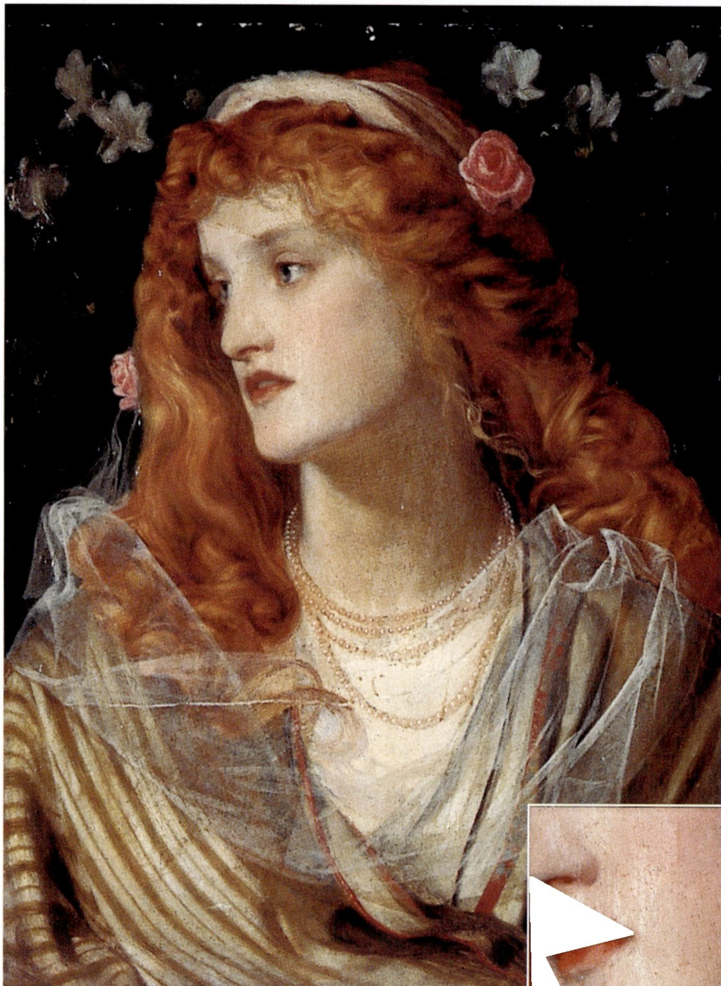

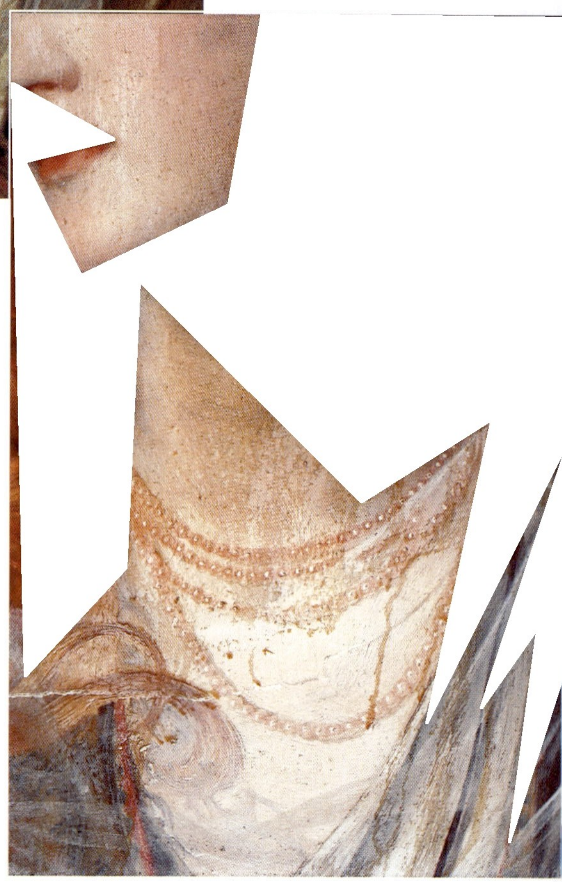

Case History 7.4, Figures 7.4.1 and 7.4.2
Frederick Sandys, *Portrait of Miranda* (oil on paper, nineteenth century) (see pp. 150, 151)

Case History 6.1: Albion Bicknell, *Painting of a Prize Cow* (oil on canvas, late nineteenth century)

The painting required both structural repair and cleaning. The cleaning was especially problematic; the painting was originally unvarnished and had apparently absorbed a substantial grime or soiling layer on its surface. At some point, the painting was varnished with a soft resin varnish; this, in time, had discoloured, and in attempting to remove it in a prior restoration, along with the underlying soiling layer, portions of the paint surface had been abraded. The surface of the painting still carried a substantial, intractable soiling layer, and remnants of the soft resin varnish. This arrangement was confirmed by cross-sections from the painting.

Staining for Pb^{+2} (with potassium iodide), suggested that substantial amounts of lead were present on, and in, the paint surface, even in design areas not predominantly pigmented with lead white. This observation was confirmed by XRF examination of the painting surface at various points. Other pigments identified in the artist's palette were (from dispersed samples under polarized light): a carbon black, ultramarine, cerulean blue, green earth, and possibly cobalt green. A small sample of the greyish soiling material was removed by scalpel, and pressed in a diamond cell, neat, for FTIR spectroscopy. The FTIR analysis suggested a proteinaceous component in the greyish material, and staining on cross-sections with FITC tended to confirm this analysis. Water alone did nothing to remove the material and only minimal effects were observed with various surfactants, pHs between 5.5 and 8.5, and saliva. The greyish material also appeared resistant to a general protease application (pepsin, pH 4.5). The following mixture did, however, rapidly remove the greyish soiling layer:

water (deionized)	100 ml
citric acid	2 g

Triethanolamine was added to dissolve the citric acid and bring the pH up to 8.0.

Triton X-100	0.5 ml
methyl cellulose (4000 cps)	1.5 g

Typically the gel would be applied to the surface of the paint film, stirred with a small brush (00) for a moment, and then wiped from the paint surface with a dry cotton swab, along with the dissolved greyish material. The surface thus treated was rinsed with deionized water, allowed to evaporate to dryness, and then rinsed again with mineral spirits.

Commentary

Soiling mixtures may, indeed, carry substantial amounts of proteins and carbohydrates as constituents. Proteinaceous materials may well have been introduced to the painting's surface as an original coating material or surface treatment as well (dilute skim milk, egg white, etc), or as a residual consolidating material (glue). Whatever the source of the material, it was clear that Pb^{+2} complexed with this proteinaceous material comprised a good deal of the greyish material, and made it intractable under normal aqueous conditions. Recall from Table 6.3 above that lead white alone had the equivalent conductivity to an 0.8 mM amount of Pb^{+2} solubilized from it on wetting; Pb^{+2} can also be present from a variety of other sources internal and external to the paint film (driers, dispersal aids, and airborne pollutants); since it was present in most sampled areas, in addition to those, like the sky, that were predominantly constructed from basic lead carbonate, its source might be suspected as coming from a drier (lead stearate or palmitate, for instance) present in the paint in general. It could be solubilized in an aqueous system, if a chelator of a sufficient log *K* for Pb could be used on the paint surface, without harm to the pigments present. Citrate-Pb^{+2} has a log *K* of 6.5; compare this to Pb^{+2} acetate (log K = 2.52) or Pb^{+2} diacetate (log K = 4.0) as examples of other simple organic acid salts of Pb^{+2}. Citrate could, predictably, bind Pb^{+2} in preference to these types of acids; the log *K* for glycinic acid was from 5.47 (Table 6.1), and this value seems typical of the log *K*s for Pb^{+2} with other amino acids (glutamic, aspartic acids). It is not surprising that citrate acted as an effective chelator in this case for Pb^{+2} and that it helped to release other organic material held on the paint surface through the metal ion. There was no apparent effect on the underlying pigments with the citrate application. But consider the log *K*s for the metals associated with the various pigments detected: only basic lead carbonate(log K = 13.13 for the carbonate, 14.93 for the hydroxide) might potentially be affected by chelation, as it is sparingly water soluble. But it would take a chelator of a much greater log *K* for Pb^{+2} than citrate to affect it (say EDTA, with a log *K* of 18.3 to dissolve lead white directly). Green earth (as the Fe, Mg, A,K, hydrosilicate, would be insoluble in water, and not prone to chelation effects), cobalt green and cerulean blue (again as the ZnO and SnO_2 complexes of CoO respectively), are insoluble in water, and not prone to chelation. Carbon black is insoluble in water, as is ultramarine (as the Na Al silicate) which would be largely unaffected by chelators.

6.4 Chelate–chelate exchange equilibria

Suppose we rewrite equation 6.13 to express the exchange of the same metal between two different chelators:

$$\mathrm{ML} + \mathrm{L}' \Leftrightarrow \mathrm{ML}' + \mathrm{L} \qquad [6.15]$$

The equilibrium constant would again be expressed as

$$K_e = \frac{[\mathrm{ML}'][\mathrm{L}]}{[\mathrm{ML}][\mathrm{L}']} = \frac{K'}{K} \qquad [6.16]$$

where again K and K' are the individual stability constants for the two chelators L and L′ for the metal M. Again, when the difference between K' and K is around 10^4 or greater (or the difference in log K' – log K is 4 or greater), we can assume that an almost complete exchange will take place of the metal M between one ligand and the other. Where metals participate in the cross-linking of polymer-bound paints and varnishes, the practical ramifications of this can be seen immediately: in aqueous cleaning preparations used to solubilize these problematic materials, in effect, the polymer binding the metal may be viewed as a general chelator with a repeated ligand unit, and a definable or measurable stability K for the association of the metal from the repeat ligand unit. A chelator with a substantially greater affinity for the metal (of the order of 4 times greater than log K) would immediately pick up or exchange the metal with the polymer, and effectively remove it as a cross-link in the polymeric system – this might thereby substantially aid in the polymer's solubilization. Polyacidic materials (proteins, degraded cellulosics, etc.), and polyhydric materials (carbohydrates, PVOH, etc.) can complex metals, and in doing so, be quite difficult to *resolubilize* in aqueous systems, even though initially they might have been very easily dissolved. The associated log Ks for these polymers and divalent metals may range (depending on the metal involved, of course) from relatively low log K values (< 5), to as high as 10 or greater. Where these values are high they can effectively cross-link certain polymers, and enormously restrict their swelling and resolubilization again in aqueous (and solvent) systems on rewetting.

Case History 6.2: J. L. Hansen, *Portrait of Hannah Holbrow* (oil on canvas, 1842)

In the 1880s the painting had been brought to the US by the sitter's daughter, rolled up. The painting was apparently restored at that point; the restoration included unrolling the painting, and lining it onto a heavyweight linen with a glue-type of adhesive. Three or four small tears in the upper left corner of the portrait were left unmended and uncompensated. The painting was essentially overpainted in the upper left corner, and varnished overall with a resin-oil type of varnish. Staining reactions on cross-sections suggested that the overpaint was bound in oil, as was the original paint; one added feature in the cross-sections were residues of what must have been the original varnish on (and in) the surface of the original oil paint. Apparently, the portrait was cleaned during the 1880s restoration, but wasn't severely 'scrubbed' in the process to remove all traces of original coating. The repaint was a badly colour-matched brown, comprised chiefly of an iron oxide or earth pigment (by XRF). The underlying background colour was olive in appearance, comprised of carbon black, yellow ochre, and a small amount of ultramarine (from examination of a dispersion in polarized light).

The cleaning proceeded in two parts: first the restoration varnish was removed and then, in the second phase, the oil overpaint. The restoration varnish was only slowly solubilized in propan-2-ol. A solvent gel based on propan-2-ol was used initially to avoid the use of more polar (and potentially more damaging) solvents:

propan-2-ol	100 ml
Ethomeen C-25	20 ml
Carbopol 954	2 g
water (deionized)	15 ml

Typically the gel was applied by brush (00), was stirred on the varnished surface for a moment, and then wiped clear along with the solubilized coating, on a dry cotton swab. The treated area was rinsed with a 1:1 mixture of propan-2-ol:mineral spirits, and allowed to dry.

The second stage in cleaning made use of an emulsion system which featured a slightly elevated pH, an alcoholic amine, and a chelating material, along with a dispersed solvent phase, to solubilize the oil overpaint:

water (deionized)	100 ml
HEDTA	2 g

The pH was adjusted to 9.0 with triethanolamine added dropwise, and then

methyl cellulose (4000 cps)	1.5 g

was dissolved into this solution. Into this aqueous gel was mixed a prepared 10 ml emulsion of xylene in water (5:3:2, xylene:water:Triton XL80N).

Typically the emulsion was applied to the overpaint surface, stirred with a small brush (00), and then removed, along with any dissolved oil overpaint, on a dry cotton swab. The area thus treated was rinsed with xylene, and allowed to evaporate to dryness.

Commentary

The cleaning proceeded in two stages because it is much easier to deal with one material at a time. The restoration varnish could be solubilized – and dispersed – in a solvent/surfactant/gel system, without having to resort to more polar solvent or solvent blends. By working from a viscous gel (20 kcps), the varnish could be removed while minimizing the swelling in the underlying oil overpaint (using it, in fact, as a barrier to the underlying original materials). The oil overpaint was more problematic; after approximately 100 years of cross-linking and oxidizing the oil binder was highly polymerized; more importantly, it was loaded with an iron oxide pigment that would have retarded its drying somewhat (as Fe and Cu can do in oil films), but would have also contributed an appreciable Fe^{+2} concentration to the film. The oil overpaint could be solubilized in an aqueous system if (1) it were swollen sufficiently and quickly enough, and (2) if it were possible to bring three important aqueous conditions to the film – an elevated pH to begin saponification, a surfactant of a high enough HLB to act as a solubilizing agent, and a strong enough chelator to remove any Fe^{+2} that might serve to cross-link, and therefore retard the swelling and solubilization of the overpaint. The emulsified xylene phase (the emulsion made separately, and then added to the viscous aqueous gel), and the choice of base (triethanolamine, an alcoholic amine) both serve as powerful swelling materials for the oil film. The pH of 9.0 was selected to increase the likelihood of swelling and saponification, but also to stay close to the pK_a of triethanolamine, to use it, in effect, as a buffer in this preparation as well as for its general solvent effect. HEDTA will be ionized sufficiently to act as a strong metal chelator above a pH of 3–4, so at 9.0, HEDTA will certainly be effective. The log *K* for the Fe-HEDTA complex is 11.6 (compare this to 3.08 for citrate-Fe^{+2}); this should be high enough to overcome the estimated log *K*s of Fe^{+2} bound to at least two carboxylate groups in the drying oil system (consider the log *K* of Fe^{+2} to diacetate is 6.1!). The (somewhat arbitrary) amount specified above for HEDTA is 0.07M; as HEDTA complexes with any available Fe^{+2}, and may be exhausted in the process, more can be brought to the unsolubilized paint film by simply adding fresh emulsion to the surface with repeated applications. The viscosity of the emulsion (4000 cps) helps to minimize swelling in the underlying original materials. Note that the original paint contains a small amount of iron oxide in the form of yellow ochre, carbon black, and ultramarine (as a sodium alumino-silicate), all of which, as pigments, would largely not be subject to chelation effects (because of their insolubility in water) save for the trace amounts of Ca, Fe, and Al present in the binder, contributed by these pigments.

The use of HEDTA in this case study helps to illustrate further the selection process for chelators; to remove a common metal (Fe) and its cross-linking role impeding the resolubilization of an overpaint film effectively, a chelator with a log *K* greater than 6.0 was required. The slightly elevated pH and the inclusion of swelling/solubilizing agents also help to 'open up' the overpaint film and increase the rate of chelation, and solubilization. The physical form of the preparation (viscosity) helps to restrict its application.

6.5 Metal buffering

Consider again the expression for the formation of a metal ML_n from a chelator L_n and a metal M:

$$M + L_n \Leftrightarrow ML_n \qquad K_n = \frac{[ML_n]}{[M][L]^n} \qquad [6.17]$$

Just as we have seen that with acidic materials we can define their maximum buffering point, or pK_a by the expression

$$pH = \log[H^+] = \log\frac{[A^-]}{[HA]} + pK_a \qquad [6.18]$$

by analogy, we can define a metal 'buffer' by the expression

$$pM = \log[M] = \log\frac{[L_n]}{[ML_n]} + \log K \qquad [6.19]$$

where K is the formation constant, and, pM = log *K* when $[L_n] = [ML_n]$. And since we have seen that $\log K = -\log K_{sp}$, (or pK_{sp}) we can derive pM data from the pK_{sp} data in standard tables. At more or less equal amounts of L_n and ML_n, it should be possible to estimate, and maintain, a constant amount of a metal in solution. Chelators can potentially be useful as metal 'buffers' in that they can be used for regulating or maintaining specific metal ion concentrations in solution, and at equilibrium (and therefore definable) concentrations. For example, a common fertilizer ingredient is the EDTA complex of Fe^{+2} (Kroschwitz 1999: 782). It is there to ensure the slow release of soluble iron to the fertilized soil 'solution' or colloidal mix. The pK_{sp} of EDTA-Fe^{+2} is 14.33, so the equilibrium concentration of Fe^{+2} would be about 1×10^{-14}M when equimolar amounts of both complex and free chelate are placed in contact with the groundwater. Both the presence of other soluble metals in the soil solution, along with a usually acidic soil pH (as low as 5), ensure that, as small amounts of soluble Fe^{+2} are depleted by soil bacteria, additional Fe^{+2} is released from the EDTA complex to maintain the equilibrium, as other soluble metals in the soil, or as H^+ ions themselves, replace it in the EDTA-Fe^{+2} complex or 'reserve'.

The inclusion in cleaning preparations of chelators as metal 'buffers' is important where specific metal ion concentrations are to be maintained during the cleaning of paint or other surfaces. Take, for example, the surface cleaning of a paint film that might include chalk as an inert material or 'filler'. The pK_{sp} of $CaCO_3$ is approximately 8.54 ($K_{sp}=3.4 \times 10^{-8}$), and indicates that, per mole of $CaCO_3$, about 1.8×10^{-4} moles of Ca^{+2} will potentially be in solution at equilibrium with a molar amount of $CaCO_3$ (remember, the K_{sp} is equal to the product of the concentrations of both ions present on dissolution, so the actual concentration of Ca^{+2} in solution would be the square root of the K_{sp}). While this undoubtedly represents a relatively small amount of the Ca^{+2} to be solubilized from this hypothetical paint film, this amount *could* potentially be lost by dilution or rinsing the cleaned paint film surface, if a constant, matching amount of Ca^{+2} were not to be maintained during cleaning operations. One strategy would simply be to include in all cleaning preparations an equal amount of Ca^{+2} ion to that which might be lost from the film itself. On a *practical* level this might be difficult to achieve, given the variables involved in wetting, swelling, and ultimately solubilizing material on, and in, real paint films, and might severely limit the types of aqueous compounds that could be used for cleaning. A metal ion reserve or 'buffer' might be a more appropriate strategy. The pK_{sp} of a Ca^{+2}-citrate complex is 4.7; its inclusion in a cleaning preparation would not tend to deplete Ca^{+2} from the chalk filler itself (since citrate binds Ca^{+2} with less affinity, that is, has a much lower pK_{sp} for Ca^{+2} than does carbonate ion). But more importantly, the inclusion in the cleaning system of equimolar amounts of both a citrate-Ca^{+2} complex and free citrate ion would ensure that a constant amount of Ca^{+2} (equal to the K_{sp} for Ca^{+2}-citrate, or 2.2×10^{-2}M) would be present during the cleaning operations, and its integrity in the paint film would remain intact, by maintaining at least at a hundredfold excess of Ca^{+2} ion on the paint film surface during cleaning.

Case History 6.3: William Mason Brown, *Landscape: View of a River* (oil on canvas, *c*.1865)

Initially, the painting appeared not to have been varnished, and then, at some later point after a small puncture was repaired in the lower left corner, the surface to the painting was varnished with what appeared to be an oil/natural soft resin mixture. This arrangement was confirmed in a microscopic cross-section. The cleaning problem seemed to be twofold: the removal of the now discoloured resin-oil varnish from the painting's surface, and then the removal of what appeared to be a tenaciously bound grime layer directly on the original paint surface. Paint had been applied with a modest impasto to the prepared white ground and fabric support. It appeared (from staining with Rhodamine B) that both ground and paint were bound with a drying oil. The oil binder was confirmed by FTIR spectroscopy. Large tracts of the composition (the green foliage, for instance, which comprised a substantial amount of the image area) appeared to contain verdigris, and the yellow pigment orpiment. The sky area of the composition seemed to contain primarily lead white, and a small amount of ultramarine. The presence of all four pigments was indicated by polarized light microscopy on dispersed samples, and by XRF. It was found that the oil-resin varnish dissolved readily in propan-1-ol:mineral spirits solution (1:1). After the varnish was removed with the solvent blend, and the surface was allowed to dry, the following mixture (gel) was applied to the painting surface to remove the absorbed greyish grime or soiling layer that was present:

water (deionized)	100 ml
citric acid (monohydrate)	2 g
$CuCl_2$	0.067 g

1M NH_4OH was added dropwise to adjust the pH to pH 6.0, then the following were added:

Triton XL80N	0.5 ml
methyl cellulose (4000 cps)	1.5 g

Typically, the gel was applied to the painting surface, stirred for a moment on the surface with a (00) brush and, then wiped away with a dry cotton swab. The area thus treated was rinsed with deionized water and allowed to evaporate to dryness.

Commentary

Once the resin-oil varnish was removed from the painting surface, it was necessary to devise an aqueous system which would remove the rather intractable grime layer on the painting's surface. No matter how well the surface was 'cleaned' of resin-oil varnish, small traces would remain to complicate the removal of the residual soiling materials. A surfactant of a sufficiently high HLB number would aid in this case, and given the pH, and the presence of Cu^{+2} ions in this particular cleaning mixture, a nonionic would be preferable; hence the use of Triton XL80N (HLB 13.5). At a slightly acidic pH (6.0), the oil film is minimally swollen in contact with an aqueous system. Citrate at a pH of 6.0 is a fairly strong buffering material, but citrate is also a chelating agent, and, in this case, a potential metal buffer as well. Soiling materials should be substantially released in these situations, if a chelator with a sufficiently high stability constant is brought to the surface. The presence of verdigris (a basic copper acetate) as a pigmenting material in the paint film would contribute to an appreciable Cu^{+2} ion concentration on the painting's surface, and in areas of design that contained the pigment, so we should anticipate Cu^{+2} salts of organic acids to be present as part of the soiling composition. Using citrate as a metal buffer allows us to present both chelator and a steady state amount of Cu^{+2} to the paint surface, without expecting to deplete any from the pigment loaded paint surface itself.

At the stated concentrations, Cu^{+2} (0.067g) is 0.005M ; citrate (2g) is 0.01M. At this ratio, a buffer for Cu^{+2} is established at about a concentration of 2.2×10^{-4} M (pK_{sp} Citrate-$Cu^{+2} = 4.35$; $K_{sp} = 2.2 \times 10^{-4}$). Now the pK_{sp} of $Cu(COOH)_2$ is 3.2 ($Ksp = 1.58 \times 10^{-3}$), and for $Cu(OH)_2$ the pK_{sp} is 19.66 ($K_{sp} = 2.2 \times 10^{-20}$). While $Cu(OH)_2$ is virtually insoluble in water (as indicated by its extremely low K_{sp}), $Cu(COOH)_2$ is sparingly soluble in water (0.0015M) at equilibrium. Given the slightly higher pK_{sp} for citrate (4.35) relative to acetate (3.2), any appreciable amount of free citrate in solution would tend to dissolve and complex Cu^{+2} from the pigment-containing paint surface. But starting with a citrate 'buffered' specifically for this ion (i.e. already complexed with it) we should not tend to complex more of the Cu^{+2} from the pigment, and, more importantly, we should slow the dissolution of the Cu^{+2} acetate by maintaining a steady state amount of $Cu+^2$ in solution.

Orpiment (As_2S_3) has a pK_{sp} of 21.68 ($K_{sp} = 2.1 \times 10^{-22}$); basic lead white, a pKsp of 13.13 ($K_{sp} = 7 \times 10^{-14}$) and $Pb(OH)_2$ a pK_{sp} of 14.93 ($K_{sp} = 1.2 \times 10^{-15}$). Ultramarine is nonionic (it is a sodium aluminum silicate). Both lead white and orpiment are virtually insoluble in water (at a pH of 6.0, as specified in the above preparation), and would be unaffected by citrate, with log *K*s orders of magnitude greater for As and Pb than citrate. But citrate will still complex Cu, Pb and As (and Fe , Co, etc., if they are present) from other organic compounds which may be present in the soiling mixture, if their respective log *K*s are low enough. Consider Table 6.1 again; it suggests that the acetate and glycinate salts of many of the metals listed exhibit log *K*s which are quite low. While acetate and glycinate are here only presented as typical or commonly encountered weakly acidic ligands, the values for the log *K*s for the metals listed are rather typical of the log *K*s that are to be found with these same metals associated with common soiling materials (proteins, carbohydrates, etc.). For Pb, for instance, the log *K* for Pb acetate is 2.52, and predictably citrate would bind Pb in preference to acetate, quickly solubilizing it.

The use of citrate as a chelator in this case history has a twofold purpose: to complex the anticipated metals on the paint surface, as an aid in solubilizing organic materials that may be held there by them, and to function as a specific metal buffer, i.e. to provide a metal ion concentration to protect a vulnerable pigment.

7

Enzymes

7.1 Enzymes

An enzyme is a protein produced in living cells, capable of catalytic activity (Metzler 1977: 301). The normal cellular 'machinery', i.e., the metabolism or breakdown of certain compounds, and the manufacturing of others, for sustained cell growth, differentiation or specialized function, are all the result of chemical reactions catalyzed by specific enzymes (Metzler 1977: 3). In the absence of these catalytic proteins, most of the reactions needed for cell growth would be difficult, or would occur so slowly as to make life as we know it impossible under normal biological conditions. On average, there are somewhere in the neighbourhood of ten thousand or more different enzymes in a cell as the full complement of catalysts needed for the cellular machinery to work properly. In the intact cell, any given enzyme is usually present in a very small quantity. The chemical reactions enzymes accelerate are, generally, thermodynamically favourable reactions, accompanied by a decrease in free energy. But even in very small quantities, enzymes can vastly accelerate the rates at which these reactions occur, and usually independently of product and reactant (substrate) concentrations, as might be the case in 'mass action' directed chemical reactions.

Enzymes can be isolated outside cellular structures, and perform their catalytic functions in the laboratory. Inside the cell, enzymes are in a rather protected environment and can function almost indefinitely without degradation. Enzymes are not distributed evenly throughout the cell, but are usually localized in those sub-cellular components or portions of the cell where the chemical reactions they catalyze are of most use (Metzler 1977: 3). Enzymes that help synthesize ATP for instance (adenosine triphosphate, a compound used to store chemical 'energy' for other cellular functions), are located in the mitochondria. But once extracted from the cellular matrix, enzymes are prone to a range of degradative effects (as are most

close proximity (even though they are not next to each other physically in the amino acid sequences of the protein, by folding the overall protein in just the right way in solution, they are brought together so as to allow them to interact intimately). But rather than forming an ion pair, the serine and histidine are bound together with a hydrogen bond. As a proton acceptor, the histidine, under certain conditions, can take on the proton shared by them, leaving the serine with an oxygen able to act as more of a nucleophile than it might ordinarily be, to help break other bonds. This molecular 'architecture' describes a number of proteases that share this histidine/serine mechanism at their active site.

The active site of an enzyme may also include molecular 'architectural' features (in addition to those elements needed for actually breaking bonds like the serine/histidine arrangement described above), which can help recognize and bind specifically certain substrates. Chymotrypsin and trypsin are both proteases that share the serine/histidine mechanism at their active site (Metzler 1977: 374). But chymotrypsin specifically catalyzes the breakdown or hydrolysis of peptide bonds in proteins next to aromatic amino acids in particular; trypsin catalyzes the hydrolysis of peptide bonds adjacent to basic amino acids. The active site of chymotrypsin also includes a sequence of neutral amino acids (leucine, isoleucine) that create a flat hydrophobic 'pocket' adjacent to the serine/histidine residues, which can locally exert a strong attractive force through London or dispersion types of interactions with other hydrophobes, especially flat planar hydrophobes such as aromatic substituted amino acids (phenylalanine, tryptophan). In trypsin, a pair of quite acidic amino acids (glutamic and aspartic acids) are very near the serine/histidine structure, and hence give it its ability to bind preferentially basic amino acids, in particular, in close proximity to the serine/histidine mechanism. In chymotrypsin and trypsin we can see two elements that make the 'architecture' at their active sites so special. The first is the ability to bring together sometimes disparate elements in the protein in just the right way, so as to create an especially reactive group to facilitate a chemical reaction. But the second is equally important; bringing elements together that will 'recognize' (bind preferentially) only certain chemical structures, and lend a high degree of specificity to the reactions that can take place there. If a co-enzyme is required for catalytic or chemical activity to occur, then active sites of enzymes will exhibit architectures that accommodate these small molecules as well. In a sense, the overall protein structure of an enzyme tends to create the local or active site architecture; the peptide chains contain sequences of amino acids, and fold in solution, to yield ultimately a structure with a unique arrangement of very disparate elements at a very special and chemically active small site on the larger macromolecule. The general solution conditions around the enzyme can affect the active site; as the pH, temperature, or ion strength change in the general or bulk solution, the shape of the protein can change; sometimes these changes can translate to enough of a change at the active sites to disrupt the enzyme's ability to carry out catalysis effectively. In trypsin, for example, its specificity for peptide bonds adjacent to basic amino acids can be destroyed at low pHs, when the charges are taken away from the glutamic and aspartic acid residues at its active site (Metzler 1977: 374). At high pHs (> 9–10), the hydrogen bond between the serine/histidine residues required for catalysis is disrupted, and the hydroxyl oxygen on the serine is no longer a strong nucleophile.

7.4 Enzyme kinetics

The velocity of uncatalyzed chemical reactions generally tends to increase linearly if the concentration of the reactants is increased. This is not the case with enzyme-catalyzed reactions; the rates of enzyme-catalyzed reactions, on the other hand, tend to approach a maximum as substrate concentration increases (see Fig. 7.1). Michaelis and Menten proposed, as early as 1913, a theoretical explanation for this observation (Jencks 1969). It primarily assumes that the rates of these reactions involve the formation of an intermediate complex of both enzyme and substrate, and it is the tendency both to form and unform that limits the rate at which an enzyme-catalyzed reaction can occur:

$$E + S \underset{k_2}{\overset{k_1}{\Leftrightarrow}} ES \overset{k_3}{\rightarrow} E + P \qquad [7.1]$$

where here E is the enzyme molecule, S is the substrate, ES is the complex of the two as an intermediate, and P is the product (or products) of the enzyme catalysis. k_1 is the rate constant for the formation of ES, k_2 for the unformation of the ES complex, and k_3 is the rate constant for the reaction producing the product of the catalyzed reaction. When the enzyme concentration is kept low compared to the amount of substrate, as substrate concentration is increased, the concentration of ES increases rapidly until a steady state is reached where the formation of ES exactly matches the amount unforming. Such a steady state is reached within a few moments (seconds usually) of combining substrate and enzyme, and during this time the reaction velocity is essentially constant. The velocity, which may be measured by the amount of product formed, is usually designated as the initial velocity, or v_o, for the reaction. Combining the separate rate equations for the three separate reactions involved, the relationship between v_o and substrate concentration at this point has

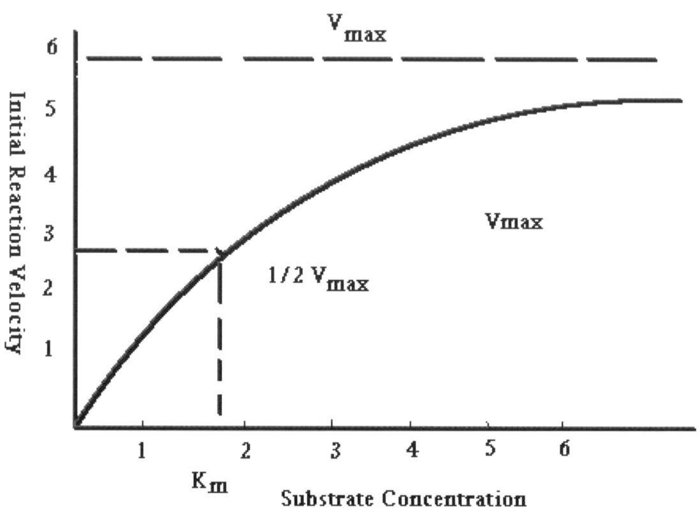

Figure 7.1 Michaelis–Menten relationship

to be expressed by the combined equation:

$$v_o = \frac{k_3[E_t]}{1 + \frac{k_2 + k_3}{k_1[S]}} \qquad [7.2]$$

where E_t is the total enzyme concentration (E + ES). It should be obvious from equation 7.2 that, for any given substrate concentration, the initial velocity is directly proportional to the total enzyme concentration. If the substrate concentration is essentially kept in large excess (infinite), then the initial velocity approaches a maximum value (v_{max}); where

$$v_{max} = k_3 [E_t] \qquad [7.3]$$

and equation 7.2 can be simplified to:

$$v_o = \frac{v_{max}}{1 + \frac{K_m}{[S]}} \qquad [7.4]$$

where K_m is defined as a combined constant for $(k_2 + k_3)/k_1$. This is the so-called Michaelis–Menten equation. K_m is called the Michaelis constant for an enzyme; in Fig. 7.1 above it would be equal to the substrate concentration where the velocity of the enzyme-catalyzed reaction was exactly one half of v_{max}. When k_3 is small compared to k_2, K_m approaches the value of the dissociation constant for the enzyme and substrate complex. The Michaelis–Menten equation describes a hyperbolic relationship between substrate concentration and velocity, and very much describes the observed relationship between these two parameters for enzymes that catalyze a reaction with a single substrate molecule; however, the relationship between substrate concentration and velocity is more complicated when more than one substrate molecule is involved.

7.5 Temperature and pH effects on enzyme reaction rates

The Arrhenius relationship describes the effect of temperature on many chemical reactions; that is, reaction rates double for every 10°C rise in temperature. For enzymatic reactions however, the observed relationship is somewhat more complex: as the temperature is increased, enzymatic activity usually increases, reaches a maximum, and then decreases with further rises in temperature. Consider the following temperature versus activity curve for a lipase (a lipid triglyceride esterase), Fig. 7.2. The maximum activity is exhibited at a temperature around 45°C, but then falls off again above that point. As was pointed out above, enzyme structures are generally folded peptide chains; these chains are held in a 'native' or particular shape mainly through weak secondary forces between the peptide chains, and between the peptide chains and the aqueous environment that surrounds the

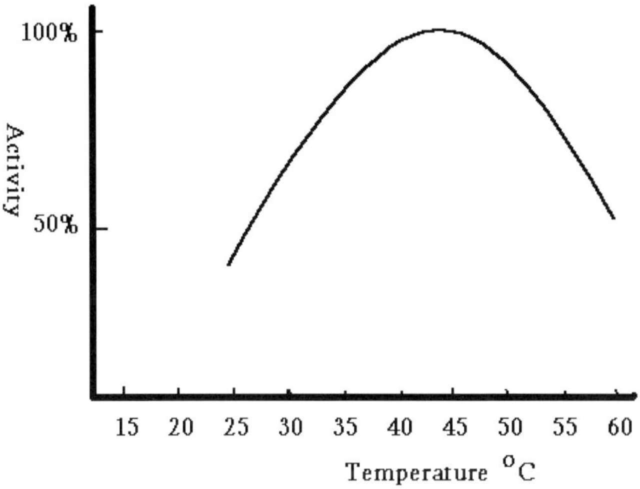

Figure 7.2 Activity versus temperature for Lipase Type VII

enzyme. As the temperature is increased above the maximum for enzyme activity, more and more of the intra-chain bonds are broken and replaced with water, changing the shape of the molecule or 'denaturing' it overall, and the active site in particular. Below the maximum, and other configurations or shapes to the enzyme molecule begin to be possible (since they are favoured energetically), and again, the active site may change as a result.

The same general relationship between pH and enzyme activity can be observed as with temperature (Kroschwitz 1950). At, or close to, a certain pH, enzymatic activity reaches a maximum, above or below this point and the activity falls off dramatically. Again consider the activity versus pH curve for the same lipase as above (Fig. 7.3). In this case, two maxima can be seen close to about 6.0, and then again at about 8.5. Enzymes are ionic species in solution, and the acidic and basic functional groups that are ionized on their surfaces at any given pH help define the shape the enzyme will take in solution. As the balance of charged or ionized groups changes, so too will the shape of the molecule, and again, ultimately these changes may affect the shape or architecture at the active site. In the case of the lipase in Fig. 7.3, the activity maximum at a pH of 8.5 corresponds to the particular shape the lipase assumes at that pH; long chain fatty acid derived triglycerides are held at the active site, and hydrolyzed to produce free fatty acids and glycerol (Godfrey 1983: 488–9). The second maximum around a pH of 6.0 corresponds to a second, not quite as active conformation to the enzyme that preferentially binds shorter chain length fatty acid triglycerides, and hydrolyzes them (Godfrey 1983: 488–9). The higher pH (8.5) conformation to the enzyme clearly allows for more hydrophobic amino acids to be available at, or close to, the active site. In this conformation these hydrophobic groups can preferentially bind the longer fatty acid chain triglycerides. At a pH of 6.0, fewer hydrophobic groups are exposed at the active site, and only shorter chain fatty acid triglycerides can bind preferentially there.

Changes in pH can affect the active site directly by determining the charged or ionized state of the amino acid groups which directly participate in the catalysis. In

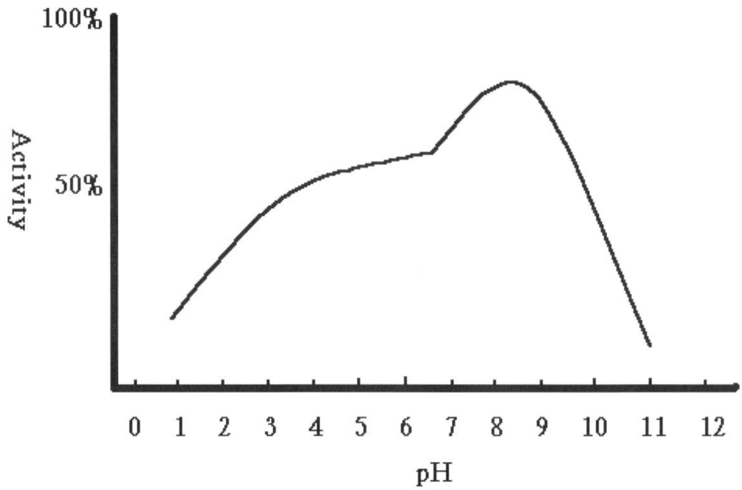

Figure 7.3 Activity versus pH for Lipase Type VII

most lipases, the imidizolic group on a histidine residue at the active site is the key to their ability to hydrolyze an ester linkage (Godfrey 1983: 289). At a pH of 6.0, the imidazole (pK_a 6.7–7.0) is protonated, and can act as a hydrogen ion donor (general acid) to help hydrolyze the ester linkage; at a pH of 8.5, the imidazole may act more as an unprotonated species in concert with a serine residue (in a similar manner to some protease active sites) to effect the hydrolysis of a triglyceride ester linkage. The exact mechanism of catalysis is pH determined in lipases, therefore, along with enzyme conformation.

7.6 Enzyme purification and isolation

Enzymes are generally extracted from their native biological sources for use and characterization. The extraction methods reflect the range of techniques available currently for protein isolation and identification. Typically, an initial step in the isolation of a particular enzyme would be to free it from the cell structure or organelle with which it is associated. Cell fractionation can be accomplished through a variety of means: grinding, freeze/thaw cycling, or sonic (ultrasound) methods. But whatever the means, because enzymes are such fragile structures, with a particular specific chemical or catalytic ability associated with them, their isolation requires a great deal of care to avoid doing irreparable harm to their structure during the isolation process. From the cell fractionate, an enzyme can be isolated from other proteins and cellular components by a variety of means: selective precipitation, adsorption onto specific materials, chromatographic techniques, or through electrophoretic means, to name just a few methods. Enzymes that are pure enough can even be crystallized. By whatever isolation means, the activity of the enzyme, i.e., its ability to catalyze a certain reaction, is as important a property as the amount of protein isolated.

It is often part of 'tracking' or measuring the degree of purity of an enzyme to assay or test, at various stages of purity, the *specific activity* of a partially purified enzyme. The specific activity of an enzyme is the unit activity per weight at any stage of purification. A standard unit of enzyme activity is taken, by convention, as the amount of enzyme required to produce 1 mg of product (or products), per minute at a standard temperature and pressure (25°C and 1 atmosphere). When this convention is not followed, usually manufacturers will state the assay conditions under which the enzyme activity was measured or reported. A cell fractionate may contain a low amount of a lipase, for instance, 1 unit of lipase activity per gram weight of cell protein extract. As the purity of the enzyme is increased (as it is freed from other contaminating proteins), and assuming that the activity that was there initially is not lost at the next purification stage, then the specific activity of the enzyme should increase. If 90% of the contaminating proteins are removed through a selective precipitation process, then there would still be a measured 1 unit of lipase activity per 100 mg of protein, or a specific activity of 10 lipase units per gram of protein after the precipitation stage. We want the highest specific activity we can get with a particular enzyme, i.e., the highest amount of activity *and* protein purity. But it isn't always necessary (or desirable) to have an absolutely pure enzyme to be of practical use. Enzymes that are only substantially free of other contaminating proteins may suffice in certain applications. It is also possible to *over*-purify an enzyme – by isolating it completely from other cellular materials we may in fact remove small ions, activators or co-enzymes which are required for its activity, and the specific activity would drop with further isolation stages.

7.7 Enzymes important to conservation

The following three sections describe the important features of those enzymes that have found conservation applications.

7.7.1 Lipases

Lipases are enzymes that catalyze the hydrolysis of triglycerides into their constituent fatty acid and glycerol components. Usually the C1 and C3 fatty acid chains on the glycerol 'backbone' are hydrolyzed first by the enzyme (see Fig. 7.4); the C2 fatty acid monoglyceride is somewhat harder to hydrolyze effectively in the intact triglyceride due to steric concerns. Some biological sources for lipases show a marked affinity in the lipases they produce for the glycerol C1 and C3 fatty acid chains; only when they have been completely hydrolyzed, will these lipases they produce begin to hydrolyze the C2 fatty acid chain. Different biological sources produce lipases which tend to show greatest activity against specific chain length fatty acids, while they exhibit a general ability to hydrolyze triglyceride fatty acid esters. C_8 or shorter fatty acids are preferentially hydrolyzed by certain bacterial lipases; in pre-gastic lipases in ruminants shorter chain length fatty acids are preferentially cleaved (see Table 7.2).

The action of lipases on triglycerides is complicated by the general insolubility of the substrate itself. Triglycerides of fatty acids greater than two or three carbons in

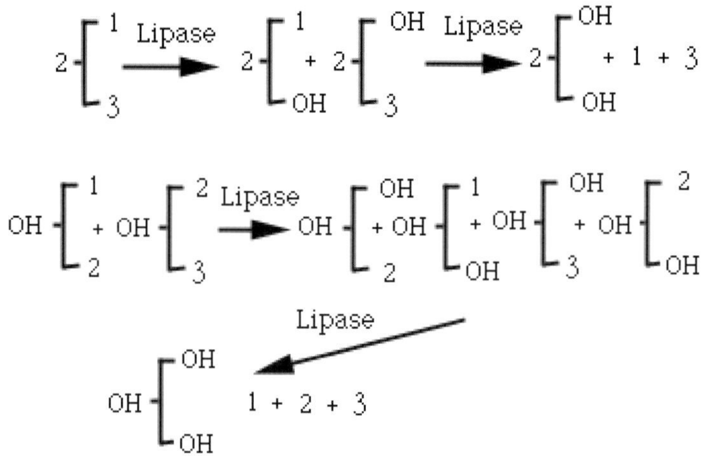

Figure 7.4 Hydrolysis of a triglyceride by lipase

Table 7.2 A comparison of the physical characteristics, and specificities of lipases derived from three different sources

	Pancreatic lingual	Duodenal	Bacterial
Inactive pH 3	No	Yes	Yes
Trypsin sensitive	No	Moderate	–
Chain specificity	4 > 6 > 8 >> 18	4 > 6 > 8 > 18	8 ≥ 18
Position specificity	1 > 2	1 >> 2	1 = 2
pH optimum	4–8	6–9	4–9
MW	40–50K	500K	120K

length are generally water insoluble. Recall from the Michaelis–Menten equation that the maximum velocity of an enzyme is a function of the substrate concentration ($\frac{1}{2}v_{max} = K_m$). The action of a lipase is on the surface of the triglyceride, and it is difficult to imagine reaching the levels of substrate concentrations to make the enzyme reach its maximum velocity. In order to have the maximum amount of substrate available, the triglyceride needs to be emulsified to increase the surface area available. While many surfactants might be able to emulsify effectively a particular triglyceride structure in water, the surface active nature of most surfactants would preclude their use in this regard; as surfactant collected at the interface between triglyceride and water phase, to lower the surface tension between lipid and water, the surfactant would in effect become the new surface, and obstruct the enzyme from performing its catalytic activity. In mammals, bile acids are made by these organisms for just this purpose: to emulsify lipids, especially triglycerides; to facilitate their transport in the bloodstream and gut, and across

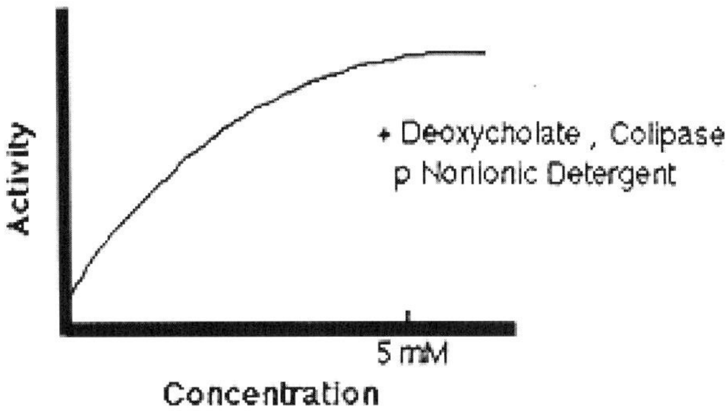

Figure 7.5 Lipase activity with co-factors present

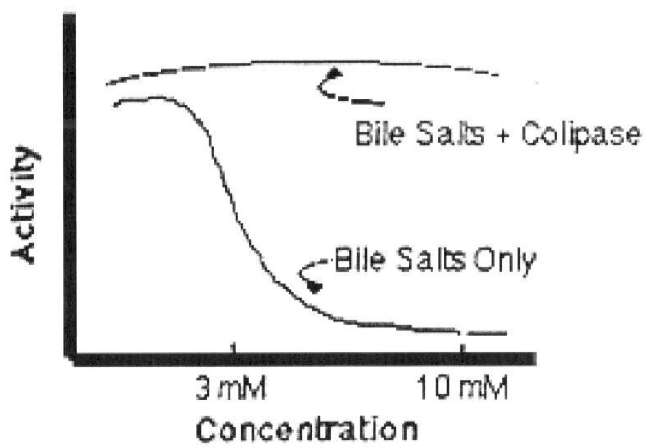

Figure 7.6 Activity of lipase with bile salts, co-lipase

absorption membranes. The bile acids bind cooperatively with lipases present in these organisms to allow the enzyme access to the emulsified triglycerides so that they can still be hydrolyzed effectively by the enzyme, and then metabolized further. Figure 7.5 shows graphically this cooperative relationship between the bile acid deoxycholic acid and a pancreatic lipase. At 5 mM (the CMC of this surfactant) of deoxycholate, the maximum lipase activity is reached in an aqueous solution.

It should be pointed out that lipases also exhibit an absolute requirement for both Na^+ and Ca^{+2} ions in solution (the equivalent of 4 Ca^{+2} ions per lipase molecule is needed for full activity), and require a co-lipase (a 70 amino acid peptide) for activity (Fig. 7.6) (Brockerhoff & Jensen 1974). The role of the co-lipase in particular is still under study (Borgström & Brockerman 1984); it may help act as a 'spacer' molecule, or bridge, that helps the lipase molecule penetrate the deoxycholate monolayer surrounding an emulsified triglyceride, or it may simply bind to the lipase at some point to give it the exact shape it needs overall to have a proper active catalytic architecture. Whatever the exact arrangement, the ratio of 1:1 of co-lipase to bile acid seems to be the optimum to effect the hydrolysis of substantial amounts of triglcerides. Figure 7.6 suggests that at much greater concentrations than the CMC, deoxycholate may not form cooperative structures with the enzyme; but when the co-lipase to deoxycholate ratio is maintained (1:1), even at higher levels of the

clear coating (a material with a bright white autofluorescence, which was positive for a natural resin component with antimony pentachloride), had collected a soiling layer; and then had been recoated with what appeared to be a layer of oil (it was positive with Rhodamine B) which had also collected a substantial soiling layer. The apparent use of an essentially pure drying oil coating over an older natural resin implies that the painting had been 'oiled-out' at some point in its past. The fact that the oil layer had been added later suggested that it would be desirable to remove it. The paint was consolidated as needed with PVA AYAA, 20% in toluene. To deal with the oil on the surface of the painting without disturbing the lower resin layer, an enzymatic/detergent system was formulated. The formula for the lipase gel that was used was:

water (deionized)	100 ml
Tris-HCl (Trizma pre-set buffer, pH 8.4)	0.66 g
hydroxypropylmethyl cellulose (4000 cps)	1.6 g
Triton X-100	0.1 ml

and to this 'stock' gel was added as a dry lyophilized powder, a lipase (Sigma Type VII, *candida cylindracea*, 700 – 1500 units/mg, 30% lactose as an extender)

lipase (type VII)	1 g

Typically, the lipase gel was applied to the painting surface (see Figs 7.1.2 and 7.1.3), stirred for a moment with a synthetic bristle brush (00), and then wiped away along with any dissolved oil and soiling material that was solubilized. The area thus treated was cleared with a saliva rinse, air dried, and then rinsed with mineral spirits and allowed to evaporate to dryness (see Figs 7.1.4 and 7.1.5).

Commentary

There were actually three complicating materials on the surface of this painting: two soiling layers, and an 'oiling' out layer or coating that had been applied at some point in the painting's history. The essentially 'pure' nature of the oiling out layer on the painting surface inspired the idea of using an enzyme (lipase) to help solubilize it. After all, extremely polar solvents had little apparent effect on the coating, or if they did, it was at the expense of the underlying natural resin coating, and paint layers. By hydrolyzing the oil, we can reduce it from a cross-linked polymer to smaller more manageable pieces which can be water dispersed or solubilized. Lipases are especially effective in these kinds of situations, where the oil is on a surface (accessible), and largely unadulterated (unpigmented, and without the addition of resins, etc).

The lipase chosen in this case was Sigma's Type VII. Recall that lipases generally require Ca^{+2} for activity. The requisite Ca^{+2} is provided in this case by the manufacturer, in the form of a substantial amount of Ca^{+2} lactate added as an 'extender' (stabilizer). For long chain fatty acid triglyceride structures (> 8 carbons), lipases derived from certain biological sources may show an increased affinity/preference for hydrolysis. The yeast *candida cylindracea* derived lipase shows an increased activity against triglycerides with long chain fatty acids, especially at a pH of around 8.0. The

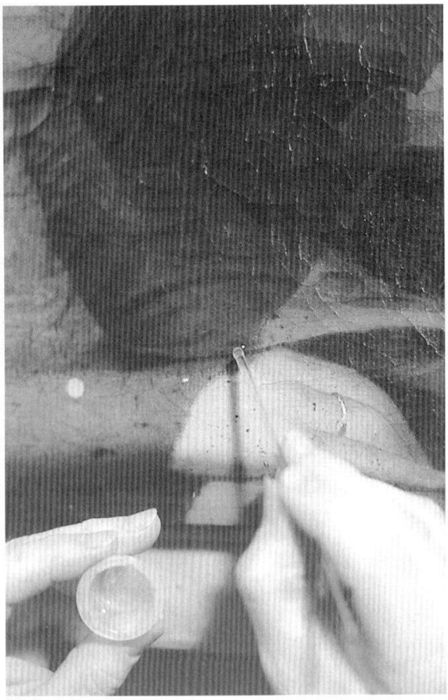

Figure 7.1.2 (see colour plates)

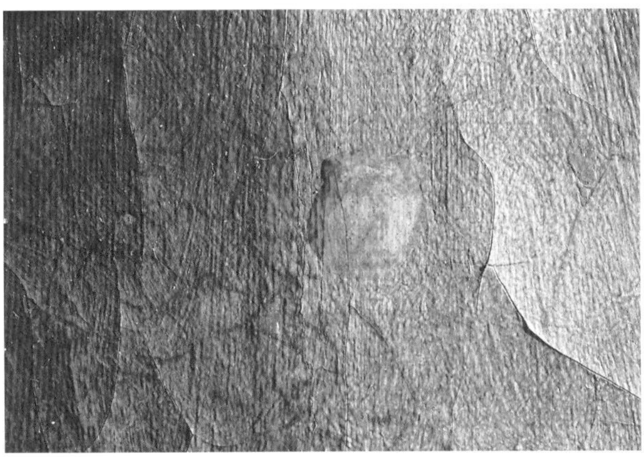

Figure 7.1.3
(see colour plates)

choice of the particular enzyme in this case is appropriate for the type of substrate likely to be present (polymerized linseed oil; linoxyn; with fatty acids of palmitic, stearic, oleic, linoleic, and linolenic acids, C chains lengths of between 16 and 18). The specific activity in this case (700–1500 units/mg) is rather low in the Type VII material; it should signal to us that the enzyme preparation is not highly purified. While this level of activity is sufficient for our needs in this case, it is also important to note that the more highly purified an enzyme preparation is, the greater the likelihood that essential co-factors or activators might be lost in the separation of an enzyme from other proteins.

Remember that lipases also require a co-lipase, a 70 amino acid peptide, for activation. We can assume that it is probably still present in this preparation, since it is not highly purified – or we can, of course, add it to our lipase gel, if necessary, to ensure that it is present (Sigma sell a co-lipase preparation; no. C 3028). At room temperature (25°C), we may lose up to 50% of the stated activity for the Type VII lipase. Sigma reports its activity at between 700–1500 units/mg at 37°C, at pH 7.7. Using olive oil as a test substrate, and employing the lipase at its optimum pH (or close to it, e.g. 8.4) at room temperature means that we can expect to have about 350–750 units of activity per mg of enzyme. At the stated concentration (10 mg/ml of gel), that means we can nominally expect to have 3500–7500 units of activity in solution per ml under these conditions. A target amount of activity for these kinds of applications is about 1000 units/ml of activity; at this level of activity we can see a

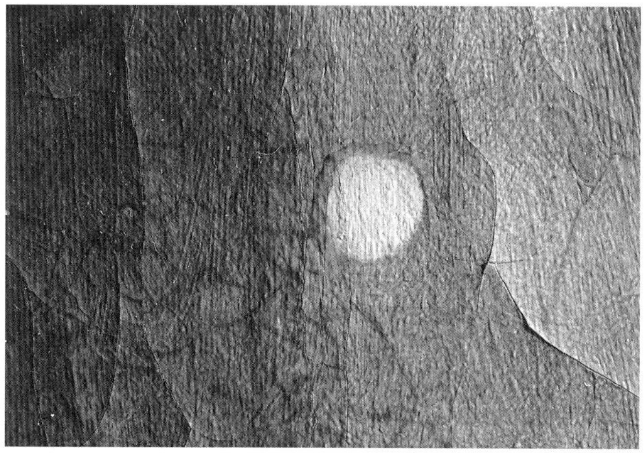

Figure 7.1.4 (see colour plates)

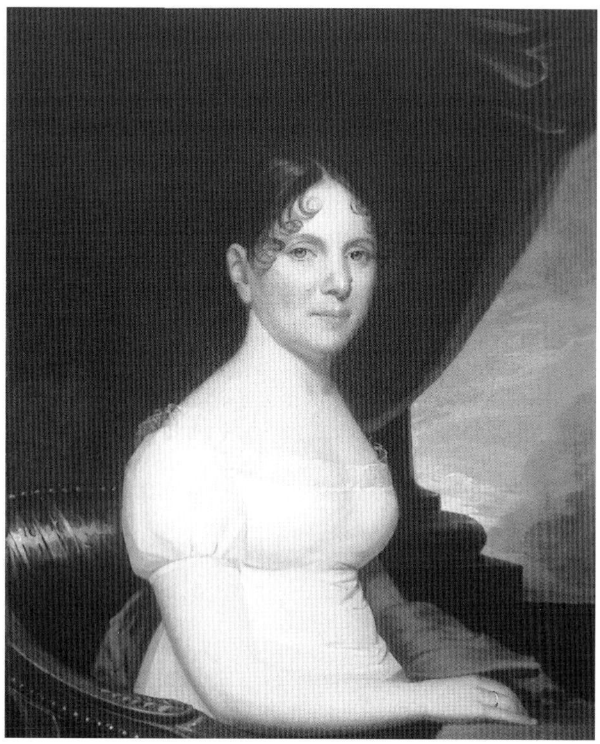

Figure 7.1.5 (see colour plates)

rapid effect on substrates – usually within a moment or two, oily substrates will begin to break up and dissolve. We can probably realize most of the expected activity under our use conditions because lipases work well on substrates which are surfaces (i.e. not in solution). The velocity of enzyme-catalyzed reactions is largely determined by substrate concentration (Michaelis–Menten equation), but lipases are unusual in that they act more efficiently on substrates (i.e. oils) which are out of solution, or present at boundaries, or in surface arrangements.

Now, the only potential problem is the use of Triton X-100 in the system described above. There are two substantial grime layers to be solubilized along with the oil coating. Triton X-100 was added at 0.1 % (MW = 624, so this is equivalent to a 1.6 mM concentration, or 7 × CMC for Triton X-100) ostensibly for these other complicating materials. A good deal of the Triton X-100 will be adsorbed on the soiling material(s); while this represents a slight excess of the surfactant beyond its CMC, we may in fact be very close to the CMC, practically speaking, at this concentration. Recall that many surfactants (including Triton X-100) suppress the activity of lipase, especially in the absence of co-lipase. At, or close to, the critical concentration of Triton X-100 (0.23 mM), about 50–60% of the activity of lipase/co-lipase potential activity is lost, so our 'nominal' activity of between 3500–7500 units/ml may be more of the order of 1000–1500 units/ml (still close enough to our target amount to work in this case). In the absence of a substantial soiling layer, the Triton X-100 concentration would be kept much lower, closer to its CMC level, or, as in Case History 7.2 below, deoxycholate or another bile acid might be used as a more compatible surfactant with lipase, and at higher concentrations. Low CMC surfactants are generally inappropriate with lipases, and especially at high concentrations, because they occlude an oily surface (by dissolving in it, if their CMCs are low enough, and forming a new surfactant-rich surface) and prevent a lipase from accessing and hydrolyzing the oil beneath.

The Trizma pre-set pH buffer material was chosen in this case for convenience; the metered buffer, on dissolving in deionized water, gives the stated pH (8.4) without the addition of added acids or bases. The amount used is equivalent to about a 40 mM amount of buffer, which is more than enough capacity for this system.

Hydroxypropylmethyl cellulose was used as the thickener in this system to produce a gel of a viscosity (4000 cps) high enough to restrict the application of the lipase to limited areas only. It can also act as a suspension aid, as a more hydrophobic cellulosic polymer for the solubilized oily material liberated by the enzyme.

The clearance procedures in this case are, first, to remove water-soluble materials (with saliva); the saliva will work because it is largely water itself, and because it contains a small amount of protease, to denature and degrade whatever lipase may remain on the treated surface. Second, the mineral spirits are applied to remove any Triton X-100 residues that remain.

Case History 7.2: Unattributed, *Christ Washing the Feet of the Disciples* (oil on canvas, nineteenth century)

The image was barely discernible through a thick brownish-black coating that covered the surface of the painting. In near UV, the coating appeared rather dark in terms of autofluorescence, exhibiting a deep orange-brown colour. The reverse of the canvas was deeply stained with varnishing materials and the painting appeared as if it had been cleaned and recoated at least once in its lifetime. Discrete solvent tests were conducted on the painting's surface; very polar solvents (methanol, DMF), and extremely alkaline preparations (1% NH_4OH, pH 10–11) were required to swell and/or remove the uppermost brownish-black coating. In the test cleaned areas, the removal of the brownish-black coating revealed a much brighter surface to the paint beneath; these cleaned test areas seemed to fluoresce in near UV with a bright yellowish-white autofluorescence. A small sample was removed from damage (a tear) on the face of the painting, mounted, cross-sectioned, and examined with the microscope. It revealed a light grey oil ground (which was positive with Rhodamine B); an oil paint layer (which was positive with Rhodamine B); the remnant of a natural resin coating (recognized by its autofluorescence), and a thick, essentially pure, oil coating (positive with Rhodamine B, and with no apparent autofluorescence). The cross-section seemed to confirm the observation that the painting had originally carried a natural resin varnish on its surface, and then at some point, was cleaned, and 'oiled'. The following mixture was made specifically to remove the oil coating:

water (deionized)	100 ml
glycine (free base)	0.4 g
deoxycholic acid (free acid)	1.0 g

The pH was adjusted to 8.5 with 1M NaOH, and then the following was added:

hydroxypropylmethyl cellulose (4000 cps)	1.6g

To this 'stock' gel was added as a dry lyophilized powder, a lipase (Sigma Type VII, *candida cylindracea*, 700–1500 units/mg, 30% lactose as an extender)

lipase (type VII)	1g

Care was taken not to mix the lipase into the stock gel with too much air 'whipped' into it, so as to not denature the enzyme. The activity of the enzyme gel was checked each day against a standard preparation of an olive oil emulsion in water (Sigma lipase substrate no. 800 – 1); typically a few drops of the creamy white emulsion were placed on a clean glass slide, an equal volume of the lipase gel added to it, and the mixture stirred and watched. If the emulsion cleared within a short amount of time, then the enzyme preparation was active enough for use on the painting. From simple testing like this, it was determined that the 'shelf' life of the enzyme once it was mixed in the gel was about 24–48 hours at most. While olive oil is Sigma's standard triglyceride for testing lipase activity, a better substrate in our case might have been an emulsion of fresh linseed or other nut oil (long fatty acid chain triglyceride) emulsified with deoxycholic acid in a water emulsion.

Typically, the lipase gel was applied to the paint surface, stirred for a moment with a synthetic bristle brush (00), and then wiped away along with any dissolved oil and soiling material that was solubilized. The area thus treated was cleared with a saliva rinse, air dried, and then rinsed with mineral spirits and allowed to evaporate to dryness.

Commentary

This is actually a very similar situation to Case History 7.1 above, in that it involves the removal of a drying oil coating from a painting that still carries the remnant, at least, of a natural resin coating underneath it. However, there is not the added complication of a substantial soiling layer; the lipase is the Type VII material from Sigma again, but it is combined with deoxycholic acid as the surfactant. The HLB number of deoxycholic acid is approximately 17.6, compared to Triton X-100 at 13.5, so in this case deoxycholic acid has a slightly stronger solubilizing power than Triton X-100. It also works cooperatively with the lipase to facilitate the enzymes' hydrolysis of lipids. At the stated concentration (1 g/100 ml) we are working at about 5 × the CMC for deoxycholic acid (CMC = 5 mM). The fact that there is a resinous layer under the oil coating is fortuitous, because as long as the pH is not so high as to rapidly solubilize the more polar or acidic portions of the resin coating, it is only slowly affected by the applied enzyme solution. The 'resin coating' is in fact, that portion of an earlier or original coating that was on the painting surface. It had been 'cleaned' with solvent applications at some point in the past, meaning that most of the lower molecular weight, less polar portions of it were brought into solution by general solvent action, and those more polar fractions of it, or the portions of the resinous coating that were intermixed with the surface of the painting itself (i.e., contained a substantial oil concentration), would only be affected slowly by the applied lipase. Lipases work quickly against pure oil coatings but more slowly as the oil is adulterated with pigments, driers, resins, and the like. In this case, the residual resin-rich surface to the paint film itself was a poor substrate (and good barrier) to the enzyme, to keep it from reaching and affecting the paint surface itself.

7.7.2 Carbohydrases

Carbohydrases catalyze the hydrolysis of carbohydrates into short polysaccharide or individual sugar units (Metzler 1977: 364–9). The most important carbohydrase is α-amylase which breaks down starch into glucosyl units. α-amylase specifically hydrolyzes the 1→4 linkage in starch at random points over the longer linear portions of the polymer; β-amylase is a related enzyme that cleaves off the end maltose units at the non-reducing end of the polysaccharide chains. Gluco-amylase is yet another starch-hydrolyzing enzyme that cleaves at both the 1→4 and 1→6 linkages in the starch molecule, at the non-reducing ends of both long and short chain sections of the polysaccharide. These three carbohydrases, while they act to hydrolyze different portions of the same molecule, have markedly different pH optima, thermal stabilities, and co-enzyme requirements. For instance, α-amylase exhibits an absolute requirement for Cl^- ion in solution for activity to occur. Some microbial α-amylases are active to 100°C or more and are typically used to reduce quickly the molecular weights of whole starch molecules, and have to reduce their high viscosity in heated slurries. β-amylase is rapidly denatured above about 63°C. α-amylase is used alone where dextrins (shorter chain polymers of glucose with some limited branching in the polymer chains) are the desired product; dextrins are used in adhesive, and certain food processing (brewing) applications (Norman 1982). For the production of individual glucose units from whole starch molecules, both α-amylase and gluco-amylase are used in concert with one another; the α-amylase rapidly breaks the larger starch molecule into shorter pieces at the 1→4 linkages, and the gluco-amylase ('de-branching' enzyme) continues the process by cleaving the starch molecule at its branching or 1→6 linkages. In this dual use of both enzymes the conditions for maximum activity of each must be met during their use. For example, in a typical industrial application, a 30–35% starch-in-water suspension would be made, the pH adjusted to 5.5 and the α-amylase added; the starch enzyme slurry could then be heated to 85°C, and held there for 40 minutes (both this temperature and pH are the optimum for α-amylase to work) (Norman 1982: 342). The pH could then be dropped to 4.5, and the temperature lowered to 63°C for 72 to 96 hours for the gluco-amylase to start to work.

Case History 7.3: Unattributed, Wallpaper Fragment, Corbett-Sharp House, Odessa, Delaware (paper, early nineteenth century)

A small fragment (Fig. 7.3.1) of what appeared to be an important early wallpaper was retrieved from behind a moulding in the Corbett-Sharp House. The paper appeared to be a wove, high rag content paper, and carried a multiple block printed floral pattern on its surface. The printing inks were relatively stable in small aqueous tests, and it was hoped that the fragment could be bathed to remove soiling and paste residues from its surface to recover the clearest possible representation of the block design. The fragment was to be used as a model for reproduction paper to be reinstalled in the room in which it was found (see Fig. 7.3.2). The fragment was bathed in the following enzymatic bath:

water (deionized)	100 ml
bis-Tris (bis(2-hydroxyethyl-imino-tris(hydroxymethyl) methane	1.4 g
NaCl	0.3 g

The pH was adjusted with the addition of 1M HCl to 6.0, and the above used as a stock solution. As needed, the following was added to it:

α-amylase (Sigma Type II-A, *Bacillus 4* × crystallized; lyophilized; 1500–3000 units/mg protein)	1g

The α-amylase was folded gently into the stock solution of buffer and NaCl; care was taken not to 'whip' air into the dissolving lyophilate to avoid air-denaturing the enzyme. The activity of the α-amylase was checked by removing a few drops of the enzyme and stock solution bath and putting them on a clean glass slide; to this was added a few crystals of amylose azure (Sigma A 3508); if the amylose azure crystals softened and dissolved in a few moments, the enzyme was deemed sufficiently active to free the wallpaper from the residual adhesive.

The wallpaper fragment was immersed in the stock solution plus enzyme and the residual adhesive material was lightly brushed from the surface of the paper with a small synthetic bristle brush (00), as it softened and/or dissolved in the enzyme and stock solution bath. The fragment was then raised on a screen, transferred to a tapwater rinsing bath, and then finally to clean blotters and weights.

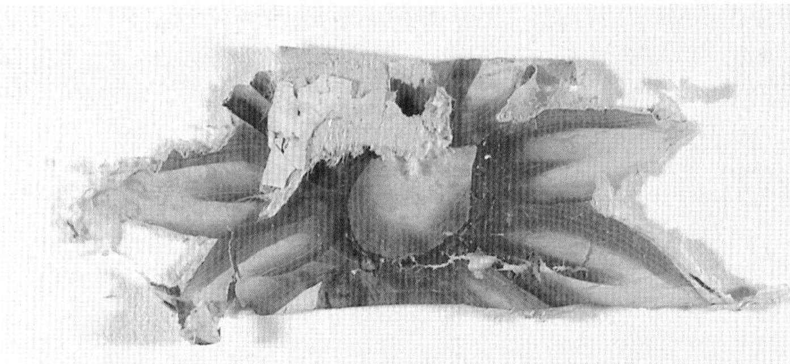

Figure 7.3.1 Unattributed, *in situ* view of wallpaper at Corbett-Sharp House, Odessa, Delaware (paper, early nineteenth century) (see colour plates)

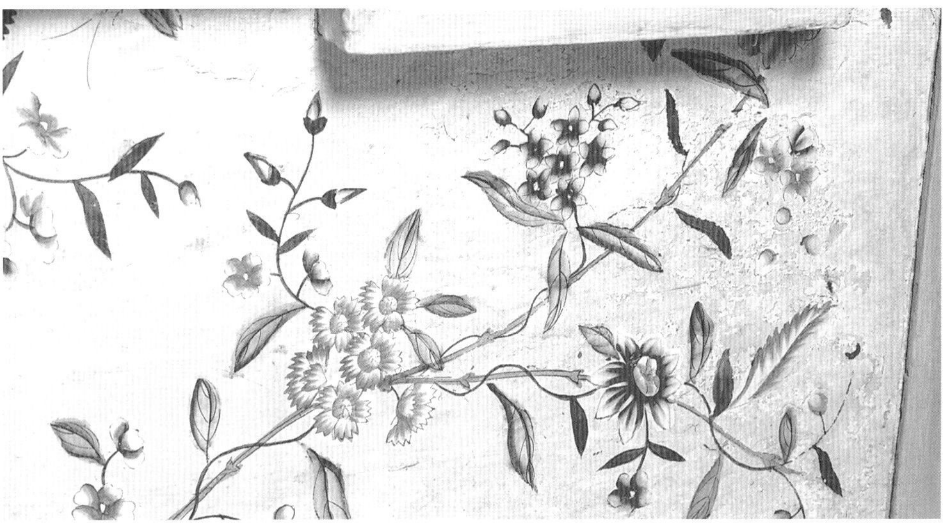

Figure 7.3.2 (see colour plates)

Commentary

The α-amylase used in this case was intended to facilitate the removal of the residual paste adhesive and soiling materials from the wallpaper fragment; only α-amylase was used (essentially 'float' washing), because it was sufficient to reduce the paste quickly to a dispersible form, not completely hydrolyze it to individual glucosyl units (so a second 'de-branching' enzyme, gluco-amylase, was not part of this formula). α-amylase requires Cl^- hence the addition of NaCl (50 mM) to the deionized water. The specific activity of α-amylase (1500–3000 units/mg protein) is close to the practically realizable amount in this system; Sigma's α-amylase assay is at 20°C and at a pH of 6.9, and under these conditions the 'units' are reported. This buffered system is at a pH of 6.0 with bis-Tris (pK_a = 6.5, but is useful over the range of 5.8–7.2). The bis-Tris is used at a 50 mM concentration, and should provide enough of a buffering capacity for the acidic material likely to be present in this substrate/ wallpaper fragment. This stock preparation did not contain a thickener (e.g. methyl cellulose 4000 cps), because diffusion into the paste/wallpaper, and rinsing away the residual enzyme afterwards, would be slow or difficult with a viscosity control agent such as this included.

7.7.3 Proteases

Proteases are enzymes which hydrolyze proteins into smaller peptide, or individual amino acid units (Metzler 1977: 370). There are so many commercially available proteases that describing and classifying them all in the present context would be difficult. They can generally be characterized by the location of the peptide bond they act on in a protein; i.e., an *exo-protease* hydrolyzes terminal amino acids from a protein; an *endo-protease* hydrolyzes peptide bonds in the middle of a protein chain. Proteases can be found and extracted from plant, animal, bacterial, and fungal sources, and this also helps to distinguish them. The mechanism at the active site of a protease can also be used to distinguish one protease from another. In a manner similar to that described for the active site of a lipase, chymotrypsin and trypsin utilize two amino acids in particular (serine and histidine) at their active site as acidic and basic functional groups to achieve catalysis. A large number of proteases have an -SH or thiol group at their active site, as a proton-donating group. Still another group of proteases have a divalent metal ion at their active site, which functions as a weak Lewis acid during catalysis. The pH optimum for maximum activity can also be a useful way of distinguishing different proteases: proteases that have their maximum in the acid range find greatest commercial use in the clotting of milk; those that have a neutral maximum in brewing (malting); and alkaline proteases have been exploited for laundry detergent preparations. Suffice it to say, that depending on the specific activity, pH optimum and range, heat sensitivity, and inactivation mechanisms, many proteases can (and have) found application in conservation techniques.

The most likely mechanism for catalyzing the hydrolysis of a peptide bond by a protease probably involves a displacement reaction through the protonation of the carbonyl oxygen in the peptide bond (see Fig. 7.8) by an acidic group on the protease at its active site (Metzler 1977: 370–1). We have seen that serine can function this

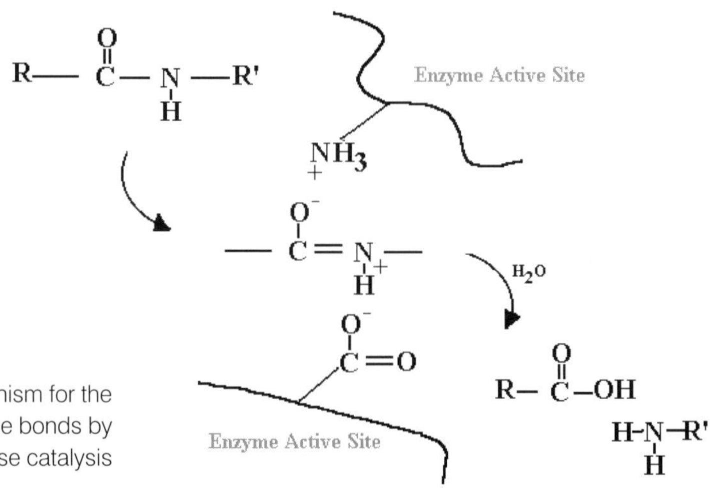

Figure 7.8 The mechanism for the hydrolysis of peptide bonds by concerted acid/base catalysis

way in chymotrypsin and trypsin; cysteine (a thiol substituted amino acid) can be a hydrogen ion donor in enzymes like papain, and metal ions can act as weak Lewis acids at the active sites of certain proteases like carboxypeptidase A (which contains a single Zn^{+2} ion at its active site). By protonating the carbonyl oxygen, this greatly increases the positive charge on the adjacent carbon through a type of resonance, and would make attack by a nucleophile at the carbon all the more likely. It also stabilizes a tetrahedrally bonded intermediate which may be formed during the catalysis.

The activation and deactivation of proteases is especially interesting and active site specific; with proteases that contain a metal ion at the active site, removal of the metal ion by chelation can suppress all enzymatic activity (Metzler 1977: 378). The enzyme can be reactivated in some cases by reinserting the metal ion in the enzyme structure. Cyanide generally inhibits metal-containing proteases (Metzler 1977: 362). Since most proteases have an acidic- or proton-donating group at their active sites, they tend to exhibit relatively narrow activity curves with regard to pH changes; chymotrypsin has an optimum between 8 and 9, for instance, with very little activity above or below this range. Bromophenylacylbromide or diazo reagents can also react with these acidic functional groups, and, in most cases, completely inhibit protease activity. In some cases Nature has also provided an interesting array of enzyme inactivators or inhibitors. Trypsin, for instance, is manufactured in the pancreas as a *zymogen* or 'pre-enzyme' in a larger, inactive form (Metzler 1977: 370). It is activated on secretion from the pancreas by another enzyme that cleaves off a long peptide that restricts it from being activated (assuming its native conformation) too soon. The pancreas also secretes a small peptide along with the zymogen (a 650 MW peptide) that binds tightly to the active site of the protease (with a binding constant of $K = 1 \times 10^{12}M$) as a second added precaution to premature activation (as an active protease, trypsin would hydrolyze and destroy other enzymes inside the pancreas if it were not protected in this way).

Case History 7.4: Frederick Sandys, *Portrait of Miranda* (oil on panel, nineteenth century)

The *Portrait of Miranda* by Frederick Sandys was ostensibly a representation of the artist's wife painted in the pre-Raphaelite tradition. The painting was executed on a mahogany panel support. Consistent with the existing information on Sandys' technique, the panel support seemed to be coated with multiple thin layers of a gesso-like material, which were burnished to a high polish. A drawing was apparently transferred to this prepared surface using either a rose-tinted crayon or pencil. As with many pre-Raphaelite paintings, the composition was probably completed area to area rather than overall. Sandys apparently worked in oils, wet-into-wet in any one area to virtual completion, and then moved on.

Structurally, the painting was in extraordinary condition (see Fig. 7.4.1). The panel had a slightly convex warp but was unchecked and unsplit. The paint, ground, and surface coatings were well secured to the support with only a hint of brittle crackle present on the painting surface. The latter had what appeared to be an initial, uniform varnish layer overall that was grimy and slightly discoloured. Under normal light, it

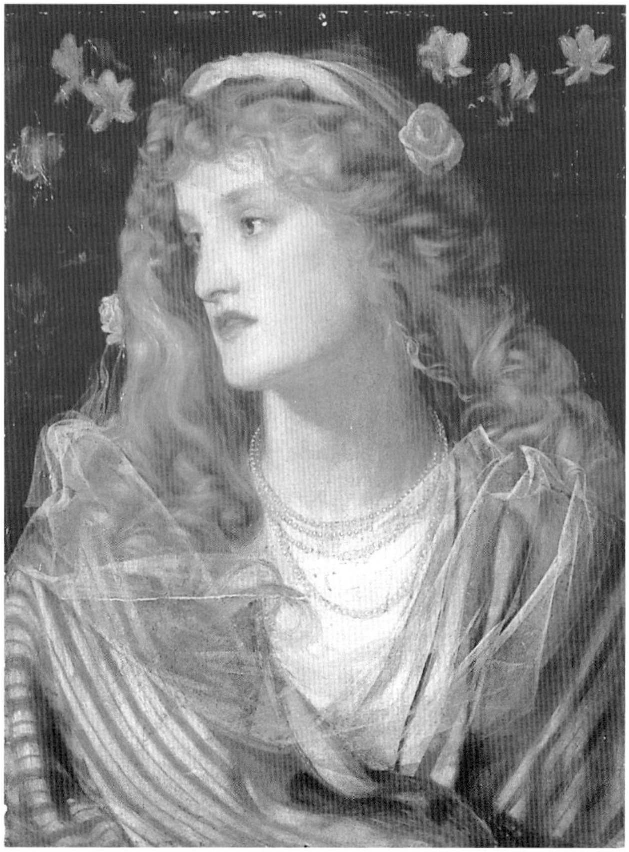

Figure 7.4.1 Frederick Sandys, *Portrait of Miranda* (oil on paper, nineteenth century) (see colour plates)

was also obvious that a second, additional coating material had been selectively applied to the face, hair and neck areas of the portrait. This material was very yellow and had obviously dripped through the highlight portions of the neck (see Fig 7.4.2). A small sample was removed from the painting for cross-sectional examination under the microscope. It was noted that in an area of flesh-coloured paint there was indeed a white ground of multiple layer applications (positive with both Rhodamine B and Lissamine Rhodamine sulfonyl chloride, suggesting both an oil- and protein-containing binding system). The sample also appeared to contain a single layer of an oil-bound flesh-coloured paint (positive with Rhodamine B); a yellowish transparent coating on top of the paint (positive with antimony pentachloride); and a second clear coating that had a distinctly brilliant blue-white autofluorescence, and stained with Lissamine Rhodamine sulfonyl chloride, and (in spots) Rhodamine B. A rather diffuse boundary between the initial transparent coating and the oil-bound paint below suggested that this coating had indeed been applied while the oil was still fresh. However, the fact that the uppermost, dripped, coating stained positively for both protein and oil was rather odd. This layer was well adhered to the original varnish beneath, but there was no diffusion layer between the two layers – the boundary was extremely distinct. Significantly, no grime layer was evident between the two coating layers. What evidence was available led to the speculation that Sandys might have used an emulsion such as egg white to varnish then further elaborate some areas of

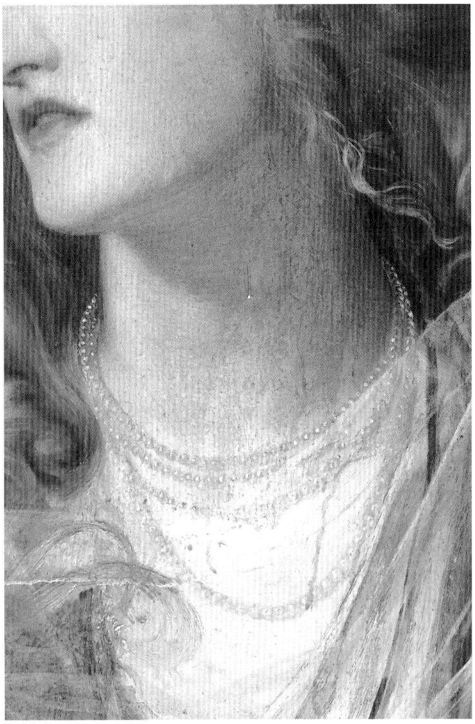

Figure 7.4.2 (see colour plates)

the portrait. Time and deterioration had then militated to produce a now obvious discolouration in this second coating material.

The owners of the painting were concerned with the visual impact of this now discoloured material. While it might represent an inherent flaw in the artist's selection of materials, it was, of course, part of the original presentation of the painting and therefore a part of the original structure. The purpose of the presumed egg-white coating was probably to give a clear, 'enamel-like' coating. The difficult decision was taken to remove the egg-white layer, or at the very least, substantially reduce it and then reappraise the recovered surface.

To remove the proteinaceous clear coating layer, an enzymatic gel system was decided upon, because its application to specific design areas could be restricted by the viscosity of the gel. A proteolytic enzyme or enzyme/detergent preparation could be used to break down the protein-containing egg white and not affect the continuous resin coating beneath. The painting would not be subjected to prolonged water-based treatments (and in particular, highly alkaline solutions). The formula used was as follows:

water (deionized)	100 ml
sodium acetate	7.5 g

Acetic acid (glacial) was added to bring the pH to 5.5, and then

Brij 35	0.1g
methyl cellulose (4000 cps)	3g

were added. The above ingredients formed a 'stock' gel; to this, as needed on a day-to-day basis, the following would be added, proportionally:

pepsin (Sigma P7125; porcine stomach mucosa; 600 – 1000 u/mg protein)	1g

To prepare the stock gel, the sodium acetate was dissolved in half of the water, the Brij 35 was added to the remaining 50 ml of water and stirred on a stirring hot plate until dissolved. The solution was cooled and added to the acetate buffer solution. The pH was checked and adjusted with the acetic acid. Preparing the enzyme gel involved mixing about 10 mg of pepsin as a dry powder per ml of the stock gel as needed. The enzyme lyophilate was mixed in carefully by 'folding' it gently into the aqueous gel; care was taken not to allow air into the mixture during mixing. The *in situ* activity of the pepsin was tested by placing a few crystals of hide powder azure (Sigma H9134) on a clean glass slide, along with some of the enzyme-gel; if the pepsin were indeed active to a level useful for removing the proteinaceous coating it would take only a few moments to dissolve the hide powder azure on the slide.

The enzyme gel was applied under the stereo-binocular microscope to areas covered with the proteinaceous coating material. It was stirred for a minute or two with a synthetic bristle brush. As the coating dissolved, it was rolled off the surface with a dry swab. Saliva was used to clear the treated area. After air drying, the enzyme-treated area was then additionally rinsed with mineral spirits and allowed to evaporate to dryness.

The surface of the overall varnish layer recovered from beneath the egg white remained saturated. The surrounding areas that carried only the initial natural resin coating were still substantially weathered and soiled. Therefore, a second stage of cleaning was initiated, intended to take up the soiled and weathered surface from the initial varnish layer only, with the goal of leaving the bulk of the film as intact as possible. The cleaning system used was:

water (deionized)	50 ml
Tween 20	10 ml
triethanolamine	4 ml

The pH was adjusted to 8.0 with 1M HCl, and then was shaken with

mineral spirits (Shell Solv T)	300 ml
Brij 35	10 g

to form the emulsion. Typically the emulsion would be applied to the surface of the soiled areas of the painting with a small brush (00), stirred for a moment on the surface, and then wiped away on a dry cotton swab. The area thus treated would then be rinsed with mineral spirits and allowed to evaporate to dryness (see Fig. 7.4.3).

Commentary

The solubilization of a proteinaceous material generally requires an aqueous system or, at the very least, a substantial aqueous component in a cleaning system.

Solvents, even very polar solvents or solvent blends, cannot solubilize to any great degree a material as large and as polar as a protein. But while a proteinaceous material may require water in one form or another for its solubilization, by hydrolyzing it with a protease – that is, breaking it into smaller pieces – the rate at which it can be resolubilized can be increased enormously. This can be accomplished enzymatically by using a protease in a water-based preparation which is compatible with the other materials present in the painting structure. In the initial step of cleaning, pepsin was chosen as the specific protease for several reasons. First, it functions optimally in an acidic range (its optimum is actually at a pH of 2, but fully 50% of the activity of this particular protease is still present in the pH range of 4–6, which is the usual optimum for most acidic proteases). Working at an acidic pH means that we can minimize the swelling effect of the cleaning preparation on oil- and resin-containing substrate materials (as already stated, both of these materials begin to swell dramatically above a pH of 6.7 (resins) and 8.5 (cross-linked oils)). The specific activity of the pepsin preparation chosen was 600–1000 units/mg of protein; at a working concentration of 10 mg/ml of enzyme gel, at the optimum temperature (37°C) and pH (2) that would mean we could expect about 6000–10000 units of enzyme activity per ml of gel. Now we can never obtain quite this level of activity for several reasons. We need to work at room temperature (25°C) and a much higher pH (5.5). While both of these conditions are off the maximum for pepsin, there is still between 30 and 40% of the stated activity with the enzyme (say, 1000–3000 units of pepsin activity per ml of gel). If we can maintain on the order of 1000 units of enzymatic activity on a substrate surface, the dissolution of the substrate can be achieved within a few moments.

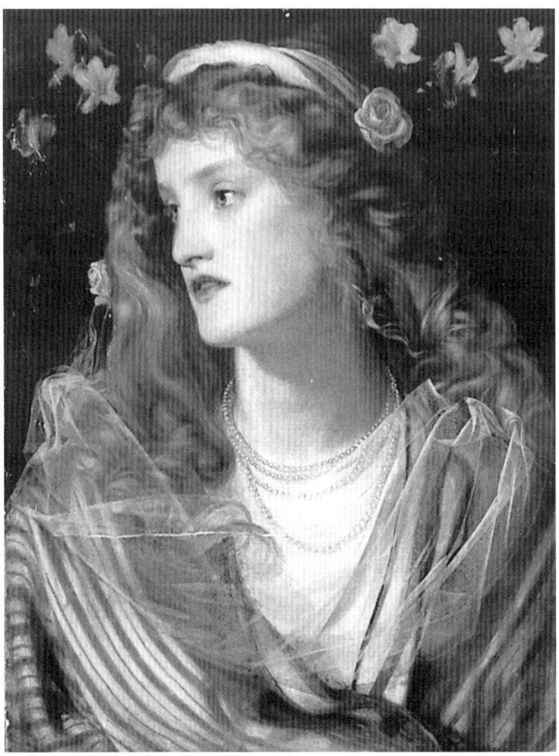

Figure 7.4.3

Pepsin is an endo-protease, meaning that it cleaves at peptide bonds in a protein chain in the middle of the chain, rather than the ends. Because of this, endo-proteases are more effective at rapidly reducing the size of a protein (and therefore solubilizing it more quickly). Fortunately, pepsin does not require any other small molecules for activation. We still need to maintain as much activity on the protein film surface as possible because of the initial non-solubility of the protein. The Michaelis–Menten equation 7.1 tells us that enzyme velocity is related to substrate concentration; but in this case, the substrate concentration is extremely low (as a solid film with a minimal surface area). A nonionic surfactant (Brij 35, in this case) can help water to wet onto the coating surface, allow the enzyme to reach the surface, and even sequester the products of the enzymatic hydrolysis which are still too large to be soluble in water. The amount of Brij 35 (POE 23 lauryl ether, MW 1182) used is equal to an 0.8 mM concentration, which is just slightly above its CMC (4 × CMC). At higher concentrations, a huge excess of the surfactant would only get in the way of the enzyme, or denature it. For detergency purposes, the fourfold excess of the surfactant is probably more than enough for wetting and solubilization purposes. The HLB of Brij 35 is 16.9 (well above the 7–9 minimum required for wetting, and high enough for detergency 13–15). Brij 35 as a nonionic will not precipitate or denature the enzyme as another ionic species surfactant might, and recall that the adsorption of surfactants onto soils and oily surfaces is determined by the amount of ethoxylate structure present in the surfactant. Brij 35, as the POE (23) lauryl ether is less likely to be adsorbed onto an oily (or oleo-resinous surface, in this case like the coating beneath the proteinaceous one) than other nonionics because of the substantial ethoxylate portion to it, and concomitantly it is more easily cleared from these surfaces.

It was not necessary in this case to inactivate the pepsin or worry about some small amount of residual activity on the recovered surface because the physical removal of the enzyme gel, and the mineral spirits rinse afterwards, were sufficient to remove all of the applied pepsin, or denature completely what small amount of it might be left. But it would be possible to include in the rinsing stage of treatment (say deionized water at a pH of 5.5 with acetate as the buffer), a small amount of pepstatin A as a specific inhibitor to pepsin, if complete clearance of the enzyme were not possible or likely. Pepstatin A (Sigma P 4265) is a small peptide (MW = 685), that, as a peptide itself, binds to the active site on the pepsin molecule; the binding or formation constant is so great that it essentially binds irreversibly in the active site, to the exclusion even of water. To inactivate the amount of pepsin applied to the surface of the coating completely (1×10^{-5}M enzyme) would require only about 10 mg/ml of pepstatin A.

Finally, the preparation was thickened (gelled) with methyl cellulose (4000 cps), both to restrict the spread of the preparation and to slow the diffusion of moisture from the water-based preparation into substrate materials.

The second preparation used to clean the remainder of the surface of *Miranda* was essentially an emulsion of water (with the pH slightly raised with the addition of TEA) in mineral spirits. The continuous phase was mineral spirits, the dispersed phase water. The proportions were purposely chosen to produce a W/O type of macroemulsion. As the continuous phase, and as a poor solvent for the underlying materials, the mineral spirits would have little effect on the substrate materials. The water phase would, on the other hand, have a better ability to pick up the accumulated materials on the painting surface (the grime or deposition material). Raising the pH in the water phase would only encourage degraded (i.e. oxidized, and acidic) materials to go into solution in that phase. The choice of two surfactants was a matter of convenience; whether we select a single surfactant of an appropriate HLB number to make our emulsion (in this case anything beyond about 4–6 would produce a stable W/O type of arrangement), or blend two surfactants to arrive at the same equivalent HLB number (Brij 35 is about 16.9, Tween 20 about 16.7, and the weight-proportioned HLB would be about 16.8, which is a far greater HLB number than needed to produce a stable emulsion), we can successfully emulsify water into mineral spirits. It was actually easier to dissolve the Brij 35 (a waxy solid at room temperature) into the mineral spirits, and the Tween 20 into the water phase, and then combine the two by shaking, than to dissolve the Brij 35 into the water first with stirring and warming. The advantage of using two surfactants may be, in this case, economy (the Tween 20 is a little less expensive than the Brij 35). Also, by using more than one detergent type, we can increase the range of material types that we can pick up (solubilize) with our surfactants.

7.8 Other enzymes of special note

While commercially a variety of other enzymes are of note, to date few have found their way into use in conservation applications. The enzyme glucose oxidase, though, might find use in certain paper and textile applications. It catalyzes the following reaction:

$$\begin{array}{ccc} \text{glucose} + O_2 + H_2O & \rightarrow & \text{glucono} - \delta - \text{lactone} + H_2O_2 \\ & & \downarrow \\ & & \text{gluconic acid} + H_2O \end{array} \qquad [7.5]$$

The production of hydrogen peroxide by glucose oxidase can be accomplished at a neutral pH, rather than at the elevated pHs required for bleaching or oxidizing with peroxide alone. Glucose oxidase is rapidly (10 minutes) inactivated at even a modestly elevated temperature (65°C). Commercially, glucose oxidase is used in either of two ways – as a steady source for peroxide for oxidation reactions, or as a way to remove either oxygen from packaged goods (the 'head volume' of air in soft drink containers has oxygen removed from it by adding the enzyme and glucose to the drink before capping it off), or as a way of removing glucose from food preparations for increased shelf life (Kroschwitz 1950).

Xylanase, hemicellulase, mannanase, are all carbohydrases worthy of note for their specific activity in degrading xylan, hemicellulose and mannan, which are prone to discolouration when they occur in paper systems. De-sizing enzymes may find use in textile cleaning applications (Kroschwitz 1950: 739). Recent laundry detergent formulations have included cellulases, which are active under alkaline conditions, as replacement materials for traditional bleaches in these applications (Kroschwitz 1950: 740). Commercial cellulases are interesting because they work very rapidly to hydrolyze cellulose derivatives like carboxy methyl cellulose, but (ironically) do not work (or work very slowly) on native cellulose.

advantageous in all situations. The repeated application of water, for rinsing purposes, may not be a good strategy for the efficient removal of certain applied materials (even those soluble originally in water), and where other potentially water-sensitive materials are close at hand or are part of a paint film. Given the seemingly infinite variety of materials combined or used in decorative and fine art materials, all paint films are not identical in their ability to swell in, adsorb, and desorb applied materials, from aqueous solutions. The emphasis should be put on the analysis or characterization of the surface materials present. Clearance of applied materials may be made much easier by characterizing the materials present in (and on) a surface to be cleaned, by whatever analytical means available or practical. We can then not only design an appropriate cleaning system(s), but we can also reasonably understand our options (in addition to water alone) for clearance.

8.2 Properties of paint surfaces

Before a treatment is carried out, the more information that can be gathered about the materials present, the better. While we can generally characterize paints initially as to film type (e.g. oil, casein, distemper), we often need more information about the specific components present, and their relative amounts, to understand the surface(s) we are dealing with, and the nature of soils retained on them, in order to design appropriate cleaning systems. We assume, for instance, that a given paint film may be bound with a drying oil, based mainly on our visual appraisal of that surface, or simply our experience in the past with similar-looking paint films. But depending on when we intercept an oil-bound film for cleaning, the exact condition of the film may be quite different. As ageing or exposure advances, so too does the degree of oxidation of the film. Initially, oxygen combines with a drying oil (or unsaturated triglyceride) in the form of peroxides or hydroperoxides; in time, this initial oxidation gives rise to the formation of more permanent cross-links, triglyceride to triglyceride, which characterize such films. Superimposed on this basic chemical 'drive' towards cross-linking and polymerization is the secondary general oxidation that characterizes the deterioration of many hydrocarbons (not just oils or fats); the inclusion of oxygen in the form of alcoholic, ketone, aldehyde, and carboxylic acid functional groups also occurs steadily on exposure. Hydrolysis, or auto-hydrolysis can take place in time, de-esterifying, and de-polymerizing these films. Undoubtedly, the more exposure occurs, the more oxidation; the more oxidation, and the more polar these surfaces become, shifting from hydrophobic to substantially hydrophilic. As the surfaces of these films degrade, they undoubtedly attract and retain soils through increasingly polar interactions. As they become acidic, the formation of salts must occur on contact with external or internal sources of alkaline materials. The higher the solubility products of these salts are, the more they will tend to form hygroscopic salts, and exert added physical forces to these surfaces; the lower the solubility product salts that are allowed to form, the more intractable soil will appear on contact with water or aqueous systems. As they contain or manifest more acidic functional groups, increasingly raising the pH on the surface of these films will undoubtedly have a pronounced swelling effect, especially as we go much above the pK_as of the acids present. These chemical processes might be said to characterize most drying oil films which are largely unadulterated with other materials. But what if other components are present? Resins, fatty acid soaps, gums, carbohydrates, proteins, and other 'non-drying' components have been added to paint binders, for a variety of chemical and rheological purposes, and will undoubtedly influence the chemistry of these films internally and on their surfaces. The addition of polar materials like gums may act to change (increase) the viscosity of some oil paints to allow for brushmarking or impasto effects but undoubtedly will also, at high enough concentrations, affect the nature of the surface(s) of these films, making them more polar from the outset, and liable to attract soiling materials more strongly. Pigments present in paint films also substantially contribute to surface chemical phenomena when they are physically prominent on paint surfaces (as they might be in leanly or underbound paint films), and through the contribution of soluble ionic material to these surfaces, where they include soluble salts.

How oxidized or polar is an oil film? What components are present? Are they present in sufficient quantity or disposition within the paint film to influence the surface chemistry? What pigments are present? Are any of them comprised of soluble salts that are likely to create insoluble salts? In some of the case histories presented throughout this book, information has been given on the examination and/or analytical technique used to appraise the condition of a painted surface. Applied microscopy techniques have been useful in this regard (see Appendix 1 in particular) for broad classes of materials (microscopic staining for organic binders such as proteins, carbohydrates, oils, and resins, for instance; and polarized light examination of dispersed samples in defined mounting media for characterizing pigments). Specific organic materials have been identified using infrared (FTIR), or GC-mass spectrometry techniques; and inorganic materials have been characterized with x-ray fluorescence (XRF), x-ray diffraction (XRD), or energy dispersive analysis coupled to scanning electron microscopy (EDX-SEM). We need to bring only those materials or conditions to these surfaces that are necessary and sufficient to perform a cleaning task.

Depending on when we intercept an oil film for cleaning, a substantially different set of conditions may exist on ageing or exposure. It was suggested in Chapter 2 that on oil films of any age or degree of oxidation, a relatively narrow pH range for aqueous solutions would be appropriate (5.5–8.5). But depending on the specific age, or more importantly, the *degree* of oxidation and exposure on a paint film surface, this range might be narrowed further still to 5.5–7.0. In this range we are closer to the pK_as of the fatty acids present (or likely to develop in an oil film), and are therefore less likely to swell or dissolve them. Adjusting the pH in a case like this – and including a buffer to do so – would be an important aspect or component of a cleaning system for this type of surface.

As an oil film becomes more oxidized, its surface becomes more polar – less hydrophobic – and it may not require a surfactant to wet water onto it at all; the surface tension between water and paint surface may be so low as to make unnecessary the use of a surfactant. The same may be said of paints that are constructed from or contain substantial amounts of more polar materials (e.g. gum, glue-oil, or casein oil films). Surfactants may not be necessary in these situations for surface wetting. Conversely, as oil films become more oxidized, acidic, and liable to the formation of salts, ionic effects such as raising or lowering the pH (H^+, OH^- ions), or specific ions (Na^+, K^+, etc.), may become more useful, even required, on these films. So too would chelating materials on films where pigments (lead white, for instance) might be present and contributing a small but steady state amount of metal ions (Pb^{+2} ion) to the paint and paint surface, to form insoluble complexes or salts with weakly organic acidic material.

8.3 Properties of varnished surfaces

Is the bulk of a surface accumulated material, or soil, water soluble? Or can it be made soluble or dispersible in water with a simple combination of surfactant, complexing agent, and buffer? If, empirically or analytically, the answer is no, then perhaps another method is required or justified. When the bulk of a degraded varnish layer of dammar or mastic is acidic – i.e. when most of the molecular moieties present are oxidized to the point of carrying at least one carboxylic acid functional group on them – by raising the pH above the pK_a of the resin acids present, most can be readily solubilized or swollen in water; the remaining material can probably be dispersed with a surfactant of sufficiently high HLB in water. In other words, on a very degraded dammar film it might be sufficient simply to raise the pH and add a weak surfactant to dissolve and disperse the coating. If the dammar film were much younger – less oxidized – the bulk of the film material would still be relatively insoluble in water (at any pH), and might be more efficiently dissolved with a tailored solvent system.

8.4 The design of cleaning systems with clearance in mind

We need to design cleaning systems that are made with appropriate amounts of materials for the cleaning task at hand. Obvious as it might seem, by simply bringing an appropriate amount, and no more, of a cleaning material to a surface, we can make the job of clearance much easier in the long run. For example, it was deemed necessary in Chapter 3 for a surfactant to be at its critical concentration (CMC) to begin to form micelles, wet water on hydrophobic surfaces, form emulsions, and act, in general, to lower the interfacial tension between two materials of widely differing surface energy. Practical detergent preparations incorporate surfactant levels at slightly higher concentrations than this: if we were to be at the CMC for a particular surfactant, the moment one molecule of a surfactant was absorbed onto a surface, the surfactant concentration would drop below the CMC, and it would cease to act to form the micellular structures and the surface aggregates we need. In Chapter 4, it was suggested that detergent preparations for laundry applications might typically be formulated at 4 to 5 times the surfactant critical concentration, to make sure that a sufficient amount of surfactant is maintained in solution at any moment to work. It seems reasonable that for painted surfaces that require surfactants as cleaning aids, that the same, or similar, slight excess of surfactant be maintained throughout the cleaning process for the same reason. The CMC for Triton X-100 is

0.23 mM; to reach this level, we only have to dissolve 0.144 g of it in a litre of water; five times this would be 0.72 g/l. Applying higher concentrations of Triton X-100 would add nothing to the cleaning effect, and simply require more work in terms of clearance after cleaning.

Using the same logic, it might be reasonable to expect that certain soiling layers, and degraded paint surfaces, have an appreciable soluble salt concentration in or on them. As an example, Pb-containing paints (and sources of lead may include pigments, driers, dispersal aids, etc.) may manifest on their surfaces appreciable Pb salts on exposure or ageing. If the solubility products of these Pb salts are high enough (or log pK_{sp}s low enough) to be complexed preferentially to chelating materials of lower formation constants (or higher pKs of formation), then soluble complexes of Pb-chelate should form. The 'completeness' of complexing or chelating of a metal is a function of the magnitude of the difference between the formation constant between the chelator and metal, and the solubility product of the metal salt. The bigger the difference (by orders of magnitude), the greater the 'driving' force to form the metal-chelate complex, and to effect the solubilization of the original metal salt. A better strategy is probably to find a chelator of sufficiently low formation constant (two or three orders of magnitude less than the solubility product), and use less of it, than to bring more of a chelator closer in formation constant to the solubility product of a given metal salt, and then have difficulty in removing it from a surface by repeated rinsing.

Typically, when a degraded oil paint film is wetted with water the surface conductivity observed might be only on the order of between 0–300 µS. 'Hypertonic' solutions (solutions where the concentration of a specific ion has been increased for ion exchange purposes, or to provide a specific counter-ion to produce an electrically stable surface) might thus be reasonably only one or two orders of magnitude greater than this intrinsic amount observed. For general soil removal from 'hard' surfaces (e.g. paint films that are relatively uniform and non-porous), it may never (or seldom) be necessary to raise the conductivity of an aqueous preparation beyond about 3000 µS.

The amount of buffer required in an aqueous solution might also be directly related to the intrinsic pH of a surface. If the pH of a degraded oil film is measured to be 6 on wetting with water, the hydrogen ion concentration is nominally 1×10^{-6}M. This represents the amount of acid that would be contributed to any aqueous solution applied to this surface. Again, whatever the specific capacity of a buffering material might be, a concentration of buffer two, three, or four orders of magnitude greater than this amount might suffice to maintain a pH at or close to the pK_a of the buffer. A 10 mM buffer solution (1×10^{-2}M) might provide more than enough buffering capacity for the amount of hydrogen ions anticipated on wetting this hypothetical surface. Many of the case histories cited in this book that feature buffers fall in the range of 10–50 mM amounts of these materials; added buffering material would add more material to clear from a cleaned surface, and also increase needlessly the ionic strength of a cleaning solution.

We can substitute materials of similar performance with those that are more rinsible, or are rinsible under a specific set of conditions from a given surface. Again, using the example of CMC: the CMC of Triton X-100 is 0.23 mM which is sufficiently low that it would probably be strongly adsorbed onto hydrophobic (e.g. oily) surfaces and also, given its relatively low solubility in water to begin with, it would be difficult to rinse with water as the sole rinse solvent or aid. At an HLB of 13.5, Triton X-100 is just strong enough to exhibit some detergency or solubilization effects. But any surfactant of an equivalent or close HLB could potentially act as a similar, albeit weak, solubilizing agent. Tween 21 (the polyethoxylate (4) of lauryl alcohol) has an HLB of 13.3, and could be used in place of Triton X-100. It also has a CMC of about 0.2 mM; the problem with many nonionics is that they generally exhibit rather low CMCs. Tween 21 would be just as likely to be absorbed onto an oily surface, and be just as difficult to remove by rinsing with water. Generally, surfactant structures that exhibit CMCs less than 2 mM are more solvent soluble than water soluble. It makes sense that, where the surface material will allow for it, rinsing these materials away in a solvent much less polar than water (in many cases aromatics, or even aliphatics with some aromatic content, are sufficient), is a better strategy for the efficient removal of these materials by dilution, than bringing copious amounts of water to try to remove them slowly from these surfaces. Stated another way: the HLB of Brij 700 (the polyethoxylate (100) of stearyl alcohol) is 18.8; that of triethanolamine (TEA) lauryl sulfate is 20.0. Both surfactants are about the same 'strength', i.e., have the same ability to solubilize oily materials. But their CMCs are very different: for Brij 100, it is about 0.2 mM, for TEA lauryl sulfate it is about 8 mM. The TEA lauryl sulfate might be more advantageous to use on an oily or hydrophobic surface if water is to be used as the rinsing material; the Brij 700 would be more strongly absorbed onto an oily surface, and be much harder to rinse with water alone, given its low (less than 2 mM) CMC. Conversely, while the Brij 700 might be more difficult to rinse with water, a much less polar solvent than water could be used to remove it. This might actually represent an advantage on a painted surface (e.g. an easel painting structure, with concomitant water-sensitive materials such as the ground; the fabric's support, etc.) which might be more easily damaged by repeated water rinses.

Lauryl sulfate, as the TEA salt in the example above, was noted to have an HLB of 20; sodium lauryl sulfate was said earlier (Chapter 5) to have an HLB of 40. The difference in HLB number is due to the counter-ion or particular salt form of the linear hydrocarbon sulfate. The sodium and potassium salts of anionic surfactants generally have higher solubility products – are more soluble – in water than other salts of these surfactants. For a slightly less water-soluble salt of lauryl sulfate (the TEA salt, for instance), the stronger the association with the sulfate group of the counter-ion, the less hydrophilic the sulfate group is, and, on balance, the lower the HLB. The CMC remains about the same (8 mM) for the sulfate ion in solution, but for the TEA salt, the HLB is reduced significantly, and, more importantly, the solubility (and rinsibility) in water would change: TEA lauryl sulfate would be, as a salt, more soluble in solvents less polar than water than the equivalent sodium or potassium salt of the same structure. In some cases, it might be that 'rinsing' this structure from a painted surface would be more efficient (and less potentially damaging to the treated surface) with a solvent rinse than with water alone.

Recall from Chapter 3 that many solution factors can affect the observed CMC of a surfactant: raising the concentration of salts can have the effect of depressing the CMC, while adding long chain alcohols, amines, or other water-miscible solvents to aqueous systems can raise the observed CMC. If the CMC is largely a measure for retention on oily or hydrophobic surfaces (which has been suggested here) – so that low CMC surfactants are retained more strongly, and are rinsed with more difficulty with water from oily surfaces – then any solution factor that affects the CMC in the applied aqueous solution, or subsequent rinse, will be of consequence here. Added salts will depress the CMC, and undoubtedly encourage a stronger retention of any surfactant on a hydrophobic or oily surface; accordingly it has to be advantageous to minimize ionic strength in some cleaning systems. Concomitantly, if solvents miscible with water tend to raise the observed CMC, these same mixtures may also encourage the clearance of strongly retained surfactants. In many of the case histories cited throughout the text, where low CMC surfactants were used, they were generally cleared in a two-step process: first the water-soluble materials were removed with a water rinse, and then, on drying, the more solvent soluble (e.g. low CMC surfactants) were removed with a solvent rinse.

This idea of a sparingly water-soluble material being rinsed more efficiently in a solvent less polar than water can also be extended to other aqueous materials. Triethanolamine as a buffer is certainly soluble in water, but it is also soluble in a range of solvents (e.g. alcohols, aromatics). It may be far more efficient to use TEA as a buffer (pK_a 7.9) in an aqueous system, and then rinse with a solvent, than to use an equivalent inorganic acid of similar pK_a (e.g. dihydrogen phosphate) which, in some cases, would be rinsible *only* in water.

Some of the longer aliphatic ethers of cellulose – propyl methyl cellulose, hydroxy propyl methyl cellulose, etc. – may have a slightly increased affinity for oily or hydrophobic surfaces over shorter aliphatic ethers such as methyl cellulose. The choice of a viscosity controlling agent or gelling material for some aqueous systems must be guided by clearance concerns as well; the more hydrophobic the surface, the more likely it is that methyl cellulose would be chosen for its decreased affinity for hydrophobic surfaces, and its increased likelihood of water rinsibility.

We can recognize that certain situations or arrangements of materials reasonably preclude the use of solutions or solutions containing certain materials. Fragile, porous, absorptive, underbound paints – i.e. paints or decorative materials that cannot be rinsed efficiently – probably preclude the use of solution methods which require rinsing. Logically, any materials in close proximity to surfaces to be cleaned, determine to some extent which methods can be brought to bear on a painted surface. Using an ammoniated solution on a painted surface next to a brass fitting or inlay, or a bronze powder painted element would be a poor application or choice of material for inclusion in an aqueous cleaning system.

8.5 Residual material remaining after cleaning

We can substitute materials of similar performance with those which might, if they are left as trace residues on a painted surface, degrade in a specific fashion. The deterioration chemistry of ethoxylated materials is very interesting. It has been observed in the author's laboratory that, on exposure, many nonionic structures degrade in a similar manner. The ethoxylate portion of these structures tends to hydrolyze very quickly on exposure, producing ethanol and glycol fragments (volatile), and degrading rapidly to the homologous fatty alcohol, or fatty acid as the starting material. In other words, Triton X-100 degraded to nonyl phenol, Brij 35 to lauryl alcohol, or lauric acid, etc. Concomitantly, certain surfactant structures seemed to remain very stable (e.g. lauryl sulfate) on exposure. Given the choice between, say, TEA lauryl sulfate (HLB 20.0) and Brij 700 (HLB 18.8), the Brij 700 is more attractive for usage because if a small amount were to remain on a surface, it would break down into stearyl alcohol, or stearic acid – a component of normal oil films on deterioration.

8.6 Substitution of less toxic materials for cleaning

We can certainly substitute less toxic materials for more toxic ones, where performance is similar. Triton X-100 degrades on exposure to nonyl phenol. Nonyl phenol, as an endocrine disrupter, has been linked to a variety of ecological problems, and may be associated with human diseases including breast cancer. It seems prudent to substitute this material with another surfactant of equal performance (i.e. HLB) in certain applications. Triton XL-80N is a linear ethoxylated hydrocarbon of the same HLB and in certain applications could be used to replace Triton X-100. Disposal of nonyl phenol derived nonionics (Synperonic N; Triton X-100) should be through proper disposal methods (i.e. incineration) for toxic solvents and solid waste. Synperonic N and NDB have been banned from domestic use in the UK (in fact the European Community) since 1998, and were banned from industrial use throughout the European Community from the beginning of 2000. This will affect their availability in European countries immediately. It remains legal (in 2000) in the European Community to use remaining stocks, and to dispose of small quantities to drains by dilution. Some alternative products have been suggested: Synperonic 9/16 (ICI) for painted surfaces and Synperonic A7 (ICI) for the cleaning of textiles are currently being investigated by the British conservation science community (Fields 2000). These materials are not likely to be banned from use in the near future, so their production is likely to be continued world-wide. The use and production of nonyl phenol derived products such as Triton X-100 might be regulated in the future in the European Community, and perhaps eventually in the USA.

8.7 Specific clearance conditions

We can remind ourselves that special materials adapted for special purposes may require specific clearance conditions. The solvent-surfactant gels cited in Chapter 4 are an example of this. By carefully adding or coupling a specific functional group to a polymer – the Ethomeens as surfactants to polyacrylic acid, for instance – we could use these surfactants in solvents of a wide solubility parameter range. As cationic materials they could form complex salts with the polyacidic material Carbopol, with the addition of a small measured amount of water. Their nonionic character, once coupled to the polymer, allows them to function as surfactants in solvent systems (with their relatively low aggregation numbers), and still be soluble in a wide range of solvents – it also allows them to be rinsed in an equally wide range of solvents. Gels made with Ethomeen C-12 could be rinsed with solvents as non-polar as mineral spirits (see Appendix 2); gels made with Ethomeen C-25 require relatively more polar solvents or solvent blends for rinsing. But, while Ethomeen C-12 might be used to make a gel of xylene, it could be rinsed with mineral spirits; it might be used to add surfactancy or to gel a specific solvent or solvent blend, but be rinsible in a less polar solvent. The same might be true of gels made with Ethomeen C-25, i.e. they might gel acetone as a solvent, for instance, but be rinsible in a much less polar solvent or solvent than pure acetone. Remember, neither gel type was rinsible in water because depending on pH, either the Ethomeens (as basic materials) or the polyacrylic acid itself (as a poly acidic material) are insoluble, and a residue would form on the 'rinsed' surface.

APPENDIX **1**

Examining and staining paint cross-sections

The research microscope has been used for some time as an examination tool for the type of materials present, and their arrangement, in small samples removed from paintings and painted artefacts. Both visible and ultraviolet illumination have been used. Most of the work cited in the case histories in this text involving cross-sections was done with a laboratory grade instrument, a Nikon Labophot microscope equipped for epi-illumination with two separate lamp housings, one for visible light with a 15W Osram lamp, and a second for ultraviolet work, an HBO 100W lamp, with a separate regulated power supply. Usually light from the Osram lamp was polarized for easier viewing of the sample in normal or white light. The ultraviolet light from the HBO lamp could be filtered one of two ways. Generally, a filter set with a 360 to 420 nm excitation filter, a dichroic mirror with a 425 nm cut-off wavelength, and a 430 to 700 nm emission filter was used to view the primary and secondary fluorescence from most samples. A number of natural and synthetic artists' materials as well as a good number of the synthetic fluorescent dyes discussed in the text can be excited by this filter set, with an excitation filter designed to permit a broad band of wavelengths in the near UV, violet, and blue regions of the light spectrum onto the sample. The Labophot, and most other similar microscopes, contain a second filter slot to tailor the illumination conditions to better accommodate viewing specific materials or dyes.

Many common natural binding materials either fluoresce or develop fluorescence with age. Materials not visible in normal light can sometimes be made more apparent with ultraviolet illumination. This phenomenon has been an aid to conservators during the routine examinations of artefacts. Certain molecular arrangements or species commonly give rise to fluorescence. For example, every glucosyl unit in a cellulose molecule has an oxygen atom in a closed six-membered ring with five carbon atoms. Many compounds that contain these sorts of closed heteroatomic cyclic rings in their structures will fluoresce. Cellulose is just one of a number of naturally occurring materials that fluoresce brightly when exposed to near ultraviolet light excitation. Proteins, gums, natural resins, and drying oils (if the last are oxidized enough) can fluoresce very intensely under broad band near UV excitation. Some metal oxides can also appear brightly fluorescent in near UV. A common mechanism in most compounds that fluoresce intensely is the possibility for electrons to be momentarily excited to a higher energy state by absorbing incident light energy of a specific wavelength (and associated energy); on returning to their original 'ground state' i.e. original energy level, they give up the absorbed light energy in the form of light (and a little heat), reradiating light at their characteristic emission wavelength.

In addition to looking for the presence of certain binding materials by their primary or autofluorescence characteristics, it is possible to apply to cross-sectioned samples, direct, reactive dyes or fluorochromes to help mark out or indicate specific materials with fluorescent dyes as a secondary or ancillary phenomenon. Several such reactive secondary fluorochromes have found their way into use in conservation, primarily as adaptations from analogous uses in the biological sciences. As with primary or autofluorescence, secondary fluorochromes have specific conditions under which they will be visible, i.e., specific excitation and emission wavelengths. As chemical moieties capable of reacting with certain compounds, or functional groups, they can be of use in further characterizing the presence of certain materials in a sample. As with any chemical reactions, these methods usually have to be carried out under a specific set of conditions for them to occur.

Presented here is a short summary list of fluorescent dyes or stains that were mentioned in some of the case histories, which are currently used to mark specific types of materials found in traditional binding media in easel paintings, through specific chemical reactions. The functional groups they react with, or the mechanism of staining is given under each dye heading, along with pertinent working characteristics, chemical structure, etc.

A1.1 Carbohydrates

Triphenyl tetrazolium chloride (TTC)

Other names: Tetrazole Red, Tetrazolium Red

Sigma Catalogue No.: T8877 (1990), (5 g/$US 5.85)

Concentration: 4% in the delivery solvent. Sigma sell a pre-diluted 'TLC' or thin layer chromatography spray reagent kit (T 9386) which contains a 4% solution of TTC in methanol (as well as a small amount of NaOH, which might not be needed), if the user wants to avoid handling or measuring small amounts of the stain.

Solubility: water (hazy), alcohols, acetone, and blends of solvents that are substantially polar in character, but which can include aromatics.

Other information: Formula weight (FW) 334.81. MP 250°C

C. Merck Index 11,9658. Light-sensitive.

Indicates: reducing sugars, plant gums, and other reducing compounds. The range of materials detected with this reagent can be explained as follows: TTC is an organic molecule with the following structure:

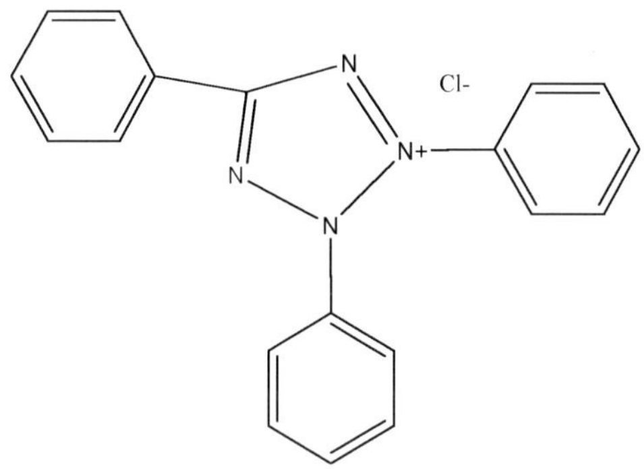

It is particularly susceptible to being reduced, i.e., the boldface nitrogen in the tetrazole ring accepts a donated hydrogen from another organic molecule. The tetrazole ring opens, and the resulting reduced form of TTC, triphenyl formazan (TF), a highly coloured material, is formed:

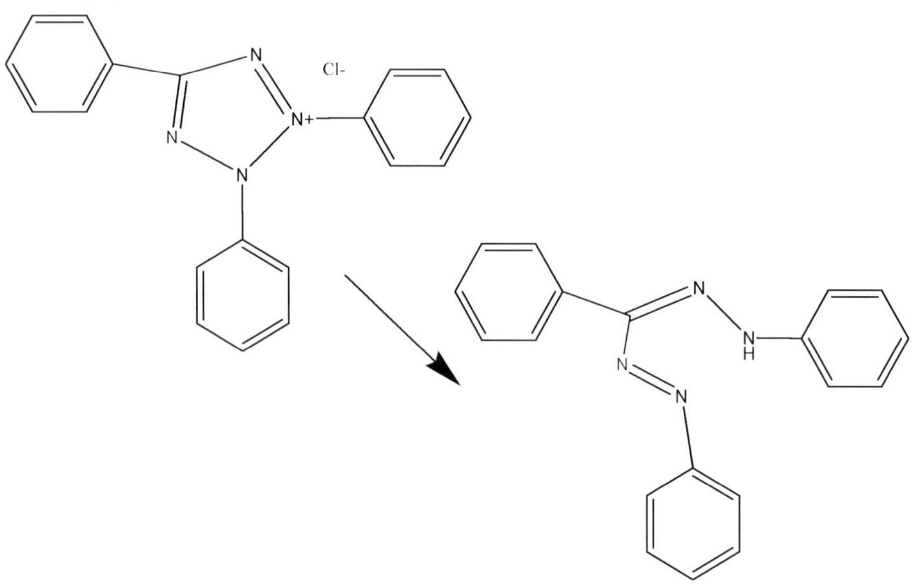

In normal light, TF appears to be a dark reddish compound; under near UV violet-blue illumination (360–430 nm), it appears a very dark reddish brown to black. The advantages of this type of stain are that it is quite sensitive to small amounts of reducing sugars, and can stain them a 'colour' quite distinct from the natural blue-white autofluorescence often encountered in carbohydrate-containing materials.

When TTC reacts, or is reduced, to TF, a reaction has taken place in the dye; the highly coloured formazan product is left to indicate the presence of a carbohydrate within a sample, but is not bound to the sample in any permanent fashion. If the application of the TTC (and more importantly, its delivery solvent) has not disturbed other materials in the sample, the TTC and TF material present can be washed off the sample, and other stains applied, without regrinding the sample.

Since at the heart of this staining procedure is a reduction type of reaction, water, at least in part, must be present for the reaction to take place. TTC is delivered to the sample to be characterized in a volatile solvent, but no reduction will take place until the solvent has evaporated away, and moisture is applied, or reaches, the TTC-charged surface of the sample. Typically, a drop (50 ml) of a 4% solution of TTC is delivered to a sample; the delivery solvent (methanol, for instance) is allowed to evaporate from the sample surface, and the TTC left in place on the sample surface. The sample is left purposely uncoverslipped to allow atmospheric moisture to be taken up on the dye-laden sample surface; after a few moments, the sample is examined at the microscope for any reaction that may have occurred. If the sample were coverslipped immediately with mineral spirits, or another similar hydrophobic medium, water would be precluded from the sample surface, and no reduction of the dye would occur. Conversely, if the sample were coverslipped with an aqueous preparation, a reaction might occur, but, solubilization and disruption of the sample might occur as well, as the sample dissolved in the mounting medium.

A variety of carbohydrate-bearing materials can effect the reduction of TTC to TF, as well as certain other reducing compounds. Generally speaking, we are taking advantage of the reducing potential of sugars as hemi-aldehydes to accomplish this:

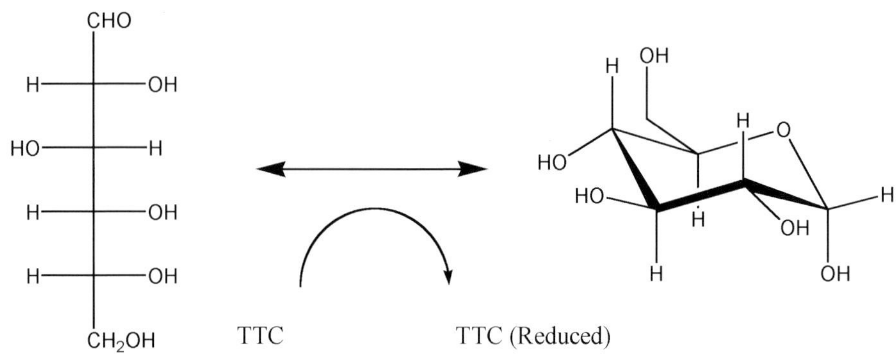

The proton made available through the ring closure of the aldehyde end of a hexose or a pentose can be used to reduce other organic molecules (including TTC). Individual hexoses or pentoses can act in this fashion, as can the 'end' groups on larger carbohydrate molecules. In nature, a wide range of carbohydrate-bearing materials exist. The chief structural component of most plants is of course cellulose, a polymeric form of glucose. Starches abound in nature, and have been used as adhesives in art; certain complex mixtures of carbohydrates (gums) comprise the binders of some water-based paints. In nature, it is also possible to find complex combinations of carbohydrates and other natural products; proteo-glycans, or protein-bound carbohydrates can be found in milk, eggs, saliva, blood etc. Lipoglycosides or complexes of steroids and carbohydrates ('saponins', for instance) also occur in nature.

Thickened paints and varnishes can have carbohydrates as ingredients. Carbohydrates have been used to thicken or change the viscosity of water-based or emulsion types of preparations at least since the Second World War.

It should be noted that any compound or material with a strong enough reduction potential in a sample could conceivably react with TTC and produce a 'false positive' test for carbohydrate. Borohydrides, and other similar reducing reagents used as chemical bleaches in conservation processes might conceivably give a 'false positive' test for carbohydrate in a sample.

TTC is only one of many compounds that contain a tetrazolic structure; it should be possible to find other similar compounds that have slightly different oxidation-reduction potentials, which might be sensitive only to certain types of carbohydrate. Further, depending on the type of groups substituted onto the tetrazole, differing colour reactions might be possible where the colour or appearance of the sample complicates an unequivocable reading of the staining pattern (Tetranitro Blue Tetrazolium (TNBT), Tetrazolium Blue, Thiocarbamyl Nitro Blue Tetrazolium, etc.).

Samples that may contain carbohydrate moieties should, as noted above, not only be mounted in resins that are not likely to extract water-soluble materials, but they should be ground and polished without water as well.

Storage: Screwcap vial; protect from light. The shelf life of the solution has been observed to be 1 to 2 years under these conditions in the author's laboratory.

A1.2 Proteins

Tetramethyl rhodamine isothiocyanate (TRITC)

Other names: Texas Red isothiocyanate (which is a misnomer; "Texas Red" usually refers to a Sulfo-Rhodamine derived material)

Sigma Catalogue No.: T5646 (mixed isomers) (5 mg/$US 26.70)

Concentration: 0.2% in delivery solvent. The delivery solvent must not contain any alcoholic or free amino groups, and must be water free.

Solubility: generally, a wide range of polar solvents including water, acetone, and alcohols. However, the reactivity of the isothiocyanate functionality precludes the use of certain solvents as noted above. A 0.2% solution of TRITC in dry acetone is very nearly a saturated solution in that solvent.

Other information: FW 443.53 Extremely moisture sensitive (see McKinney *et al.* 1966)

Indicates: protein-containing samples. TRITC is a bright red colour in normal light, and an increasingly bright reddish fluorescent colour when viewed under near UV, blue, or green light respectively. The mechanism of this reaction centres on a single reactive isothiocyanate group present on a highly coloured or fluorescent dye molecule (see eosin isothiocyanate, EITC, or fluorescein isothiocyanate, FITC, for similar reactions). The isothiocyanate group can react, in the absence of water, with any free amino group, and to a lesser extent, alcoholic groups available on other organic molecules to form a covalent or permanent bond with the sample:

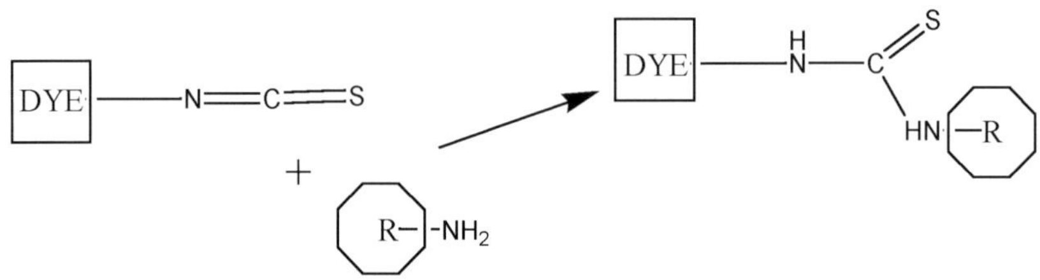

TRITC can thus react quite rapidly to form a permanent adduct to proteinaceous materials through this mechanism. Solvent selection can be critical with this stain however; water by itself or in trace quantities in other solvents can also react with TRITC, competing with the sample for reaction with the stain. Sample preparation (grinding, polishing) should either be done in the absence of water, or if water is employed, the sample should be allowed to dry thoroughly before the stain is applied. It should also be noted that the delivery solvent should be substantially free of water as well. Alcohols, acetone, and other water-miscible solvents should either be obtained in dried form ('spectral' grades are likely to contain a minimum of water), or dried prior to mixing with TRITC by passing the solvent over anhydrous sodium sulfite, or some other similar desiccant. Molecular sieves or zeolites capable of selectively absorbing water from these solvents could also be used for this purpose. If the isothiocyanate group is allowed to contact water, the usefulness of this particular stain is destroyed – its ability to mark protein-containing materials will be lost.

Typically, a 50 µl volume of a 0.2% solution of TRITC in acetone is applied to a sample; the reaction with the sample is immediate. The sample is then rinsed quickly with a little free acetone to 'sweep' any excess and unreacted TRITC from the sample surface, and then it is coverslipped with mineral spirits and examined at the microscope. The TRITC-tagged material in the sample should remain behind through all of this; unless the sample is ground and polished further, or subjected to a solvent that would extract the labelled material (water, for instance) the tagged material will last, even through subsequent staining procedures.

It was noted above that 'free' amino groups would react with TRITC. Amino groups are certainly found on proteins through some of the basic amino acid side chains (lysine, asparagine, and glutamine, for instance) present in these materials. But they can be present not as free bases, but rather in salt forms or paired with oppositely charged ions. Such salts of these basic amino acids (chlorides, etc) will not react with TRITC, and consequently will not be tagged and visualized by this staining technique. Pre-treating the sample with a basic solution, or gently warming the sample may help in recovering or making available more free amino groups to the stain.

Materials that are highly substituted with hydroxyl or alcoholic functional groups will also react with TRITC. While the rate of this competing reaction is not as fast as with available free amino groups, nonetheless it can occur. At sufficiently high concentrations, polyhydric materials will also appear to stain with TRITC (shellacs, gums, etc.). To resolve such discrepancies, further staining or other analytical techniques may be needed to characterize a material more fully. It is also possible that some synthetic materials that contain free amino groups will react with TRITC, for example, materials as seemingly divergent as cationic detergents (in cleaning formulations, and emulsion preparations), and 'aminoplast' or urethane types of synthetic resins.

Storage: protect from both moisture and light. A typical storage method is to aliquot the sample (divide it into small, more manageable portions) into 1 ml 'stock' solutions in brown glass vials, under nitrogen. The vials can even be the injection type with teflon septum tops that allow the user to remove some of the staining solution into a syringe without constantly opening and closing the stock vial.

Fluorescein 5 isothicyanate (FITC)

Other names: None

Sigma Catalogue No.: F7250 Isomer I (50 mg/$US 10.60)

Concentration: 0.1% in delivery solvent. As with TRITC noted above, the delivery solvent must not contain any alcoholic or free amino groups, and must be water free.

Solubility: generally, a wide range of polar solvents including water, acetone, and alcohols will dissolve FITC; but the reactivity of the isothiocyanate functionality precludes the use of solvents that contain a reactive functional group (amines, alcohols), or solvents with appreciable amounts of water in them. A 0.1% solution of FITC in dried acetone is very nearly a saturated solution in that solvent, and a typical delivery solvent.

Other information: FW 389.4 Extremely moisture sensitive (see Riggs *et al.* (1958)

Indicates: protein-containing samples. FITC is a bright yellowish colour in normal light, and a bright yellowish-green fluorescence colour when viewed under near UV, blue, or green light respectively. As with TRITC described above, the mechanism of this reaction centres on a single reactive isothiocyanate group present on a highly coloured or fluorescent dye molecule. The isothiocyanate group can react, in the absence of water, with any free amino group, and to a lesser extent, alcoholic groups available on other organic molecules to form a covalent or permanent bond with the sample. See TRITC notes above for solvent selection and preparation. Typically, a 50 μl volume of a 0.1% solution of FITC in dry acetone is applied to a sample; the reaction with the sample is immediate. The sample is then rinsed quickly with a little free acetone to 'sweep' any excess and unreacted FlTC from the sample surface, and then it is coverslipped with mineral spirits and examined at the microscope. The FlTC tagged material in the sample should remain behind through all of this;

unless the sample is ground and polished further, or subjected to a solvent that would extract the labelled material (water, for instance), the tagged material will last, even through subsequent staining procedures.

The same limitations for cross reactivity apply to FITC, as noted above for TRITC: specifically, that materials that contain free amino groups (other than proteins), or substantial amounts of free hydroxyl groups, will react with FITC.

Storage: protect from both moisture and light. A typical storage method is to aliquot the sample (divide it into small, more manageable portions) into 1 ml 'stock' solutions in brown glass vials, under nitrogen. The vials can even be the injection type with teflon septa tops that can allow the user to remove some of the staining solution into a syringe without constantly opening and closing the stock vial.

Eosin 5– isothiocyanate (EITC)

Other names: None

Sigma Catalogue No.: E200S (10 mg/$US 19.30)

Concentration: 0.1% in delivery solvent. As with TRITC noted above, the delivery solvent must not contain any alcoholic or free amino groups, and must be water free.

Solubility: generally, a wide range of polar solvents including water, acetone, and alcohols will dissolve EITC; but the reactivity of the isothiocyanate functionality precludes the use of certain delivery solvents that contain reactive functional groups (alcohols, amines), as well as solvents containing appreciable amounts of water. A 0.1% solution of EITC in dry acetone is very nearly a saturated solution in that solvent, and acetone is often used as the delivery solvent.

Other information: FW 705.0 Extremely moisture sensitive (see Cherry 1976)

Indicates: protein-containing samples. EITC is a bright red colour in normal light, and an increasingly bright reddish fluorescent colour when viewed under near UV, blue or green light respectively. As with TRITC described above, the mechanism of this reaction centres on a single reactive isothiocyanate group present on a highly coloured or fluorescent dye molecule The isothiocyanate group can react, in the absence of water, with any free amino group, and to a lesser extent, alcoholic groups available on other organic molecules to form a covalent or permanent bond with the sample. See TRITC notes above for solvent selection and preparation. Typically, a 50 μl volume of a 0.1% solution of ElTC in acetone is applied to a sample; the reaction with the sample is immediate. The sample is then rinsed quickly with a little free acetone to 'sweep' any excess and unreacted EITC from the sample surface, and then it is coverslipped with mineral spirits and examined at the microscope. The ElTC tagged material in the sample should remain behind through all of this; unless the sample is ground and polished further, or subjected to a solvent that would extract the labelled material (water, for instance), the tagged material will last, even through subsequent staining procedures.

The same limitations for cross reactivity apply to EITC, as noted above for TRITC: specifically, that materials that contain free amino groups (other than proteins), or substantial amounts of free hydroxyl groups, will react with EITC.

Storage: protect from both moisture and light. A typical storage method is to aliquot the sample (divide it into small, more manageable portions) into 1 ml 'stock' solutions in brown glass vials, under nitrogen. The vials can even be the injection type with teflon septa tops that can allow the user to remove some of the staining solution into a syringe without constantly opening and closing the stock vial.

Fluorescamine (FLUR)

Other names: Fluram

Sigma Catalogue No.: F9878 (1990) (25 mg/$US 6.85)

Concentration: 0.05% in acetone. A stock solution at this concentration is sold by Sigma (D 6756) as a preprepared material.

Solubility: same conditions and restrictions as noted for TRITC

Other information: Weigele, *et al.* (1972)

Indicates: reacts with free amino groups exclusively to form a fluorescent compound. Fluorescamine will react with amino acids, peptides, and proteins. The reaction that takes place is:

Fluorescamine forms a water-clear solution with acetone; as an unreacted material, it is not fluorescent. Upon addition to an amino group, the new compound has a bright blue-white fluorescence under blue light illumination. While fluorescamine is more specific than isothiocyanates or acid halides in terms of tagging only

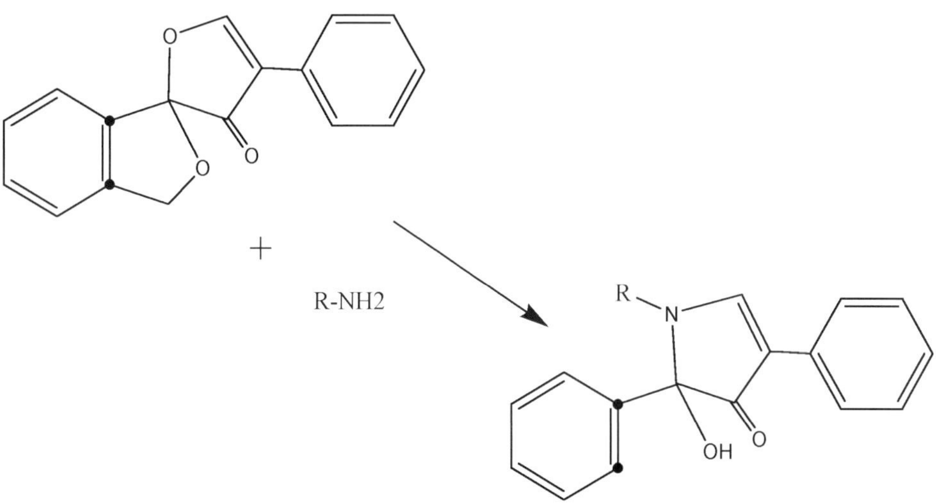

proteinaceous materials, its chief drawback is the colour of the fluorescent compound produced. The blue-white fluorescence produced is hard to distinguish from the autofluorescence intrinsic to most proteins, which is also a blue-white colour in appearance.

The typical procedure for application of fluorescamine to a protein-bearing sample would be to grind and polish the sample in mineral spirits on increasingly finer grits of bonded abrasive cloths or papers, or dry on cushioned abrasive paper (to avoid washing away any water-soluble protein). Then approximately 50 μl of a 0.05% solution of fluorescamine in acetone would be delivered to the sample. Once the acetone is entirely evaporated away, the sample can be coverslipped in the usual fashion with mineral spirits, and examined at the microscope.

Storage: avoid light and moisture. Aliquot the dye into smaller portions or solutions if possible.

Lissamine rhodamine sulfonyl chloride (LISSA)

Other names: Sulforhodamine B sulfonyl chloride

Sigma Catalogue No.: Sigma does not produce Lissamine. It is produced exclusively by Kodak under licence from ICI. The Kodak cat. no. is 1361401 (1987–88) (1 g/\$US 58.00)

Concentration: 0.2% in the delivery solvent. A typical solvent for usage would be acetone. Alcohols and amines would react with this dye and would not be suitable for this purpose.

Solubility: same as noted for TRITC, including exceptions

Other information: MW 577.11

Indicates: proteins. That is, Lissamine will react essentially with the same functionalities noted for TRITC above, but with a slightly different mechanism:

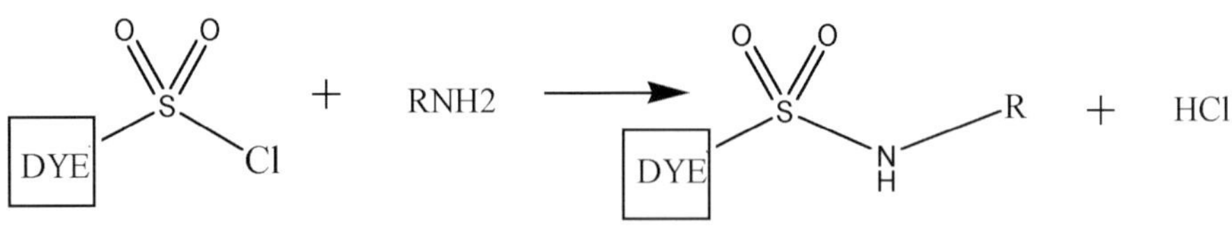

As an acid halide, it can react with free amino bearing materials, more slowly to alcohols, and to a very much more limited degree, compounds containing carboxyls. Both the delivery solvent and sample must be as dry as possible; as with the sensitivity of isothiocyanates to water noted for TRITC above, acid halides are rapidly broken down in the presence of water. Typically, 50 μl of a 0.2% solution in acetone is applied to the test material; the acetone is allowed to go to dryness, the sample is briefly rinsed in acetone, coverslipped with mineral spirits, and examined at the microscope. The slightly wider range of reactivity of this particular fluorochrome derivative makes it a little less useful for fully characterizing a protein-containing sample; however, its bright (red-orange) fluorescence under UV-blue-green illumination conditions makes it particularly easily seen over most autofluorescing materials. Pre-treatment of the sample with alkaline preparations or heat can increase the likelihood of any primary amino groups present in a sample being available (not in a salt form) to react with the applied stain.

Storage conditions: identical to those of TRITC

A1.3 Lipids, oils and fats

Rhodamine B (RHOB)

Other names: Tetraethyl Rhodamine, Brilliant Pink B, Rhodamine O, Basic Violet 10

Sigma Catalogue No.: R4252, as a preprepared TLC spray reagent. R6626 as the dry powder (25 g/$US 7.15). The premixed TLC spray reagent comes as a 0.2% solution in ethanol.

Concentration: generally Rhodamine B is used in the range of 0.02–0.2%

Solubility: Rhodamine B is soluble in a fairly wide range of polar solvents, as well as blends of non-polar solvents mixed with polar components. A typical preparation of Rhodamine would be in a fast-evaporating solvent such as ethanol; it could be 'diluted' with increasing amounts of xylene to adjust the solubility parameter of the delivery solvent blend to the solubility range of the substrate at hand. Since, in many cases, we should like to be able to stain for oils that may have been included in resin or clear coatings, the choice of delivery solvent is critical; most resin coatings are at least in part soluble in solvents as polar as ethanol.

Other information: FW 479.02, Mutagen! Handle with care

Indicates: drying oils. As with most lipid stains Rhodamine B literally 'dissolves' into a lipid-containing material and stains it a bright red in normal light. The following reaction takes place (see overleaf).

In a polar environment, Rhodamine B can exist as an ionic species or salt; bright red in normal light, but not fluorescent when illuminated by UV blue-green light. In the relatively non-polar environment of a lipid, however, its structure changes slightly to produce a molecule capable of fluorescing under the right excitation conditions. If viewed in green light in particular, Rhodamine B fluoresces a bright orange-red colour; everywhere it is non-specifically deposited it appears dark under these illumination conditions. For most purposes, there will be enough 'excitation' of Rhodamine B in the blue portion of the visible light spectrum to produce this fluorescence; viewing a sample under UV or blue light increases our ability to see more clearly autofluorescing materials in a sample, and locate oil-stained materials contextually within the sample.

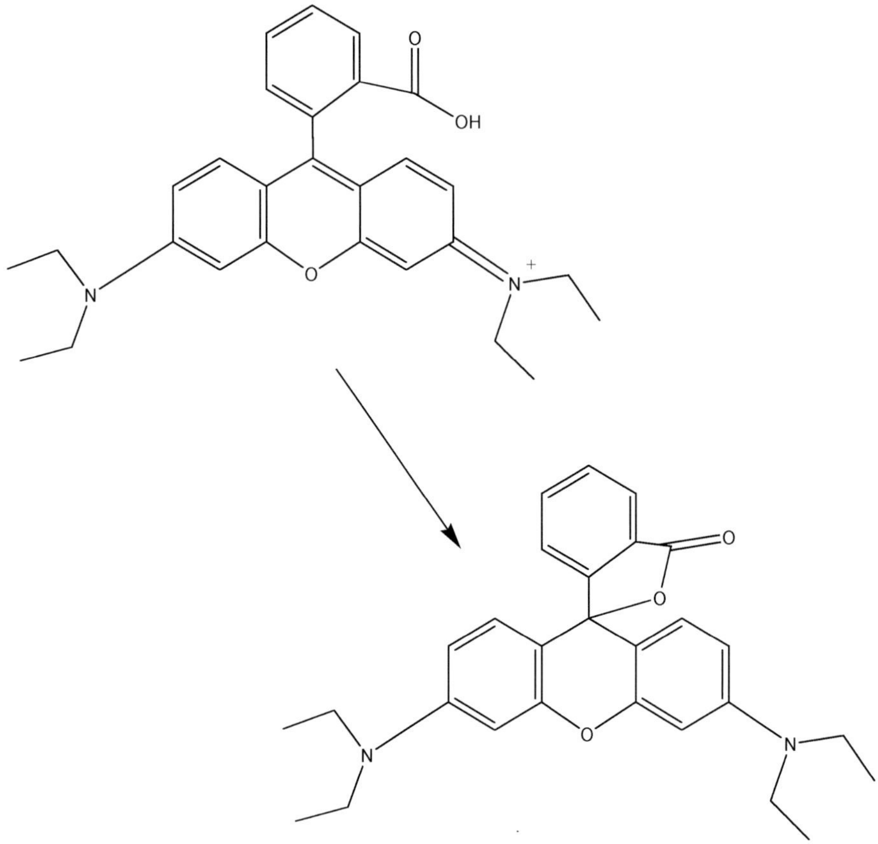

As mentioned above, while Rhodamine B is soluble in a wide range of solvents, care must be taken to deliver the dye to a substrate without dissolving or disrupting it (to do so would be to destroy the contextual information available to us). We might start with a relatively high concentration of Rhodamine B in a fast evaporating solvent (i.e., the TLC spray reagent, up to tenfold, and at the same time make the delivery solvent less polar by blending e.g. xylene, with it). The purpose of a carrier or delivery solvent is simply to solubilize the dye, get it to a lipid-containing substrate, and evaporate from the substrate surface, leaving the dye to dissolve into (and mark) the lipids (or triglyceride structures, i.e., drying, and non-drying oils). Solubilizing the substrate, or leaving solvent behind in it even momentarily might confuse the results of our staining.

In terms of specificity, Rhodamine B should 'dissolve' in lipid-containing materials. The triglycerides present in drying oils such as linseed oil, or in non-drying oil foodstuffs, such as cooking oils, would pick up Rhodamine B. It is also conceivable that certain oil-modified materials (alkyds, urethanes, etc.) might also pick up Rhodamine B if these polymers were densely substituted with fatty acid functional groups. Soaps, and certainly detergents may be present in sufficiently concentrated amounts in some samples to pick up Rhodamine B (e.g. latex or emulsion paints).

One other aspect of specificity might be the relative age of an oil-containing substrate. Initially, drying oils are quite unsaturated in character; it is this unsaturation that allows them to cross-link and eventually form a polymeric network. But in time, the character of drying oils changes further; oxidation reactions undoubtedly occur in this material, as they do in most weathering organic materials. Hydrolytic reactions can occur to break down the polymer. Kept in the dark, or precluded from the normal amounts of oxygen, light, and moisture, drying oils can even increase in their relative unsaturation again. Rhodamine B 'dissolves' in triglyceride structures. There comes a point when most of this material is consumed in a polymerized paint film; as other organic structures tend to develop within these films, staining with Rhodamine B becomes increasingly difficult. We need to 'stain' for other types of structures likely to be present at this point. Consider the structure of **Rhodamine 123**:

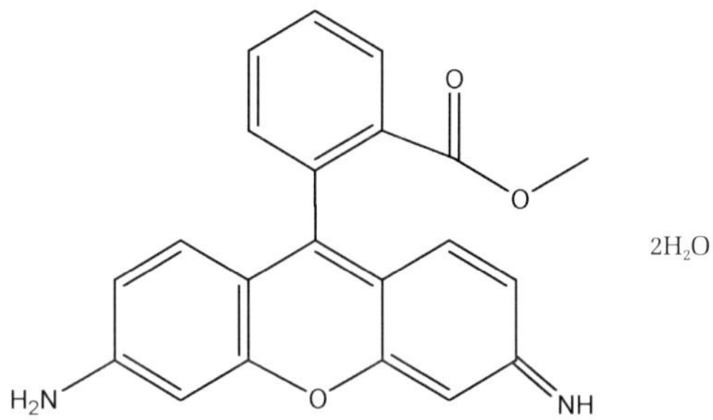

In Rhodamine 123, the ethylenic groups (on the boldface nitrogens) present in Rhodamine B have been completely reduced, thereby making Rhodamine 123 a relatively more polar molecule at this end than Rhodamine B. Rhodamine 123 can 'dissolve' in slightly more polar lipids than Rhodamine B (i.e. more weathered, or oxidized). **Rhodamine 6G** is structurally more polar than Rhodamine B, and could be used in a similar manner. 2,7- dichlorofluorescein can stain both saturated and unsaturated lipids, and may be of some use in either marking very 'young' oil films (that still contain a good deal of unsaturation), or 'older' oil layers that have reincurred some degree of unsaturation on ageing.

2,7 -dichlorofluorescein (DCF)

Other names: None

Sigma Catalogue No.: D 6132 (5 g/$US 13.00), as a dry powder. Sigma also sell DCF as a premixed TLC spray reagent, D 5013, as a 0.2% solution in ethanol.

Concentration: same concentration range and related remarks for Rhodamine B

Solubility: same remarks for solubility as for Rhodamine B

Other information: FW 401.2

Indicates: saturated and unsaturated lipids (drying, non-drying oils in particular). The structure of DCF is shown overleaf.

While there is no change in the DCF molecule when it 'dissolves' in a lipid-containing material as with Rhodamine B, the lipid environment surrounding the

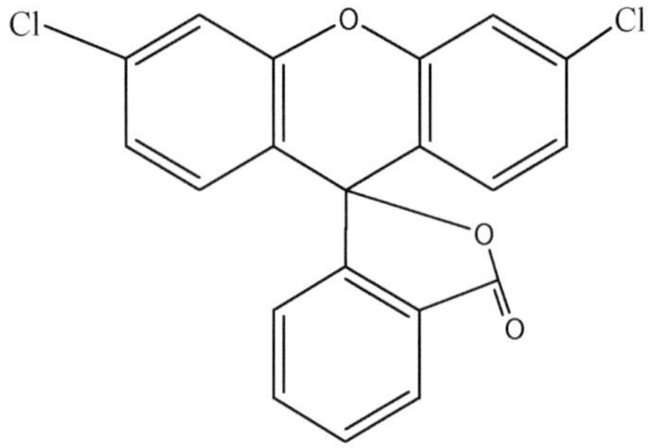

DCF molecule can affect its fluorescence colour, ranging from pink (in relatively saturated lipids), to a bright yellow (in unsaturated lipids). DCF is also quite sensitive to changes in pH; in an aqueous (water-based) delivery system, or on a 'wet' sample DCF can change from a yellow to a colourless material in the pH range of 3–5. Again, as with Rhodamine B, the choice of delivery solvent is critical; we want a solvent, or blend of solvents, which are polar enough to dissolve the dye but not so strong as to disrupt or dissolve our sample in the process. The 'ideal' delivery solvent is the one that can minimally affect the substrate, deliver the dye to the substrate surface, and then volatilize away. In the case of DCF, a relatively 'dry' solvent (i.e. water free) would be preferable to avoid the confusion that might ensue from water being present in or on a sample. As a lipid stain, delivered from a solvent, DCF in this instance can and is used as a marker for oil-containing materials.

A1.4 Resins

Antimony pentachloride (APC)

Other names: None

Sigma Catalogue No.: is only available from Sigma as a premixed TLC spray reagent, A 6653, at a concentration of 20% in chloroform

Concentration: the premixed TLC spray reagent at 20% is far more concentrated than needed; approximately 4–5% antimony pentachloride in a convenient carrier solvent would be better

Solubility: antimony pentachloride is soluble in a range of polar solvents or solvent blends; as a preprepared solution in chloroform, diluting the APC with a volatile aromatic solvent such as xylene might be preferable to applying the APC in neat chloroform, since many resinous materials and paint films can be disrupted (swollen), or dissolved in chloroform. APC cannot be diluted in 'wet' (water-containing) solvents, or alcohols.

Other information: antimony pentachloride is an extremely toxic material which should be handled and stored only in a fume hood. Gloves and other protective gear should be worn when handling or diluting this material. FW 299.02. Merck index 11,727. Moisture sensitive.

Indicates: triterpenes such as dammar and mastic; rosin and rosin esters; vitamins A, D, E, bile acids, essential oils, and steroid sapogenins. The reaction that takes place, in the absence of water or alcohols, is:

$$ROH + 2SbCl_5 \rightarrow R + SbCl_6 + SbCl_3 + Cl^- + OH^-$$

Triterpenoids like dammar contain a sizeable fraction of methyl steroid material that is substituted with one or more alcoholic groups; these sterols can react with antimony pentachloride to form a bright blue-white fluorescent adduct that signals their presence. While this 'reaction' can be difficult to see over the normal autofluorescence that develops, in time, within a natural resin-containing material, it is made easier by the fact that other materials will turn black in the presence of this stain (as the APC is reduced to metallic antimony non-specifically on the rest of the sample).

Competitive reactions can occur on the other materials listed from the outset; bile acids are 'sterols' as well, and can react with APC.

These might be found in blood, or other biological fluids. Sapogenins are plant sterol-glycosides (Fig. ii). The vitamins A, D, and E are, of course, found in a number of plant sources (Fig. iii). These other materials are simply listed here to show the range (albeit limited) of other closely related organic materials that might be present in an artefact and also react with APC.

(i)

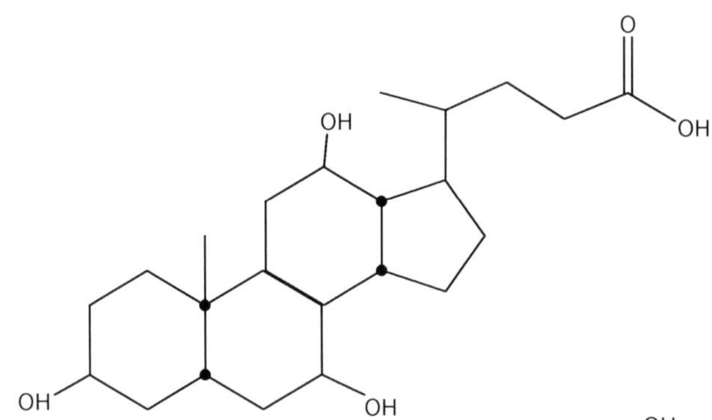

(ii)

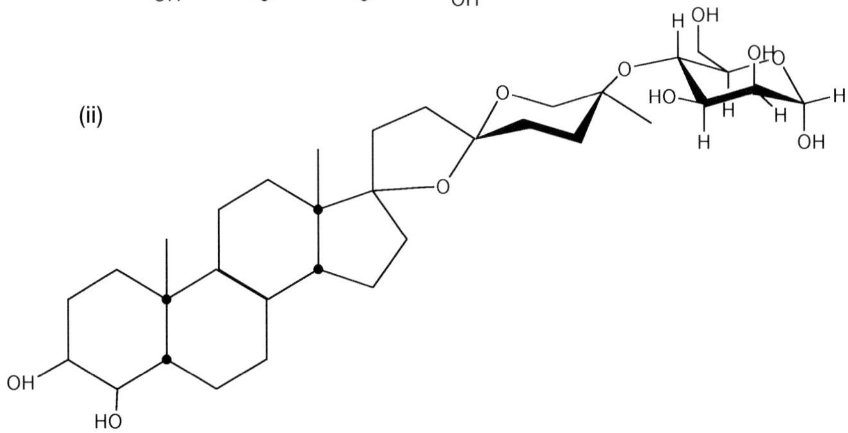

(iii)

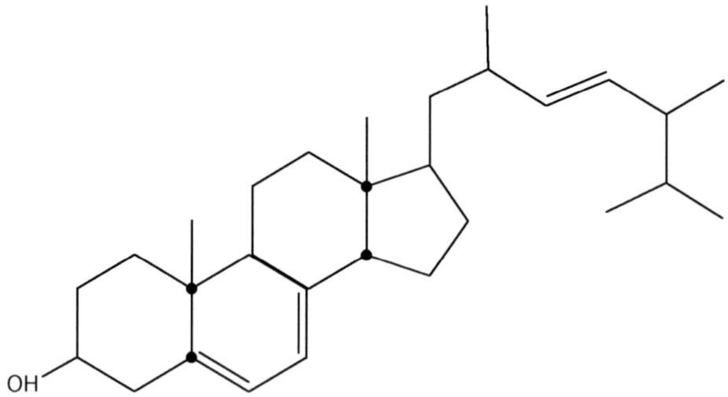

Table A.1 Common fluorochrome dyes, and their peak excitation and emission wavelengths.

Fluorochrome/Fluorophore	Mean excitation wavelength	Mean emission wavelength (fluorescence)	Exciting radiation
Diamino-phenyl oxydiazoles (DAO)	280 nm	460 nm	Ultraviolet
1-dimethyl amino naphthalene-5-sulphonic	340 nm	525 nm	
5-hydroxy tryptamine	400 nm	530 nm	
Stilben (SITS = stilben isothiosulphonic acid)	365 nm	460 nm	
Fluorescamine (FLUR)	**390 nm**	**460 nm**	
Aurophosphine G	450 nm	580 nm	Violet/blue violet
Berberine sulphate	430 nm	550 nm	
Catecholamine	410 nm	470 nm	
Eucrysin	430 nm	540 nm	
Eucrysin	430 nm	540 nm	
Primuline O	410 nm	550 nm	
Pyronine	410 nm	540 nm	
Quinacrine mustard (QM)	440 nm	510 nm	
Tetracycline	390 nm	560 nm	
Thioflavine S	430 nm	550 nm	
Antimony pentachloride	**430 nm**	**550 nm**	
Acridine yellow	470 nm	550 nm	Blue
Acridine orange	470 nm	530–650 nm	
Auramine	460 nm	550 nm	
Coryphosphine O	460 nm	575 nm	
Fluoroscein isothiocyanate (FITC)	**495 nm**	**525 nm**	
Phospine 3R	465 nm	565 nm	
Rhodamine 69	480 nm	550 nm	
Lissamine-rhodamine B200 (RD200)	**575 nm**	**565 nm**	Green
Magdala red	540 nm	570 nm	
Pararosaniline (Feulgen)	570 nm	625 nm	
Rhodamine B	**540 nm**	**625 nm**	
Acid Fuchsine	540 nm	630 nm	
Thiazine red R	510 nm	580 nm	
Tetramethyl rhodamine-isothiocyanate (TRITC)	**540 nm**	**570 nm**	
Lissamine rhodamine sulfonyl chloride (LISSA)	**570 nm**	**590 nm**	
Eosin 5-isothiocyanate (EITC)	**524 nm**	**548 nm**	
Rho123	500 nm	540 nm	

It should be noted that the boldfaced dyes represent those mentioned in the preceding section. These dyes are used as stains for common binding materials in paints or varnishes. More information on the examination of cross-sections in conservation, and the use of stains can be found in Becker (1989), Derrick *et al.* (1994), Gay (1978), Geusau and Schreiner (1992), Johnson and Packard (1971), Martin (1977), McKinney *et al.* (1966), Messinger (1992), Plesters (1955/56), Ploem and Tanke (1987), de la Rie (1982), Rinuy and Gros (1989), Rost (1992), Schramm and Hering (1988), Siegel (1993), Tsang and Cunningham (1991), Weigele *et al.* (1972), Wolbers and Landrey (1987), Wolbers (1989).

APPENDIX 2

Suppliers of materials

Sigma Chemicals

USA: Aldrich Chemical Co.
PO Box 14508
St Louis MO
Tel: 1 800 325 3010
www.sigma-aldrich.com

UK: Sigma-Aldrich Co. Ltd.
Fancy Road
Poole
Dorset BH12 4QH
Tel: 0800 717181

Aldrich Chemical Co.
The Old Brickyard
New Road
Gillingham
Dorset SP8 4XT

Ethomeen and Carbopol products

Conservation Support Systems
924 West Pedregosa Street
Santa Barbara
CA 93101
Tel: 1 805 682 9843

Micromesh polishing materials

USA: Micro-Surface Finishing Products Inc.
1217 West Third Street
Box 8181
Wilton
IA 52778
Tel: 1 319 732 3240

UK: PW Products Ltd.
64–66 Barnet High Street
Barnet
Herts EN5 5SJ
Tel: (+44) (0)181 441 4151
www.pwproducts@compuserve.com

Shellsol T (mineral spirits)

Major chemical suppliers in the UK/USA

USA: EM Industries
5 Skyline Drive
Hawthorne
NY 105332
USA
Tel: 1 914 5924 660
www.merck-ltd.co

UK: Merck Ltd.
Hunter Boulevard
Magna Park
Lutterworth
Leicester LE17 4XN
UK
Tel: 0800 223344

References

Academic Press 1978. *Enzyme Nomenclature*, International Union of Biochemistry: Nomenclature Committee (London: Academic Press).

Adam, N. K. 1937. 'Detergent Action, Wetting, and Emulsification', *Journal of the Society of Dyers and Colour Chemists* **53**, 121.

Becker, E. 1989. *Fluorescence Microscopy* (Germany: Wild Leitz GmbH).

Borgström, B. and Brockerman, H. (eds) 1984. *Lipases* (New York: Elsevier).

Bourne, M. C. and Jennings, W. G. 1963. 'Existence of Two Soil Species in Detergency Investigations', *Journal – American Oil Chemists' Society* **40**, 17.

Brockerhoff, H. and Jensen, R. 1974. *Lipolytic Enzymes* (New York: Academic Press).

Burnstock, A. and Kieslich, T. 1996. 'A Study of the Clearance of Solvent Gels Used for Varnish Removal from Paintings', in *11th Triennial Meeting, ICOM Committee for Conservation*, preprints, J. Bridgland (ed.) (London: James and James).

Burnstock, A. and White, R. 1990. 'The Effects of Selected Solvents and Soaps on a Simulated Canvas Painting', in *Cleaning, Retouching and Coatings*, J. S. Mills and P. Smith (eds) (London: IIC).

Burnstock, A. and White, R. 1993. 'Cleaning Gels: Further Studies', *Conservation Science in the UK* (London).

Burnstock, A. and White, R. 2000. 'A preliminary assessment of the aging/degradation of Ethomeen C-12 residues from solvent gel formulations and their potential for inducing changes in resinous paint media', in *Tradition and Innovation: Advances in Conservation*, A. Roy and P. Smith (eds) (London: IIC).

Cherry, R. J. 1976. 'A Spectroscopic Technique for Measuring Slow Rotational Diffusion of Macromolecules', *Biochemistry*, **15**, 3653.

Cox, M. F. and Matson, T. P. 1984. 'Cost Effectiveness Comparisons of Popular Actives in Detergent Powders', *Journal – American Oil Chemists' Society* **61**, 1270.

Cutler, W. G. and Kissa, E. (eds) 1987. *Evaluation of Detergency* (New York: M. Dekker).

Davies, J. T. 1957. *Proceedings of the International Congress on Surface Activity*, 2nd edn (London: Butterworths).

Dean, J. (ed.) 1985. *Lange's Handbook of Chemistry*, 13th edn (New York: McGraw-Hill Co.).

de la Rie, E. R. 1982. 'Fluorescence of Paint and Varnish Layers, Part I–III', *Studies in Conservation* **27**, 1–7, 65–9, 102–8.

Derrick, M., *et al.* 1994. 'Embedding Paint Cross Sections in Polyester', *Journal of the American Institute of Conservation* **33**, 227–45.

Diagnostic Kits and Reagents No. 800, General Cat., 1990, p. 1965 (Sigma Chemical Co., P.O.Box 14508, St. Louis, MO).

Erhardt, D. and Bischoff, J. 1993. 'Resin Soaps and Solvents in Cleaning of Paintings: Similarities and Differences', in *10th Triennial Meeting, ICOM Committee for Conservation*, preprints, J. Bridgland (ed.) (London: James and James).

Fava, A. and Eyring, H. 1956. 'Equilibrium and Kinetics of Detergent Absorption', *Journal of Physical Chemistry* **60**, 890.

Feiser, L. and Feiser, M. 1959. *Steroids* (New York: Reinhold).

Fields, J. 2000. 'Replacing Synperonic N', *Conservation News* **72**, 3.

Ford, B. and Byrne, A. 1991. 'The Lipid Stripping Potential of Resin Soap Gels for Cleaning Oil Paintings', *AICCM Bulletin* **17**, 51–60.

Friberg, S. E. and Larsson, K. 1963. 'Liquid Crystals and Emulsions', in *Advances in Liquid Crystals*, vol. 2 (New York: Academic Press).

Gay, M. C. 1978. 'Application of Staining Methods to Cross Sections in the Study of Media of Various Italian Paintings', in *Conservation and Restoration of Pictorial Art*, N. S. Brommelle and P. Smith (eds) (London).

Geusau, P. and Schreiner, M. 1992. 'Beitrag zur Gemaeldereinigung: Vergleichende Studien der Praktischen Awendbarkeit und Wirkungsweise von Loesungsmittelgelen, Emulsionen, Harzseifen, und Enzymen', *Zeitschrift für Kunsttechnologie und Konservierung* **2**, 260–74.

Godfrey, T. (ed.) 1983. *Handbook of Industrial Enzymology* (New York: The Nature Press).

Griffin, W. C. 1949. 'Lanolin Derivatives', *Journal of the Society of Cosmetic Chemists* **1**.

Harkins, W. D. 1946. 'Surfaces of Solids: Theory of the Reaction Loci in Emulsion Polymerization', *Journal of Colloid Science* **1**, 469.

Harris, J. C. 1959. *Detergency Evaluation and Testing* (New York: Interscience Publishing Inc.).

Hatch, G. B. and Rice, O. 1939. 'Surface Active Properties of Hexametaphosphate', *Industrial Engineering Chemistry* **31**, 51.

Hobbs, M. E. 1951. 'Effects of Salts on the Critical Concentration, Size, and Stability of Soap Micelles', *Journal of Physical Chemistry* **55**, 675.

Hsaio, L. *et al.* 1956. 'Critical Micelle Concentrations of Polyethoxylate Nonionic Detergents', *Journal of Physical Chemistry* **60**, 657.

Jencks, W. P. 1969. *Catalysis in Chemistry and Enzymology* (New York: McGraw-Hill).

Johnson, M. and Packard E. 1971. 'Methods used for the Identification of Binding Media in Italian Paintings', *Studies in Conservation* **16**, 145–64.

Kahane, E. *et al.* 1958. 'Isolation of Membrane Glycoproteins by Affinity Chromatography in the Presence of Detergents', *Biochimica Biophysica Acta* **426**, 464.

Klevens, H. 1948. 'UV Transmission Limits of Some Liquids and Solids', *Journal of Physics and Colloid Chemistry* **52**, 130.

Koller, J. 1990. 'Cleaning of a Nineteenth Century Painting with Deoxycholic Soap: Mechanism and Residue Studies', in *Cleaning, Retouching and Coatings*, J. S. Mills and P. Smith (eds) (London: IIC).

Kroschwitz, J. (ed.) 1950. 'Enzymes and Enzymology, *Kirk-Othmer Encyclopaedia of Chemical Technology*, 1st edn, vol. 5 (New York: Interscience).

Kroschwitz, J. (ed.) 1991a. 'Air Pollution', *Kirk-Othmer Encyclopaedia of Chemical Technology*, 4th edn, vol. 1 (New York: Wiley and Sons).

Kroschwitz, J. (ed.) 1991b. 'Chelating Agents', *Kirk-Othmer Encyclopaedia of Chemical Technology*, 4th edn, vol. 5 (New York: Wiley and Sons).

Kroschwitz, J. (ed.) 1991c. 'Dry Cleaning', *Kirk-Othmer Encyclopaedia of Chemical Technology*, 4th edn, vol. 7 (New York: Wiley and Sons).

Kroschwitz, J. (ed.) 1999. 'Surfactants', *Kirk-Othmer Encyclopaedia of Chemical Technology*, 4th edn, vol. 5 (New York: Interscience).

Kruyt, H. R. 1952. *Colloid Science*, vol. I (New York: Elsevier Publishing Co.).

Lang, S. 1998. 'A Review of Literature Published in Response to Wolbers' Resin Soaps, Bile Soaps, and Solvent Gels'. MA Dissertation, Royal College of Art/Victoria and Albert Museum Joint Course in Conservation, London.

Lapple, C. E. 1961. 'Fall Out Control', *Stanford Research Institute Journal* **5**, Third Quarter.

Lewis, M. 1995. 'Aquazol: The Use of Poly-2-Oxazoline As An Inpainting Medium', *Student Papers of the Twenty-First Annual Conference, The Association of Graduate Programs in Conservation* (Newark, DE: The Winterthur Museum, University of Delaware Program in Art Conservation).

Lide, D. (ed.) 1992. *Handbook of Chemistry and Physics*, 73rd edn (Boca Raton: CRC Press).

Lin, T. 1978. 'Effects of Treadmill Exercise on Plasma and Urinary Cyclic Adenosine, 3,5 Monophosphate', *Journal of the Society of Cosmetic Chemists* **29**, 120.

Long, C. (ed.) 1961. *Biochemist Handbook* (New York: Reinhold).

Martell, A. E. and Calvin, M. 1952. *Chemistry of Metal Chelate Compounds* (Inglewood Cliffs, New Jersey: Prentice Hall Inc.).

Martin, E. 1977. 'Some Improvements in Techniques of Analysis of Paint Media', *Studies in Conservation* **22**, 63–7.

McCutcheon's Emulsifiers and Detergents, 1991, vols I–II (Glen Rock, New Jersey: MC Publishing Co.).

McKinney, 1966. 'Detergents in Labeling Efficiency of Fluorescein Isothiocyanate Products', *Analytical Biochemistry* **14**, 421.

Messinger J. M. 1992. 'Ultraviolet Fluorescence Microscopy of Paint Cross Sections', *Journal of the American Institute of Conservation* **31**, 267–74.

Metzler, D. 1977. *Biochemistry* (New York: Academic Press).

Mills, J. and White, R. 1994. *Organic Chemistry of Museum Objects*, 2nd edn (London: Butterworth-Heinemann).

Mizuno, I. 1975. 'Detergency Theory and Test Methods', Part III *Surfactants Series*, vol. 5, eds Cutler and Davis (New York: Dekker).

Morgan, G. T. and Drew, H. D. 1920. 'Color Producing Intermediates', *Journal of the Chemical Society* **117**, 1456.

Mortvedt, J. J. *et al.* 1972. *Micronutrients in Agriculture* (Madison, Wisconsin: Soil Science Society of America).

Neugebauer, J. 1988. *Detergents in Biology and Biochemistry* (St. Louis: Calbiochem-Novabiochem).

Norman, B. E. 1982. 'A Novel Debranching Enzyme for Application in the Glucose Syrup Industry', *Starch/Stärke* **34**(10), 340–6.

Osipow, L. 1962. *Surface Chemistry* (New York: Reinhold).

Osmond, G. 1993. 'Accelerated deterioration of artists' oil paints: an assessment involving ultraviolet fluorescence spectroscopy', *10th Triennial Meeting, ICOM Committee for Conservation*, preprints, J. Bridgland (ed.) (London: James and James).

Plesters, J. 1955/56. 'Cross Sections and Chemical Analysis of Paint Samples', *Studies in Conservation* **2**, 110–57.

Ploem, J. S. and Tanke, H. J. 1987. *Introduction to Fluorescence Microscopy* (Oxford: Oxford University Press, Royal Microscopical Society).

Raison, M. 1957. *Proceedings of the 2nd International Congress on Surface Activity*, 2nd edn (London: Butterworths).

Riggs, H. J. L. *et al.* 1958. 'Fractionation Method for the Preparation of Fluorescein Labeled Gamma Globulin', *American Journal of Pathology* **34**, 1081.

Rinuy, A. and Gros, L. 1989. 'Liants dans le Peinture Anciennes', *Zeitschrift für Kunsttechnologie und Konservierung* **3**, 9–27.

Rost, F. W. D. 1992. *Fluorescence Microscopy* (Cambridge: Cambridge University Press).

Saubestre, A. 1975. 'Detergency Theory and Test Methods', Part II *Surfactants Series*, vol. 5, C. Cutler and R. H. Davis (eds) (New York: Dekker).

Schaefer, S. 1997. 'Fluorescent staining techniques for the characterisation of binding media within paint cross-sections and digital image processing for the quantification of staining results' in *Early Italian Paintings: Techniques and Analysis*, Tonnie Bakkenist, René

Hoppenbrouwers and Hélène Dubois (eds) (Maastricht, The Netherlands: Limburg Conservation Institute).

Schilling, M. 1989. 'The Glass Transition of Materials Used in Conservation', *Studies in Conservation* **34**, 110–16.

Schramm, H. P. and Hering, B. 1988. *Historische Malmaterialien und ihre Identifizierung* (Berlin).

Schwartz, A. M. 1949. 'Principles of Detergency and Their Application in Textile Processing', *Journal – American Oil Chemists' Society* **26**, 212.

Shinoda, K. and Arai, H. 1964. 'Selective Absorption Studies by Radio-Tracer Techniques', *Journal of Physical Chemistry* **68**, 3485.

Shinoda, K. and Friberg, S. 1975. 'Advances in Colloid and Interface Science', *Interface Science* (New York) 4, 281–304.

Siegel, A. B. 1993. *Computer Enhanced UV Fluorescence Microscopy of Aged Artist's Materials*, Art Conservation Training Conference, Buffalo, USA.

Smoot *et al.* (eds) 1983. *Chemistry: A Modern Course* (Columbus, OH: Merrill Publishing Co.).

Stulik, D. *et al.* 2000. 'Surface cleaning: quantitative study of gel residue on cleaned paint surfaces', in *Tradition and Innovation: Advances in Conservation*, A. Roy and P. Smith (eds) (London: IIC).

Tsang J. and Cunningham, R. 1991. 'Some Improvements in the Study of Cross-Sections', *Journal of the American Institute of Conservation* **30**, 163–77.

Tsang, J. and Erhardt, D. 1992. 'Current Research on the Effects of Solvents and Gelled Aqueous Cleaning Systems on Oil Paint Films', *Journal of the American Institute of Conservation* **31**, 87–94.

Wagner, E. F. 1963. 'Effects of Pyrophosphates and Triphosphates on Metal Complex Dyes', *Textil-Rundschau* **18**, 295.

Wagner, E. F. 1964. 'Effects of Detergents and Normal Electrolytes on the Energy and Sorption Behaviour of Pigments Towards Cotton', *Textil-Rundschau* **19**, 317.

Weiden, M. and Norton, L. B. 1953. 'Temperature Effects in Selected Non-ionic Structures', *Journal of Colloid Science* **8**, 606.

Weigele, M. *et al.* 1972. 'Fluorescamine: A Reagent for Assay of Amino Acids, Peptides, Proteins, and Primary Amines in the Picomole Range', *Journal of the American Chemical Society* **94**, 5947.

Wennerstrom, H. and Lindman, B. 1979. 'Micelles: Physical Chemistry of Surface Association', *The Journal of Physical Chemistry* **23**, 2931.

Wentz, M. 1987. 'Detergency in Non-Aqueous Systems', *Detergents Series*, vol. 20, W. G. Cutler and E. Kissa (eds) (New York: Dekker).

Willeke, K. and Whitby K. T. 1975. 'Comparison of Volume and Mass Distribution of Denver Aerosols', *Journal of the Air Pollution Control Association* **25**, 529.

Wirtz, G. 1977. *Handbuch der Textilhilsmittel* (Weinheim, Germany: Verlag Chemie).

Wolbers, R. 1989 & 1990. *Notes for a Workshop on New Methods of Cleaning Paintings* (Marina del Ray, CA: Getty Conservation Institute).

Wolbers, R. 1990. 'The Use of a Radio-isotopic Assay for the Direct Measurement of Residual Cleaning Materials on a Paint Film', *Cleaning, Retouching and Coatings*, J. S. Mills and P. Smith (eds) (London: IIC).

Wolbers, R. 1992. 'The Use of a Synthetic Soiling Mixture as a Means for Evaluating the Efficacy of Aqueous Cleaning Methods on Painted Surfaces', *ARAAFU Bulletin, Conservation-Restauration Des Biens Culturels*, No. 4 (December).

Wolbers, R. and Landrey, G. 1987. 'The Use of Direct Reactive Dyes for the Characterisation of Binding Media in Cross-Sectional Examinations', AIC Preprints, 15th Annual Meeting, Vancouver, B.C.

Zimon, A. D. 1969. *Adhesion of Dust and Powders* (New York: Plenum).

Index

1-methyl-2-pyrrolidinone 46, 80
2,4 pentanedione 124
abietic acid 19, 22, 39, 41, 43, 45, 48, 50, 51
acetic acid 9–13, 15–19, 21–4, 49, 67, 68, 70, 115, 151, 152
acetone 40, 42, 80, 82, 83, 84, 129, 165, 168, 171, 172, 175, 176
adjuvant 6, 7, 56
adsorption 57, 61–71, 73, 93, 94, 134, 154, 102–4, 111, 122, 139, 158, 162–4, 168, 171, 172, 176, 180, 181
Aerosol OT 72
affinity chromatography 53, 187
aggregation 30
aggregation number 35, 36, 37, 52, 74, 164
alcohols 26, 28, 34, 39, 41, 43, 45, 63, 68, 81, 82, 84, 89, 90, 99
aleuritic acid 34, 53
alkalis/alkaline 15, 45, 49, 53, 58, 61, 80, 138, 144, 148, 151, 155, 158, 177
alkanes 32–4
amines 17, 24, 25, 26, 28, 32, 34, 39, 40–49, 52, 55, 69, 70, 73, 74, 76, 78, 82, 84, 87, 88, 90, 99, 100, 101, 104, 107, 109, 115, 119, 122, 125, 129, 139, 140, 152, 156, 162, 163, 172, 176, 186
amines, primary 34, 186
ammonia 5, 15, 17, 102, 139, 163
ammoniate ion 15, 17
ammoniated solutions 5, 163
ammonium chloride 15, 17, 32, 52
amphoteric 14, 20, 28, 70
amylase, type IIa 146
amylase (alpha) 6, 145, 146, 147
amylase (beta) 145
amylose azure 146
anion/anionic 19, 20, 28, 30, 39, 58, 59, 64, 70, 88, 90, 92, 93, 95, 104, 110, 111, 113, 116, 162
Anne Ross Hopkins 139
antimony pentachloride (APC) 40, 48, 99, 140, 150, 180, 181, 183
aragonite 20
Armeen, 12D 74, 76
Arrhenius 13
Arrhenius relationship 132
Atlas Sunchex 59, 63
autofluorescence 21, 24, 80, 99, 139, 140, 143, 144, 150, 168, 169, 176, 181

benzaldehyde 38
benzalkonium chloride 49, 50, 52
benzene/benzene ring 34, 38, 61
benzyl alcohol 82, 84
Bicknell, Albion 119
bile acids 136, 137, 181
biocides 50
bituminous ground 99, 100
bleaches 71, 155, 171
borohydrides 171
Brij, 35 35, 45, 47, 107, 108, 151, 152, 154, 155, 163
Brij, 700 67, 68, 69, 162, 164
bromophenylacylbromide 149
Brönsted-Lowry 13, 14

Brown, Joan 67
Brown, William Mason 124
buffer pair 17, 18
buffers 6, 16, 123, 124, 161
  2-N-morpholino ethane sulfonic acid/2-N-morpholino ethane sulfonate (MES) 17
  acetic acid/acetate 17, 22, 23
  boric acid/borate 17
  carbonate/bicarbonate 17
  citric acid/citrate 17, 119
  diethylbarbituric acid/diethylbarbiturate 17
  ethanolamine/ethanolate 17
  formic acid/formate 17
  glycine/glycinate 17, 144
  KH_2PO_4/borate 17, 104, 106
  KH_2PO_4/$NaHPO_4$ 17
  N, N, bis (2-hydroxyethyl)glycine 17
  Na_2PO_4/PO_3 17
  N-tris (hydroxymethyl)methylglycine 17
  p toluene sulfonic acid/*p* toluene sulfonate 17
  phenylacetic acid/phenyl acetate 17
  succinate/borate 17
  succinic acid succinate 17
  triethanolamine/triethanolate 17
  tris(hydroxymethyl)aminomethane (tris) 17, 140

calcium carbonate 21
caprylate, sodium 59
carbonate, lead 99, 104, 120
carbonate, sodium 58
carbonic acid 21
Carbopol, 934 74, 76, 77, 78, 80
Carbopol, 940 82
Carbopol, 954 46, 107, 121
carboxylates 19, 27, 28, 39, 87, 11, 112, 114, 115, 122
carboxymethylcellulose, sodium 58
cation/cationic 1, 15, 20, 21, 23, 24, 28, 47, 59, 64, 70, 88, 90, 92, 104, 110, 111, 113, 114, 115, 116, 173
cellulase(s) 115, 155
cetyl alcohol 89
cetylpyridinium chloride 37
charge density 33, 36, 37
chelates/chelation 95, 109, 110, 111–114, 116, 120, 124, 161, 188
  2.4 pentanedione 110
  binding sites 110
  citrate ion 111, 124
  coordination number 110
  EDTA 60, 114, 115, 116, 120, 124
  fertilizers 109, 123
  food preservation 109
  ketonyl oxygens 110
  ligands 110–15, 120, 121, 126
  metal buffering 123
  metal cations 111, 113
  ore-leaching 109
  pH effects 111–14
  valence state 110
  water softening 109
chemical activity 130
chitin 156
chitinase 156
Christ Washing the Feet of the Disciples 143
chymotrypsin 130, 148, 149
citrate/citrate ion 17, 53, 60, 106, 111–115, 118, 120, 122, 124, 125, 126
citrate, diammonium 6, 52, 104, 106
citric acid 17, 111, 112, 119, 125
clays 73
clearance 38, 66, 67, 73, 74, 143, 154, 157, 158, 160, 161, 163, 164, 188
  by solvent means 70, 162, 163
cloud point 38, 96
coalescence, rate of 93, 94
Cobett-Sharp House, Odessa de 146
cocoalkylamine 78
collagens 53
colloids 72, 73
complexing agents 6, 26, 56, 67, 116
conductivity 26, 30, 64, 73, 117, 118, 120, 161
conjugate acid 13, 15
conjugate base 16, 24
contact point 3
corrosion 6
  control 6, 109
co-surfactant 103, 104
Coulombic forces 3, 4, 5, 56
critical micelle concentration (CMC) 30–39, 43, 47, 50, 53, 56, 57, 59, 60–63, 65–71, 73, 74, 87, 106, 108, 137, 138, 143, 145, 154, 160, 161, 162, 163
  and detergency 66, 58, 59, 60
  data 32
  depression 34
  determination of 30
  effect of chain length 32
  effect of electrolytes 33, 36
  effect of molecular structure 33
  effects of polar additives 34
  effects of temperature 34
  equations for 32
  of mixtures of surfactants 34
  of nonionics 37, 38
critical pigment volume concentration (CPC) 25, 60
cryoscopic effects 56, 63

dammar 22, 40, 42, 49, 160, 181
de-branching enzymes 146, 147

denaturation 128, 143, 144, 145, 154
deoxycholate, sodium 53, 59, 63, 64, 88, 137, 143
deoxycholic acid 35, 50, 51, 52, 53, 137, 144, 145
desorption 60, 61
detergents/detergency 55, 56–8, 60, 61, 62, 63, 64, 65, 66, 68, 69, 70, 71, 73
  and adsorption 57, 61–65, 68–71, 73
  compositions 58
  cryoscopic effects 56, 63
  effect of concentration 55, 56, 57, 59, 60, 62
  effects of electrolytes 57, 58
  electrical forces 73
  enzyme mixtures 58, 83
  mechanisms 56, 57
  in non-aqueous system 71–4
  nature of soils 55, 56–8
  rolling up 56, 57
  substrate soil bonds 56–8
dextrin 145
diacetone alcohol 99
diazo reagents 149, 183
dibutyl phthalate 38
dichlorfluorescein (DCF) 179
dielectric constant 5, 9, 14, 56
diethylbenzene 38
dimethylformamide (DMF) 41, 46, 139, 144
dipolar forces 2, 27, 28, 56, 67, 85
dispersal aids 25, 26, 52, 54, 55, 117, 118, 120, 161
dispersal system (pollution) 2, 4, 6
dissolution 6, 9, 10, 12, 13, 16, 19, 20, 49, 54, 58, 63, 66, 73, 84, 109, 117, 124, 126, 153
distempers 98, 107, 158
diterpenes/diterpenoids 22, 39, 43, 50
dodecylamine 73, 74, 76
dodecyltrimethylammonium bromide 59
dowicide *o*-benzylepichlorphenol 67, 68
dry cleaning 58, 71–3, 138, 187
drying oil(s) 12, 24, 42, 46, 68, 76, 122, 125, 140, 145, 158, 159, 168, 177, 178, 179

EDTA (ethylenediaminetetraacetic acid) 60, 114–16, 120, 122, 123, 124
egg whites 86, 119, 150, 152
Eichholtz, Jacob 119
electrical forces 3, 4
electrolyte 9, 10, 12, 20, 21, 34
electrostatic charge 24
emulsions 43, 72, 76, 85, 86, 92, 93, 94, 95–8, 100–8, 122, 123, 138, 144, 150, 152, 154, 155, 160, 171, 173, 178, 186, 188
  continuous phase 85
  discontinuous phase 85
  dual 86
  gelled 100, 101
  inverse 86
  lamellar arrangements 86
  optical properties 92
  particle size 92
  preparation 100, 102, 103
  stabilty 92, 93, 94, 107
  ternary systems 96–8
  type 85, 86
entropy 110
enzymes 127–38, 140–45, 147, 148, 149, 154, 155, 156
  active site 129, 130, 133, 134, 138, 148, 149, 154
  active site amino acids 129, 130, 147, 148
  as catalysts 127
  assays 135, 138
  charge transfer 138
  definition of unit activity 129
  denaturation 135
  de-sizing 155
  hydrolysis 129, 130, 134, 135, 137, 138, 140, 145, 148, 154, 158
  inhibition 149, 154
  kinetics 131
  Michaelis-Menten relationship 131, 132, 136, 143, 154
  pH vs. activity curves 133, 134
  preparation/isolation 155–156
  specific activity 135, 141, 147, 148, 153, 155
  structure in solution 126
  substrate interactions 128–30
  temperature vs. activity curves 133–4
  velocity 131, 132, 136, 143, 154
Eosin 5-isothiocyanate (EITC) 172
equilibrium 4, 9, 10, 11–14, 16, 17, 20, 21, 24, 65, 98, 109, 113, 116, 120, 123, 124, 126
equilibrium constant 13, 17, 116, 120
essential oils 126
Ethofat, 242/25 49, 50
Ethomeen C-12 107, 164, 165
Ethomeen C-25 46, 47, 77, 78, 79, 80, 82, 84, 121, 164, 165
ethylene glycol 88
ethylene oxide 37, 38, 50
ethylenediaminetetraacetic acid (EDTA) 60, 114–16, 120, 122, 123, 124

faux graining 81
ferrous hydroxide 15, 16
flocculation 93
floor tiles 63

Fluorescamine (FLUR) 76, 175, 176, 186
fluorescein isothiocyanate (FITC) 119, 172, 183
fluorescence 21, 24, 80, 139, 140, 143, 144, 150, 159, 167, 168, 169, 175, 176, 177, 180, 11, 183, 186
fluorescent dyes 167, 168, 183
  excitation and emission data 183
fluorochromes 1, 21, 168, 177, 183
force of adhesion 2, 45
free acid 10, 16, 24, 41, 43, 52, 70, 74, 78, 90, 144
FTIR 24, 119, 125, 159

Garnsey, Elmer 107
gelatin 4
gels 22, 24, 25, 26, 35, 39, 41, 42, 46, 47, 49, 50, 52, 53, 58, 67, 70, 71, 74–83, 96, 98, 100, 102, 104, 105, 107, 108, 119, 120, 121, 122, 123, 125, 128, 129, 140, 141, 142, 143, 144, 151, 152, 153, 154, 159, 162–165, 175, 186, 188, 189
George Washington (trade sign) 98, 100
gesso 104, 149
gilding 98, 104, 106, 149
  compo 104
  bole 104
  gesso 104, 149
  water 98, 106
  oil 104, 106
  with other metal leafs 106
glass transition temperature (Tg) 4, 187
gluconic acid 129, 155
glucose 129, 145, 155, 170, 188
glucose oxidase 129, 155
glue 4, 40, 48, 53, 106, 119, 121, 121, 159
glycerol 84, 89, 133, 135
gouaches 98
graphite 63

Hansen, J. L. 121
hard surfaces 63
HBO lamps 78, 79, 114, 122, 123
hemi-aldehydes 170
hemicellulose 155
hexametaphosphate, sodium 58
HLB 34, 39, 43, 47, 50, 51, 53, 68, 69, 70, 79, 84, 86, 87, 88, 89, 90–92, 94, 95, 96, 101, 102, 106, 108, 122, 125, 145, 154, 155, 160, 162, 164
  by group number 87, 88, 89
  for nonionics 89, 90
Hobbs equation 33, 187
hydrocarbons 5, 27, 28, 29, 31, 32, 33, 34, 37, 38, 39, 50, 52, 53, 54, 56, 63, 67, 68, 69, 71, 72, 85, 87, 88, 89, 91, 94, 95, 102, 103, 104, 158, 162, 164
hydrochloric acid (HCl) 13, 16, 25, 32, 41, 45, 46, 48, 52, 53, 83, 100, 107, 140, 146, 152
hydrogen bonding 2, 27, 56, 67, 130
hydrolases 128, 129
hydrolysis 15, 19, 58, 129, 130, 134, 135, 137, 138, 140, 145, 148, 154, 158
hydronium ion 10, 12
hydrophile-lipophile balance number (HLB) 34, 39, 43, 47, 50, 51, 53, 68, 69, 70, 79, 84, 86, 87, 88, 89, 90–92, 94, 95, 96, 101, 102, 106, 108, 122, 125, 145, 154, 155, 160, 162, 164
hydrophilic 2, 28, 29, 30, 32, 33, 39, 53, 86, 87, 88, 89, 92, 95, 96, 98, 158, 162
hydrophobic 1, 4, 5, 63, 68, 69, 70, 90, 91, 128, 130, 133, 143, 158, 159, 160, 161, 162, 163, 170
hydroxylpropylmethyl cellulose 41, 43, 48, 70, 140, 143, 144
hypertonic 161

ICI 176
In Defense of the Barricade 80
infrared spectroscopy/spectrum 24, 159
interfacial tension 85, 91, 95, 160
iodide, potassium 99, 119
ionic forces 9
ionic strength 35, 53, 66, 72, 92, 102, 113, 161, 163
ionization 17, 19, 20, 72
ionization constant 11, 14, 18
isoelectric point 19, 20
isomerases 129
isothermal adsorption 62, 65
isothermal phase diagram 98
isotherms 61, 62, 65

K_a, pK_a 12–19, 22, 23, 26, 32, 33, 34, 39, 40–42, 45, 49, 50, 51, 53, 58, 61, 64, 70, 80, 90, 111, 113, 122, 123, 129, 134, 138, 144, 145–8, 151, 155, 158, 159–61, 163, 177, 186, 187
K_b, pK_b 13, 15, 16, 19, 42, 43, 71, 101, 111, 135
Krafft point 37
K_{sp} 20, 21, 114, 117, 123, 124, 126, 161

Labophot microscope system 167
lauryl sulfate 35, 59, 86, 87, 89, 92, 162, 164
lauryl sulfate, sodium 35, 59, 87, 89
lauryl sulfate, triethanolate 162
law of mass action 10, 20, 127
Le Chatelier's principle 10
leaching 61, 109, 155
lead white/basic lead carbonate 52, 99, 101, 104, 117–20, 125, 126, 139, 160
lecithin 86

ligands 110–15, 120, 121, 126
  monodentate 110
  bidentate 110
  tridentate 110
  polydentate 110
ligases 129
light scattering 35, 36, 73
  low angle X-ray 35
linseed oil 4, 12, 19, 22, 42, 141, 144, 178
lipase 6, 83, 135–8, 140–44, 147
  action on triglycerides 135, 136, 143
  assays for 138, 142
  bacterial 138
  calcium requirement 137, 138
  Candida cylindracea 140
  co-lipase 137, 138, 141, 142
  duodenal 137
  effects of detergents 137, 138
  pancreatic 137
  type VII 140, 142, 144, 147
lipophilic 28, 29, 30, 53, 86, 87, 88, 91, 95
liquid crystal 95, 96, 188
lissamine rhodamine sulfonyl chloride 40, 99, 150, 176, 183
lithocholic acid 51
lyases 129

macroemulsion (O/W) 76, 92, 95, 102, 103, 104, 107
macroemulsion (W/O) 95, 102, 103, 104, 107, 154
macroemulsions (water-in-xylene) 76, 92, 95, 102, 103, 104, 107, 154
mannanase 155
Mary Morris Jones 21
Massachusetts hinged writing desk 74
mastic 22, 40, 160, 181
McCutcheons Emulsifiers and Detergents 54, 87, 187, 188
Merck index 169, 181
metal buffering 123, 125, 126
metal surfaces 28, 63
methanol 13, 76, 82, 144, 168, 170
methyl cellulose 22, 25, 26, 41, 43, 45, 46, 48, 50, 52, 58, 67, 68, 70, 78, 94, 105, 119, 122, 125, 140, 143, 144, 151, 154, 155, 163
micelles 29, 30, 32, 34, 35, 37, 72, 73, 93, 94, 95, 96, 102, 160
  inverse 56, 71, 72
  size 92, 102
  charge 72, 93
Michaelis-Menten relationship 131, 132, 136, 143, 154
microchemical tests 25, 99
  carbohydrates 168, 169, 170
  oils lipids, fats 177, 179, 180
  proteins 175
  resins 180, 181
microemulsion(s) 72, 76, 96, 97, 98, 102, 103, 104, 106
mineral oil 58, 59, 86, 87, 91, 95, 102, 103
mineral spirits 22, 23, 25, 26, 40, 41, 42, 45, 46, 48, 70, 74–81, 83, 107, 108, 119, 122, 125, 140, 143, 144, 152, 154, 155, 164, 165, 170, 172, 176, 185
molality 37
molarity/molar/mole 10, 11, 20, 24, 43, 76, 84, 102, 113, 116, 117, 118, 124
molecular forces 2, 3, 4
morpholine 46

n-butyl methacrylates 54
n-acetylglucoseamine 156
Naismith, William 76
naphthelene 183
natural resin 4, 19, 21, 22, 39, 40, 42, 47, 76, 80, 100, 101, 140, 144, 143, 145, 152, 181
Nikon 167
non-polar 27, 28, 42, 47, 69, 73, 81, 101, 164, 177
nonyl phenol 38, 96, 163, 164
N-pyrrole 46, 47, 80, 81

octyl phenol 68
oil–water mixtures 43, 85, 86, 90, 93, 94, 95, 96, 101, 104
oleate 58, 89, 90, 102
  potassium 89, 90, 102
  sodium 89, 90
  triethanolamine 90
oleic acid 89, 90, 102
oleo-resinous coatings 49, 50, 82, 154
optical brightners 58
oxido-reductases 129

paint
  oil 12, 22, 24, 25, 41, 42, 52, 58, 60, 63, 64, 65, 66, 68, 69, 76, 80, 101, 116, 117, 121, 139, 144, 159, 161, 186, 189
  bronze powder 99, 163
  casein 104, 158, 159
  diffusion transition region 63, 150
  soil interaction 1, 2, 4, 5, 6, 12, 21, 24, 25, 49, 50, 52, 53, 55, 56, 57, 58–63, 66, 67–76, 79, 91, 100, 101, 102, 104–8, 118, 119, 124, 125, 126, 139, 140, 143–7, 152, 154, 158, 160, 161, 188
  dispersion 4
  distemper 98, 107, 158
  latex 5, 178
paint film constituents
  driers 25, 52, 55, 117, 118, 120, 145, 161
  dyes 55, 117
  extenders 22, 55, 117, 140

pigments 22, 25, 52, 54, 55, 60, 61, 99, 104, 117, 118–23, 125, 126, 140, 145, 159, 160, 161
rheological modifiers 55
paint strippers 82
paint surface, oxidation/weathering 25, 40, 42, 52, 61, 69, 70, 79, 155, 159, 160, 168, 179
Painting of a Prize Cow 119
palmitate, lead 25, 52, 53, 120
palmitate, sodium 30, 34
palmitic acid 58
papain 129, 149
paraffin/paraffinic 4, 39, 87, 91, 96
partitioning 63, 65, 72
Pastoral Landscape 76
patina 82
Paxson's Hollow 52
Peale, James 21
pepsin 119, 152, 153, 154
pepstatin A 154
perchlorethene 71
perfumes 58, 71
petroleum ether 74
pH 4–7, 12, 14, 16–26, 28, 39, 41–3, 45–53, 56, 58, 59, 61, 63, 64, 71, 78, 79, 83, 84, 90, 94–6, 100–102, 104, 105, 106, 108, 111, 115, 119, 122–6, 128, 130, 132–4, 140, 142–9, 151, 152–5, 159–61, 165, 180
phase diagram 97, 98
phase inversion temperature (PIT) 95, 96, 97, 98
phenolic resin 5
Philadelphia tilt top tea table 81
phosphates 6, 17, 18, 58, 61, 62, 67, 127, 129, 163
phosphatidylcholine 86
photometric methods 58
photosynthesis 109
pK_a 12–19, 22, 23, 26, 32, 33, 34, 39, 40–42, 45, 49, 50, 51, 53, 58, 61, 64, 70, 80, 90, 111, 113, 122, 123, 129, 134, 138, 144, 145–8, 151, 155, 158, 159–61, 163, 177, 186, 187
pK_b 13, 15, 16, 19, 42, 43, 71, 101, 111, 135
pK_{sp} 20, 114, 117, 123, 124, 126, 161
plywood 58
POE, 10 sorbitan monooleate 89
POE, 23 lauryl ether 154
polar 2, 9, 27, 28, 29, 34, 39, 41, 42, 45, 46, 49, 56, 61, 67, 69, 71, 72, 73, 74, 76, 78, 79, 80, 81, 84, 85, 87, 91, 98, 99, 100, 101, 113, 119, 121, 122, 125, 128, 129, 140, 144, 145, 153, 158, 159, 162, 163, 164, 165, 167, 168, 171, 177–9, 180
polyacidic 17, 18, 121, 164
polyacrylic acid 73, 74, 76, 79, 80, 84, 164, 165
polybasic 17
polymers, acrylic 54, 73, 80, 81
polymers, polyurethane 81, 82, 83, 84
polymers, PVA-AYAA 140
polyoxyethylenes (POE) 38, 68, 69, 78, 79, 89, 154
polysaccharides 87
Portrait of Hanna Holbrow 121
Portrait of Miranda 149, 154
potash 6
potassium iodide 99, 119
potential difference 3
potential energy 29, 93
Pre-Raphaelites 149
propylene glycol 88, 89
propylene glycol monolaurate 89
propylene glycol monostearate 89
proteases 6, 119, 129, 130, 134, 143, 148–9, 153, 154
acidic 153
alkaline 148
endo- 148, 154
exo- 148
metal requiring 148, 149
proteins 6, 19, 20, 53, 119, 121, 126, 127, 128, 129, 130, 134, 135, 141, 148, 159, 168, 171, 172, 175, 176, 186, 187
pyridine 41, 46, 139
pyrophosphate, terasodium 58, 62, 67, 129

reaction constant 11, 13, 15, 18
reflectance measurments 58, 59
refractive index 30
Remington, Frederic 80
residence time 2
resin soap 41, 45–50, 189
nonionic 49, 50
triethanolate 41, 45–50
Rhodamine, 123 (RHO123) 179
Rhodamine, 6G (RHO6G) 179
Rhodamine B 40, 44, 45, 52, 69, 76, 99, 125, 139, 140, 144, 150, 176, 177, 178, 179, 180, 183
rinsing/clearing 22, 23, 25, 26, 41, 45, 46, 48, 50, 53, 58, 59, 67, 68, 69, 70, 73, 74, 75, 76, 78, 79, 80, 81, 83, 101, 102, 105, 106, 107, 108, 119, 122, 125, 140, 144, 152, 154, 162–5, 176
rolling up 47, 73
rosin 19, 49, 50, 181
rubber 4
Ryder, C. F. 52

saliva 6, 41, 45, 46, 48, 52, 67, 119, 140, 143, 144, 152, 170
Sandys, Frederick 149, 150

sapogenins 182
saponification 122
Schoonover, Frank 50, 58, 107
Second World War 58, 171
secondary bonding forces 27, 28, 85, 126
sedimentation force 93, 94
sedimentation rate 35, 94
sequestering, metals 21, 154
shellac 53, 81, 173
Shinoda equation 32, 39, 43, 72, 93, 187
Sigma Chemical Co. 83, 140, 142, 144, 145, 146, 147, 152, 154, 168, 171, 175, 176, 177, 179, 180, 184, 188
silicates 58, 120, 123, 126
sizes 71
soaps, fatty acid 25, 27, 32, 58, 63, 69, 102, 116, 118, 159, 178, 188, 189
soaps, sodium 32, 102
soil redeposition 72
soiling/soiling layer 1, 2, 5, 12, 21, 23–5, 49, 50, 52, 53, 55, 56–9, 61, 63, 67, 69, 70, 71, 73, 74, 76, 91, 100, 101, 104–8, 114, 118, 119, 125, 126, 140, 143, 144, 145, 146, 159, 161, 188
solubility parameter 47, 54, 73, 78, 79, 82, 164, 177
solubility product 20, 117, 158, 161, 162
solubilization 6, 35, 40, 42, 47, 55, 58, 59, 61, 63, 66, 71, 72, 76, 80, 84, 91, 95, 109, 121, 122, 152–154, 161, 162, 170
solvent gels 35, 46, 47, 78, 80, 107, 121, 188, 189
soot 67, 68, 69, 90
sorbitan 88, 89
sorbitan mono-laurate 89
sorbitan mono-oleate 89
sorbitan mono-palmitate 89
sorbitan monostearate 89, 90
sorbitan tetrastearate 89, 90
sorbitan tristearate 89, 90
span 80 89
specific activity, enzymatic 135, 141, 147, 148, 153, 155
stearate, lead 25, 52, 53, 58, 120
stearate, sodium 58
stearic acid 12, 164
stearine wax 63
sterol glycosides 181
Stokes equation 93, 94
student violin bow 49
sulfates 2, 8, 87, 162
sulfates, alkyl 32, 33, 39, 87
sulfates, sodium 5, 8, 59, 62, 162
sulfonates alkyl 17, 28, 32, 39, 87
sulfonates, alkyl aryl 34, 61, 62
sulfosuccinate, sodium dioctyl ester 72
Sunchex, Atlas 59, 60
surface energy 29, 30, 69, 160
surface tension 6, 30, 31, 37, 56, 57, 68, 71, 73, 78, 84, 90, 91, 95, 136, 159
surfactant 5, 6, 7, 25, 27–39, 45, 47, 50, 52, 53, 54, 55, 56, 57, 58, 59, 61, 62–8, 71, 72, 76, 77, 78, 79, 80, 82–92, 94, 97, 102, 103, 104, 106, 118, 119, 122, 125, 136, 137, 138, 143, 145, 154, 155, 159, 160, 162, 163, 164, 167, 187, 188
  affinity 39, 47, 49, 53, 54
  affinity, acrylic 54
  dilution effects 59
  adsorption on surfaces 59, 61, 62, 63, 64, 65, 66, 68
  builders 57, 58, 61, 67
  nonionics 38, 47, 50, 68
  fluorinated 28
  anionic 39, 58, 66
  cationic 59, 66
  radiolabeled 63, 64, 69
  in solvent blends 71, 72, 73, 76, 77, 78, 79, 80, 82, 83, 84
suspension aid 6, 23, 43, 57, 58, 73, 74, 79, 143
Synperonic N 164
Synperonic NDB 164

taurocholic acid 52
tetramethyl rhodamine isothiocyanate (TRITC) 171, 172, 173, 175, 176, 177, 183
tetra nitro blue tetrazolium (TNBT) 171
tetrazoles 168, 169, 171
tetrazolium blue (TB) 171
Tetronic 908 78, 79
Texas Red (TR) 171
The Death 48
The Prodigal Father 24
thermodynamics 27, 103, 110, 127
thiocarbamyl nitro blue terazolium (TCNBT) 171
thiols 28
titration curve 18, 19, 138
transferases 129
triethanolamine 17, 24, 25, 26, 41, 42, 43, 45, 47, 48, 49, 69, 70, 78, 90, 100, 101, 107, 119, 122, 139, 152, 162, 163
triglyceride 12, 19, 129, 132, 133, 134, 135, 136, 137, 138, 140, 144, 158, 178, 179
triglycerol monostearate 89
triphenyl formazan 169, 170
triphenyltetrazolium chloride (TTC) 168, 169, 170, 171
triterpenoids 181
Triton X-100 22, 23, 25, 26, 35, 38, 41, 43, 46, 47, 48, 65, 68, 69, 83, 84, 92, 96–8, 100, 101, 102, 104, 105, 106, 119, 122, 125, 138, 140, 143, 145, 160, 161, 162–4
Triton XL–80N 70

Trizma-HCL 52, 53, 83, 140, 143
tromp l'oeil 107
troysol CD1 54
trypsin 130, 148, 149
tung oil 4
turbidity 36, 138
Tween 20 152, 155
Tween 61 89
Tween 80 35, 89
Tween 81 89

ultraviolet light (UV) 21, 183
UV microscopy 167, 168, 186

Van der Waals forces 2, 39, 52, 56, 85, 93
varnishes 1, 2, 4, 5, 7, 12, 21, 22, 24, 40, 42, 44, 45, 46, 47, 48, 49, 52, 55, 73, 77, 84, 91, 100, 101, 119, 120, 121, 122, 124, 125, 144, 149, 150, 152, 160, 171, 183, 186, 188
Venetian Canal Scene 44
View of a River 124
viscosity 23, 30, 73, 93, 94, 107, 117, 123, 143, 145, 148, 151, 159, 163, 171
vitamins 128, 129, 181
Von Liebrach. E. 40

wallpaper 146, 147, 148
wax(es) 4, 24, 28, 45, 63, 69, 70, 74, 75, 76, 81, 85, 87, 155
wetting 6, 24, 34, 53, 54, 56, 57, 61, 66, 68, 69, 73, 86, 90, 91, 118, 120, 121, 124, 154, 159, 161
whiteners 71
whitewash 99
wine 5
Winterscape 40
Winterthur Museum 81, 98, 188
Wolstenholme, Dean 48

xylanase 155
xylene 46, 47, 50, 52, 70, 72–79, 82, 96–102, 104, 105, 106, 122, 165, 177, 178, 180

Zssar polyurethane 81
zymogen 149